Conducting Research

Social and Behavioral Science Methods

Second Edition

Lawrence T. Orcher

Pyrczak Publishing
P.O. Box 250430 • Glendale, CA 91225

"Pyrczak Publishing" is an imprint of Fred Pyrczak, Publisher, A California Corporation.

Project Director: Kyle Dump.
Editor: Danielle Dobies.

Cover design by Robert Kibler and Larry Nichols.

Editorial assistance provided by Cheryl Alcorn, Amber Avines, Wendy Baker, Jenifer Dill, Erica Simmons, Karen Sommerfeld, and Sharon Young.

Printed in the United States of America by McNaughton & Gunn, Inc.

Contents

Continued →

Detailed Contents

Notes:

Introduction

This text is designed to prepare students to conduct their first empirical research study. It provides concrete, specific advice for beginning researchers and is illustrated with numerous examples from published research reports. Both quantitative and qualitative methods are covered in detail.

Nonlinear Organization of This Text

Most beginning texts on conducting research methods are linear, starting with definitions of research and ending with how to write original research reports. In contrast, this text is divided into two overlapping sections.

Section I Writing a Preliminary Research Proposal (Chapters 1 through 11)

A unique feature of this book is that the early chapters (Chapters 1 through 11) provide a complete overview of the research process—from selecting a topic through writing a preliminary research proposal. As a result, students can prepare a preliminary proposal early in the semester, allowing ample time to get feedback, as well as to reconsider their research plans and revise them.

Section II Refining the Preliminary Proposal (Chapters 12 through 27)

Chapters 12 through 27 amplify the material in the first 11 chapters, providing additional concepts, details, and background material. As students work through these subsequent chapters, they can continually revise and improve their preliminary research proposals.

The nonlinear presentation, in which the overview in the early chapters overlaps with the more detailed material in later chapters, has three advantages.

First, the overview of the research process in the first 11 chapters provides a conceptual framework for students that will help them comprehend the more detailed material in the later chapters.

Second, writing a proposal for research early in the semester helps students develop a high level of personal involvement as they work through the more technical material in the last 16 chapters of the book. The material in these chapters helps them improve the preliminary proposals they wrote earlier in the semester.

Third, because the first 11 chapters culminate in writing a complete research proposal, students who will be expected to conduct basic research as a term project in a single semester can get started early, allowing more time to conduct the research and write and revise a research report.

Presentation of Statistical Material

Because statistical methods are an integral part of quantitative research and also have some limited applications in qualitative research, basic methods are discussed in this text. For students who have taken a course in statistics, this material will serve as a review. The calculation of statistics, however, is beyond the scope of this book.

About the End-of-Chapter Exercises

The end-of-chapter exercises have *Factual Questions* and *Questions for Discussion*. The factual questions help students review key concepts covered in the chapters, while the questions for discussion encourage students to consider specific techniques and strategies that they might use while planning and conducting their research.

About the Learning Resource Materials

The *Learning Resources* (LR) are sold as a part of this learning package, which consists of a traditional textbook, which you are now reading, and the LR that have been punched for a three-hole binder.

The LR extend beyond the materials included in traditional textbooks. For example, there are comprehensive chapter outlines to help students blend classroom discussion with the ideas presented in this book. The LR also include a full-length journal article that provides insight into conducting online surveys in research.

New to the Second Edition

A new chapter (Chapter 4) has been added to introduce the basics of citing references using the styles recommended by the American Psychological Association (APA) and the American Sociological Association (ASA). In addition, three new chapters (Chapters 21–23) have been added to give guidance to students who are planning to do survey research.

The LR described above are also new to this edition.

Contacting the Author

I encourage you to share your criticisms of this book with me. You can communicate with me via my publisher, either through the mailing address shown on the title or by e-mail at Info@Pyrczak.com.

Lawrence T. Orcher
Los Angeles, California

Part A

Getting Started

The 11 chapters in Part A of this book will take you through the complete process of preparing a preliminary research proposal, starting with selecting a research topic and ending with a written plan for research. The remaining parts of this book amplify the material in Part A, providing additional information and examples. As you work through Parts B–G, plan to revise and improve your preliminary proposal based on the information contained in them.

Notes:

Chapter 1
Selecting Tentative Topics for Empirical Research

Research is the process of systematically collecting and interpreting information. While *library research* refers to the systematic collection and interpretation of materials written by others, *empirical research* refers to making systematic observations to collect new information.[1] The information collected through empirical research is called *data*, which are analyzed in order to assist in making interpretations.

Note that in empirical research, the term *observation* is used in a broad sense. It refers not only to using the senses to directly observe overt behaviors but also the indirect processes and procedures used to collect data such as multiple-choice tests, attitude scales, and interviews.

The first step in conducting empirical research is to select a topic. For beginning researchers, it is usually best to start by identifying several broad areas of interest, often called "broad topics," and then narrowing them down to the point where they can serve as the starting point for planning a particular research project.

Everyday Observations as a Source of Research Topics

Everyday observations can be a source of ideas for research. This is especially true when something unexpected is observed. Consider an example: Suppose you observe that a new acquaintance is an occasional smoker who sometimes smokes several cigarettes in a row yet sometimes does not smoke at all for several weeks. To you, this is an unexpected observation because the nicotine in cigarettes is widely regarded as being highly addictive. The following six questions can be applied to such a behavioral observation in order to identify possible research topics:

1. *What is the prevalence of the observed behavior?* For instance, a research topic could be to determine how many and what percentage of smokers are only occasional smokers.

2. *What are the demographics of those who exhibit the behavior?*[2] For instance, a research topic might be to determine the prevalence of occasional smoking among major demographic groups, such as women and men, as well as various socioeconomic status groups.

3. *What is the cause of the observed behavior?* For instance, a research topic could be to investigate what stimuli cause occasional smokers to engage in smoking behavior.

---

[1] The adjective *empirical* is derived from *empiricism*, which refers to acquiring information using observation.

[2] Demographics are background characteristics of the individuals being studied. The role of demographics in selecting a research topic is discussed in more detail later in this chapter.

4. *What does the observed behavior cause?* For instance, a research topic could be to investigate the health consequences of occasional smoking.

5. *Is it possible to predict the behavior?* For instance, a research topic could be to determine which personal variables (e.g., ages at which individuals began smoking) predict if a person becomes an occasional smoker.

6. *What theory or theories might account for the behavior?* For instance, a research topic could be to apply reinforcement theory in an effort to reduce occasional smoking behavior.

Theories as a Source of Research Topics

Theories are statements of principles that help explain why a wide array of behaviors is exhibited and how certain types of behaviors are associated with other types. Often, a suitable research topic can be found by considering predictions based on a theory. For instance, consider the brief description of terror management theory offered by the authors of Example 1.1. They used this theory as a basis for making the predictions shown in Example 1.2. These predictions are, in effect, the specific research topics that the researchers investigated.

Example 1.1
Brief description of terror management theory (TMT)
"TMT posits that human awareness of the inevitability of death creates the potential for existential terror, which is both highly aversive and capable of undermining adaptive behavior unless effectively managed. According to the theory, people stave off this potential for anxiety by: (a) maintaining faith in cultural worldviews . . . , (b) garnering self-esteem, by living up to their culture's standards of value, and (c) maintaining close interpersonal attachments."[3]

Example 1.2
Two predictions (hypotheses) based on the theory described in Example 1.1
1. Church attendance should be up the few Sundays after the unexpected and violent death of a famous person. The death should trigger anxiety and terror, leading people to maintain faith.

2. Divorce rates should be down for several months shortly after a major disaster in which hundreds of people die. These deaths should trigger anxiety and terror, leading people to maintain close interpersonal attachments.

Testing a prediction based on a theory is, in effect, a test of the theory. For instance, if the research supports the predictions in Example 1.2, the results of the research provide *support* for (but do not prove) terror management theory. If the research results are inconsistent with the predictions, the theory, or at least some aspects of it, might be called into question.

---

[3] Pyszczynski, T., Motyl, M., Vail III, K. E., Hirschberger, G., Arndt, J., & Kesebir, P. (2012). Drawing attention to global climate change decreases support for war. *Peace and Conflict: Journal of Peace Psychology, 18(4)*, 354–368. doi: 10.1037/a0030328

Researchers are often expected to defend their selection of a research topic. This is especially true for students who are conducting research as a class project or for a thesis or dissertation. Being able to show that the topic is related to a well-known theory is a good basis for establishing the importance of the topic. Put another way, research that contributes to theory building is generally held in higher regard than nontheoretical research. This is because theories have many applications, and research that tests theories usually has more implications than research that does not explore issues from theoretical perspectives.

Availability of Participants and Topic Selection

Ideally, research topics should be selected, narrowed, and refined first, followed by identification of appropriate individuals to serve as participants. However, in reality, certain types of participants may be unavailable or very difficult to reach, which may lead to abandoning some potential research topics in the early stages of topic selection.

Before spending much time refining a research topic, make at least preliminary inquiries as to the availability of participants for a study of the topic. The following anecdote illustrates the importance of this point: When advising a master's degree student who was planning her thesis, this writer cautioned the student that obtaining permission to test a sample for her proposed study on the prevalence of depression among high school students might be difficult or impossible. Because she was already employed as a teacher while she was earning her master's degree, she felt certain that approval would be granted by the district in which she worked. After spending a month researching various measures of depression and preparing a preliminary literature review on depression, she applied to her school district for permission to conduct the research. Unfortunately, permission was denied, forcing her to pursue a different topic for her thesis.

Thus, as a general rule, researchers should never assume that access to individuals in institutions such as schools, prisons, or hospitals will be granted, even if the research topic is important.

Ethical Considerations in Topic Selection

Ethical principles require researchers to keep research participants free from physical and psychological harm. Beginning researchers would be well advised to steer clear of any research topic that has the potential for harm.

Obviously, researchers will want to avoid topics that require the administration of potentially harmful treatments to participants. However, even in studies in which there are no treatments, the mere act of asking certain questions might cause psychological distress. For instance, asking adults about childhood sexual abuse might cause recollection of painful memories and harmful psychological crystallization, which might not have been anticipated by the researcher. Thus, as a general rule, beginning researchers should avoid sensitive topics, which are better left to seasoned researchers who have the experience and resources to plan a study with minimal harmful impact on participants.

Ethical considerations in conducting research are considered in more detail in Appendix D.

The Audience's Expectations Regarding Topics

Many researchers conduct research for a particular audience, whether it is the editorial board of a journal in which they want to be published, the instructor of a research methods class, or the members of a thesis or dissertation committee.

Consulting with instructors and members of a committee while selecting a topic is highly recommended. Typically, these individuals are experienced researchers who can help in a number of ways such as (1) suggesting specific research topics within a student's area of interest, (2) identifying barriers to conducting a satisfactory study on a given topic, and (3) helping to narrow a topic to make it more manageable while maintaining the potential to generate interesting data.

One of the biggest mistakes student researchers can make is to ignore negative feedback from instructors on their selection of tentative research topics. Even mildly negative feedback should be a cause for serious concern. As a rule, it is best to work with instructors until a topic that interests the student and the instructor, without reservations, is identified.

Personal Needs and Topic Selection

Conducting research can help meet certain personal needs, such as the desire for more information on a topic on which the researchers have strong personal involvement or feelings. There is nothing inherently wrong with this as long as the involvement and feelings do not create blind spots that will make it difficult for the researchers to examine their topics fairly and be open to data that run counter to their beliefs.

Another issue arises for beginning researchers who have a strong personal need to achieve, which may cause them to select a difficult or complex topic to study when the circumstances dictate only that the research be competently executed within a reasonable timeframe. Keep in mind that in some circumstances, such as research for a class project, a higher grade can often be obtained by competently conducting basic research with a straightforward design rather than by struggling with a complex research problem and failing to satisfactorily complete it. Consultation with instructors can help resolve this issue.

Published Research as a Source of Topics

Reports of original research are usually published as journal articles. Scanning such articles can be a highly fruitful source of ideas for research topics. While doing this, consider the following three possibilities:

One possibility is to identify a study for which you want to conduct a replication (i.e., conduct the same study again using essentially the same methods and same types of participants). Replication is especially recommended for studies that had unexpected findings, such as a study that produces results that are inconsistent with a well-known theory. By conducting a replication of such a study, a researcher can help establish whether the results are reliable (i.e., can be independently obtained again). Note that some instructors may prefer that students do more than perform an exact replication.

Another possibility is to conduct a modified replication of a published study. This might entail conducting the same study with a sample from a different population (e.g., using a sample of girls if the original study used a sample of boys), conducting the same study with other measuring tools (e.g., using direct observations of behaviors instead of a self-report checklist), and/or conducting the same study with modified treatments (e.g., giving the experimental group a modified schedule of praise rewards for appropriate behaviors).

Researchers often explicitly discuss the limitations of their research in the last section of their reports, usually under the heading "Discussion." A good possibility for a research topic is to plan a modified replication that overcomes one or more of the limitations. Consider Example 1.3, which is a statement of limitations for a study that estimated the number of violations of a university's non-smoking policy from counts of cigarette butts that were littered near seven campus buildings.

Example 1.3
Statement regarding limitations (useful for planning a modified replication)
The project had several limitations. First, it was possible that the project's team members did not pick up every cigarette butt that was littered inside of the prohibited smoking areas. For instance, leaves, brush, mulch, and other material could have covered cigarette butts from the view of the team members. Second, data from the project represent cigarette butts picked up from a sample of buildings on a college campus and do not represent total smoking policy violations for the entire campus. Third, because not all smokers litter their cigarette butts, the number of littered cigarette butts should be considered a conservative estimate of the actual number of smoking violations. Fourth, because the project was conducted at only 1 university, its results are not generalizable to other universities or colleges. (p. 333)[4]

The study could be replicated with modifications to reduce the effects of one or more of the limitations, respectively, as follows:

1. In a replication, the project's team could be given tools such as garden rakes so they could look under leaves and brush.

2. Team members could observe other types of smoking policy violations in various areas of the campus.

3. Team members could observe to determine what percentage of smokers litter their cigarette butts.

4. The study could be conducted in other universities and colleges.

Near the end of research articles in journals, researchers often briefly describe future directions for research in light of the insights they have gained from their study. When recommendations for future research are included in a research report, this material

---

[4] Seitz, C. M., Strack, R. W., Orsini, M. M., Rosario, C., Haugh, C., Rice, R., Wyrick, D. L., & Wagner, L. (2012). Quantifying littered cigarette butts to measure effectiveness of smoking bans to building perimeters. *Journal of American College Health, 60,* 331–334.

is usually included under the subheading "Discussion." Example 1.4 below shows statements regarding future research directions.

Example 1.4
Statement regarding topics for future research in a journal article
. . . This study focused exclusively on accounts of heterosexual intimate partner violence. We did not investigate the nature of same-sex interpersonal violence because it was rarely mentioned by participants. It may be that nontraditional gender and sexual identities are consistent with or differ drastically from the findings presented here regarding the frequency and nature of intimate partner violence among hip-hop youth. **Future studies** [emphasis added] should investigate the prevalence of violence among homosexual couples, typically in light of the "down-low culture," which is so closely tied to urban male youth and hip-hop culture. (p. 603)[5]

When student researchers are asked to justify their choice of a research topic, it is usually helpful to be able to say that the proposed research will be conducted in a way to overcome the limitations of previous research or to say that the proposed research was suggested in a journal article for future research.

Using Demographics to Narrow a Topic

As mentioned earlier in this chapter, demographics are background characteristics. If a topic seems too broad to be manageable, it can often be made narrower by delimiting it by using one or more demographic characteristics. In Table 1.1, the first column lists some commonly used demographic variables. Note that all variables have two or more categories. The second column in the table shows a sample category for each demographic variable. To see how to use the table, consider Example 1.5, which shows a topic that is too broad for most research purposes because physicians give many different types of directions to many different types of patients. Example 1.6 is much narrower because of the inclusion of three demographic characteristics: (1) elderly, (2) male, and (3) diabetic.

Example 1.5
A research topic that is too broad
Patients' compliance with physicians' directions.

Example 1.6
Topic in Example 1.5 made narrower by including three demographic characteristics
Compliance with physicians' directions by elderly male patients who have diabetes.

Using Demographics to Make a Topic More Complex

Sometimes, a research topic can be made more complex, and perhaps more interesting, by including one or more demographic variables. Example 1.7 shows a research top-

---

[5] Hernandez, D., Weinstein, H., & Munoz-Laboy, M. (2012). Youth perspectives on the intersections of violence, gender, and hip-hop. *Youth & Society, 44*, 587–608.

ic that has been made more complex in Example 1.8 through the introduction of the two categories on the demographic variable of gender.

Table 1.1

Sample demographic variables and categories.[6]

Sample demographic variables for delimiting topics:	Sample categories that might be used to delimit topics:
age	elderly
education, classification	gifted
education, highest level of	college graduate
education, type of	vocational
employment, length of	newly hired
employment status	employed part-time
ethnicity/race	Caucasian
extracurricular activities	competitive sports
gender	male
group membership	union member
health, mental disorder	depressed
health, overall status	poor health
health, physical disease	diabetes
hobbies	gardening
household composition	intact family with children
income, household	$20,000 to $35,000
income, personal	high income
language preference	Spanish
marital status	divorced
nationality, current	Canadian
national origin	Mexico
occupation	nurse
place of birth	Korea
political activism	votes regularly
political affiliation	Independent
relationship status	divorced
religion, affiliation	Greek Orthodox
religiosity	attends religious services often
residence, place of	New York City metropolitan area
residence, type of	homeless
sexual orientation	heterosexual
size of city/town/area	large urban area

Example 1.7

A research topic that may not be sufficiently complex

The association between time spent on the Internet and completion of homework assignments by fifth-graders.

---

[6]   Table reproduced with permission from Pyrczak Publishing from Pan (2013, p. 2).

Example 1.8
Topic in Example 1.7 made more complex by including the demographic variable of gender
A comparison of the association between time spent on the Internet and completion of homework assignments by fifth-grade boys with the association for fifth-grade girls.

Staying Open to Other Topics

Avoid the temptation to quickly settle on a research topic. The final selection should be made only after a preliminary reading of the literature on the tentative topics under consideration.

The next chapter covers how to search for literature on a topic. It is best to start with two or three topics because examining the literature on them may cause one or more to be ruled out. For instance, reading the literature might reveal that a number of studies have already been conducted on a given topic and that there is a consensus on the results among researchers. Under this circumstance, conducting yet another study on the topic might not be fruitful. Also, while reading the literature on several topics under consideration, it is not uncommon to find that one that seemed less interesting than the others actually has more interesting literature on it and/or has more important implications than anticipated, which might make it more appealing as a topic for research than the others.

Exercise for Chapter 1

Factual Questions

1. The term "empirical research" refers to making systematic observations to collect what?

2. According to this chapter, everyday observations can be a source of ideas for research topics. This is especially true when what is observed?

3. Which of the following is generally held in higher regard?
   A. Theoretical research.   B. Nontheoretical research.

4. Should the availability of participants be considered only after a research topic has been refined into research purposes/hypotheses? Explain.

5. Is it safe to assume that if a researcher does not plan to administer treatments, no ethical considerations need be applied when selecting a research topic? Explain.

6. When is deciding to replicate a published study especially recommended?

7. How can a researcher's description of limitations in a published research report assist in the selection of a research topic?

Questions for Discussion

8. Name one or two tentative topics on which you might want to conduct research.

9. Consider the six questions on pages 3–4 in relation to the topic(s) you named for Question 8. Are any of the questions especially helpful in refining and narrowing the topic? Explain.

10. Are you aware of any theories that might apply to the topic(s) you named in Question 8? Explain.

11. For the topic(s) you named in Question 8, to what extent are you confident that it will be possible to locate and get permission to use appropriate participants in the research?

12. Do you anticipate any ethical problems you might encounter when researching the topic(s) you named in Question 8? Explain.

13. Try making the topic(s) you named in Question 8 narrower by introducing a category of a demographic variable from Table 1.1 in this chapter (e.g., "only males").

14. Try to make the topic(s) you named in Question 8 more complex by introducing two or more categories on a demographic variable from Table 1.1 in this chapter (e.g., "both males and females").

Notes:

Chapter 2
Locating Literature and
Refining a Research Topic[1]

After selecting one or more tentative research topics, the next step is to locate literature on the topic(s). The literature can be useful in helping to make a selection among tentative topics and to refine the one that is selected, a process that is covered near the end of this chapter.

Because original reports of research are almost always published in professional journals, this topic focuses on locating research journal articles.

Identifying Appropriate Databases

Almost all journal articles are indexed in one or more electronic databases, which are usually accessible through college or university libraries. The first step, then, is to identify databases that are likely to have indexed research on the tentative research topics being considered.

ERIC

A major database is ERIC (www.eric.ed.gov), which stands for Education Resources Information Center. At the time of this writing, ERIC contains references to more than a million records that provide citations to journal articles, books, conference papers, and so on.

When using the term *education* in its title, ERIC defines it in its broadest sense (i.e., not as a field devoted only to classroom and curriculum issues). For instance, a sociology student interested in reviewing literature on the homeless could do a *simple search* (with no restrictions to the search) in ERIC, which, at the time of this writing, retrieved references to 2,182 documents on the homeless. Restricted to only journal articles (i.e., an *advanced search*, not a simple search), 1,133 journal articles were retrieved.[2]

Likewise, a business student using the term "advertising" would find 5,795 documents by conducting a simple search. Restricting the search to only journal articles, the search retrieved 1,613. As you can see by these examples, an ERIC search will probably be fruitful for students interested in almost any topic that deals with human behavior.

Access to the ERIC system is free to all Internet users. Its home page has information about its services, its history, and how to conduct effective searches for relevant literature.

---

[1] Much of the material in this chapter was adapted from Chapter 3 of Pan, M. L. (2013). *Preparing literature reviews*: *Qualitative and quantitative approaches* (4th ed.). Glendale, CA: Pyrczak Publishing.
[2] To restrict a search to only journal articles, click on "Advanced Search" on the home page. Then click on the box to the left of "Journal Articles."

PsycARTICLES and PsycINFO

The American Psychological Association (APA) maintains two important databases. The first is the PsycARTICLES database, which contains more than 158,000 searchable full-text articles (i.e., the complete articles, not just summaries) from 42 journals published by the Association and allied organizations. The second is the PsycINFO database, which contains abstracts (i.e., summaries only) of more than 3.2 million references to both APA and non-APA journal articles and books.

Most colleges and universities subscribe to APA's databases and make them available to students and faculty at no charge.

CSA Sociological Abstracts

Published by Cambridge Scientific Abstracts (CSA), CSA Sociological Abstracts indexes abstracts of articles published in more than 250 English-language journals. Moreover, it abstracts dissertations, books, and unpublished papers. In addition to covering sociology, this database covers related fields such as anthropology, criminology, social psychology, and urban studies.

Most colleges and universities subscribe to CSA and make this database available to students and faculty at no charge.

Social Work Abstracts

Social Work Abstracts indexes abstracts of articles in more than 460 social work and human services journals. In addition to social work, other fields covered are child and family welfare, civil rights, family welfare, drug and alcohol addiction, and various human services.

Most colleges and universities subscribe to Social Work Abstracts and make this database available to students and faculty at no charge.

Google Scholar

Google Scholar (www.scholar.Google.com) is oriented toward scholarly research. Rather than searching popular media and sources such as newspapers, magazines, and Internet blogs, Google Scholar provides a convenient means to search scholarly literature across numerous disciplines. It covers many types of resources including books, abstracts, and journal articles published by universities, professional societies, and academic publishers, among others.

One particularly useful feature offered is the "Cited by" feature, which is described below under the heading "Using a Citation Index."

Google Scholar in a basic mode is as intuitive as using the general Google search engine. It also offers more sophisticated features that are explained within its "About Google Scholar" FAQ section.

Other Databases

Other useful databases include Linguistics and Language Behavior Abstracts, GenderWatch, Medline, AgeLine, Business Source Plus, Health Source Plus, as well as

MEDLINE/PubMed. In addition, there are some highly specialized databases (not listed here) that you might be able to access through an academic library. You can identify these through library handouts and/or consultation with a reference librarian.

Using a Citation Index

As mentioned above, Google Scholar has a "Cited by" feature. Specifically, for each document (e.g., journal article, book) retrieved, Google indicates how many times the document has been cited and where it has been cited.

Information on citations can be important for two reasons. First, a document that has been cited by many other authors has probably been influential, controversial, or especially useful. Second, knowing where a document has been cited may provide leads to additional literature on that topic. For instance, suppose John Doe authored a pivotal article on a tentative research topic. By referring to a citation index, a researcher can locate articles in which Doe's article has been cited. This literature might provide alternative perspectives on Doe's article; some might critique it, others might report successful and unsuccessful attempts to replicate Doe's research, while others might provide evidence for and against Doe's theory, and so on. Obviously, there is great potential for obtaining valuable information from a citation index.

Using a Database Thesaurus

If the database has a thesaurus of keywords on which it is structured, search the thesaurus for relevant terms to use in a search. For instance, in the ERIC database,[3] the thesaurus can be accessed by clicking on the "Thesaurus" tab at the top of the home page and then selecting the "Search & Browse the Thesaurus" option in the column at the left of the page.

A thesaurus can be useful in identifying search terms known as *descriptors*, which will produce the most fruitful search. Below are specific instructions on how to conduct a search using the ERIC Thesaurus.

1. On the "Search & Browse the Thesaurus" page, enter the term "problem drinking" (in quotes) in the "Search for" box and click on "Search."

2. This will produce the underlined term Problem Drinking, which is a hyperlink.

3. Click on the hyperlink, which will produce a page indicating that "alcohol abuse" should be used for "problem drinking" (i.e., "alcohol abuse" is the preferred term) with an underlined hyperlink for the term Alcohol Abuse.

4. Click on the hyperlink, which will produce a page with useful information such as the definition of the term, broader terms (BT), narrower terms, related terms, and the date that the term was incorporated into the database.

5. On the same page, click on the box with "Start an ERIC Search" using the term Alcohol Abuse as a search criterion.

---

[3] At the time of this writing, ERIC is undergoing a major renovation. The resulting website will contain a Thesaurus of ERIC descriptors. Note, however, you may need to modify the six steps described here due to the renovation.

6. On the search page that follows, select "Show only records indicating peer review." Select "Journal Articles" under "Publication Type(s)." Click on "Search," which yields 1,719 references to journal articles. Note that ERIC stores references to all types of documents, including papers submitted by authors themselves (e.g., self-publication). Restricting a search to only peer-reviewed professional journals yields the highest-quality sources of information.

Using Boolean Operators (NOT, AND, and OR) to Refine a Search

By using the Boolean[4] logical operators (NOT, AND, and OR), a researcher can broaden or narrow a search.[5] For instance, consider the results of four searches shown in Example 2.1, which were conducted in the PsycARTICLES database. The example makes it clear that the operators NOT as well as AND reduce the number of references found while OR increases the number.

Example 2.1
Number of journal articles identified using NOT, AND, and OR

Term entered in database restricted from the year 2000 to the year this was written	Number of journal articles identified
depression	6,713
depression NOT treatment	4,966
depression AND treatment	1,747
depression OR treatment	23,120

Boolean operators can also be used to delimit a search to selected demographics. (See Table 1.1, Chapter 1.) For instance, searching only for "anxiety" in the ERIC database yields 14,672 references. Searching for "anxiety" AND "children" yields 3,549 references.

Searching for Theoretical Literature

Because the development and testing of theories is a major activity in the social and behavioral sciences, it is desirable to discuss relevant theories in literature reviews on most topics. Theoretical literature can be located searching for a topic term and the term "theory" with AND as a Boolean operator. For instance, for the topic term "aging," at this writing, PsycARTICLES yields 3,501 references. Searching for "aging" AND "theory" yields 242 references, which are the ones most likely to contain a discussion of theories that relate to aging.

---

[4] The term "Boolean" is based on the name of the British mathematician, George Boole, who developed Boolean logic.
[5] To access the Boolean operators in ERIC, first click on "Advanced Search" on the home page. In APA databases, first click on "Fielded Search."

Entering the name of a theory as a search term will usually yield references on that particular theory. For instance, at this writing, a PsycARTICLES search using the term "social learning theory" yields 653 references for all years to present.

Searching in Only the Title and/or Abstract Fields

The information in databases is divided into fields, such as the author field, which allows a user to search for articles written by a particular author. Two especially helpful fields are the title (the title of the work) and the abstract (a summary of the work) fields. For instance, consider a topic that contains the word "discipline." Without any restrictions, a search of PsycARTICLES yields 1,246 articles that contain the word in one or more fields, including the body of the article where discipline might be mentioned only in passing.[6] However, if at its core an article focuses on "discipline," the keyword is very likely to be used in the title and/or abstract (i.e., summary). Searching for "discipline" in just the titles of articles retrieved 113 articles (a much more manageable number than the original 1,246). Requiring that the articles have the word "discipline" in *both* the title AND the abstract is more stringent and retrieved only 79 articles, which are probably highly relevant because the author chose to use the term "discipline" in both of these important fields.

Searching for the Works of a Particular Author

Many prolific researchers conduct research on a selected topic over a period of decades. Often, the insights on a topic gained from one study lead to the development of new hypotheses on the same topic that the same researcher investigates in subsequent studies. To locate the literature authored by such a researcher (and trace the history of that author's work on the topic), restrict a search to the author field (i.e., from the drop-down menu in the advanced search mode of ERIC, select "Author" and type in the author's name). For instance, Albert Bandura has conducted research on self-efficacy for many years. By selecting the "Author" field from the drop-down menu in ERIC and typing in "Bandura," coupled with "self-efficacy" using AND as a Boolean operator, eight journal articles that Bandura authored or coauthored on self-efficacy from 1977 through 2012 are identified.

Locating Statistics at www.FedStats.gov

At www.FedStats.gov, you can access statistics from more than 100 federal agencies.[7] Prior to establishment of this website, researchers needed to search for statistics agency-by-agency. While the FedStats site still allows researchers to do this, they can also search by *topic*, and the FedStats search engine will automatically search all agencies for relevant links to federal statistics. This is important for two reasons: (1) you do not

---

[6] By using the dropdown menu in PsycARTICLES, you can restrict the search to just selected fields such as titles, abstracts, authors, and language.

[7] Be sure to go to www.FedStats.*gov* and *not* www.FedStats.*com*. The latter is *not* a government site.

have to search each agency separately and (2) an agency that you are not aware of may have statistics relevant to a research topic.

Citing specific, relevant statistics when writing a literature review, which is covered in the next chapter, makes it more authoritative and informative. Consider, for instance, the sample statements in Example 2.2 (for a research topic related to the Head Start program) and Example 2.3 (for a research topic related to victimization of juveniles). They illustrate the usefulness of searching for statistics while searching for literature.

Example 2.2

A statement in a literature review without specific statistics (weak)

Most enrollees in Head Start are 3 or 4 years old.

A statement in a literature review with specific statistics found on FedStats (stronger)

Most enrollees in Head Start are 3 or 4 years old, with 34% being 3 and 53% being 4.

Example 2.3

A statement in a literature review without specific statistics (weak)

A number of juveniles age 12 through 17 are victims of simple assault.

A statement in a literature review with specific statistics found on FedStats (stronger)

Approximately 65 out of every 1,000 juveniles age 12 through 17 are victims of simple assault.

Keeping a Record of How the Search Was Conducted

Suppose a reviewer reaches the conclusion that "few experimental studies have been published on the XYZ phenomenon" and includes the conclusion in a literature review. Such a statement might be challenged by a professor who is familiar with relevant experimental studies that the reviewer failed to locate. By being able to state specifically which databases were searched and how they were searched, the reviewer can deflect criticism that he or she was careless in conducting the search. Example 2.4 shows a careful description of how a literature search was conducted.

Example 2.4

Careful description of how a search was conducted

We conducted a computerized literature search of PsycINFO using the terms *pride*, *proud*, *embarrass*, *shame*, and *guilt* (search terms combined with *or*). We did not include the term *gender* because it would have biased the search toward studies that reported significant gender differences. The search was restricted to empirical studies with human samples, published in English through 2010. The search resulted in 22,665 abstracts. (p. 951)[8]

---

[8] Else-Quest, N. M., Higgins, A., Allison, C., & Morton, L. C. (2012). Gender differences in self-conscious emotional experience: A meta-analysis. *Psychological Bulletin*, *138*, 947–981.

Using a Coding System When Reading Literature

An effective way to code is to use different colored highlighters. At a minimum, one color should be used for anything that is especially interesting or surprising, another for discussions of relevant theories, another for definitions of key terms, and yet another for suggestions for future research.

Considering Literature When Selecting and Refining Topics

Having located and considered the literature on several tentative topics, a researcher should be in a good position to make a selection among the topics. There are many ways in which the literature can assist in topic selection. For instance, the results reported in the literature on one topic might be more interesting than those on the others, one topic might be less researched than the others, one topic might have more practical implications than the others, and so on.

Once one research topic has been selected over the others in a tentative list, consider how the literature might be used to refine the topic. Consider, for instance, what demographics (such as age) have been taken into account in previous research. If the literature reveals that the topic has been studied only with college-age participants, the research topic could be modified to refer to some other age group.

Also, as noted in Chapter 1, consider previous researchers' descriptions of their limitations and their suggestions for future research. These can often help in identifying how a topic can be refined or modified to make it more likely to contribute to the understanding of a topic.

Exercise for Chapter 2

Factual Questions

1. "A limitation of the Education Resources Information Center's (i.e., ERIC's) database is that it only indexes literature on classroom and curriculum issues." Is this preceding statement true *or* false?
   A. True.   B. False.

2. A citation index allows researchers to search for what?

3. Broader terms (BT) can be found in the *ERIC Thesaurus*. This chapter mentions what other two types of terms that can be found there?

4. When searching a database for literature using two terms, use of which one of the following Boolean operators will identify the largest number of journal articles?
   A. NOT   B. AND   C. OR

5. Why might a researcher want to search for articles by restricting the search to only the title and/or abstract fields when using a database such as PsycARTICLES?

6. What is the name of the website that allows a researcher to access statistics from more than 100 federal agencies?

Questions for Discussion

Note: The following questions assume that you have already consulted at least one database to locate literature on one of your possible topics.

7. Name a database that you have consulted.

8. Did you consult a thesaurus for the database you named in your response to Question 7? If so, was it helpful? Explain.

9. Did you conduct a search using the word "theory" as one of the keywords? If yes, did the search locate any articles with theoretical perspectives on your topic? Explain.

10. Did you try conducting a search by restricting it to only the title and/or abstract fields? If yes, was this helpful? Explain.

11. Did you consult a citation index? Did it help you locate useful literature? Explain.

12. Did you search www.FedStats.gov for statistics relevant to your topic? Did you find any? Explain.

13. When conducting a preliminary reading of the literature, did you color-code? If yes, what colors did you use for each type of material coded? Explain.

14. Has a preliminary reading of the literature you found helped you in selecting among your tentative topics? Has it helped you in refining a topic? Explain.

Chapter 3
Preparing a Literature Review

After carefully examining the literature on the topic, the researcher's next step is to prepare a literature review that will become part of the research proposal. For a class project, a literature review might be brief and highly selective, while one for a thesis or dissertation usually would be much more comprehensive.

The literature review is an important part of a research proposal because the review helps to establish the need for the proposed study.[1] The review is also a major component in a report of completed research because it establishes the context in which the study was conducted.

Because it is assumed that research articles will be the main sources in a literature review, the term *articles* is used throughout this chapter to refer to sources. Note, however, that the suggestions in this chapter apply equally to books, material obtained from the web, papers presented at professional conferences, and so on.

Preparing a Table That Shows the Key Features of Each Article

If there are several articles on a topic, it is easy to get lost in the details of individual articles and fail to see important overall trends and outcomes. Preparing a table showing the key features of each article can help avoid this problem.

The first step in preparing the table is to give each article a unique identifier. A good identifier is the last name of the author and the year of publication. These should be listed in the first column of the table. The contents of the remaining columns may vary substantially, depending on the literature to be reviewed. Some important ones to consider are (1) type of sample, (2) number of participants in the sample, (3) measurement approach, (4) overall results, and (5) notable features. Table 3.1 shows such a table.

Examination of Table 3.1 reveals certain trends that the researcher will want to note in the literature review. For instance, (1) all studies except for Lynch (2013) found a relationship between X and Y, (2) the relationship between X and Y was strongest in the studies with college students, and (3) only one study took gender into account, which indicated a relationship for women but not men, and so on.

Inspection of such a table can also aid in the further refinement of the research topic. For instance, Solis (2013) found a weak relationship between X and Y among women but found no relationship among men. This set of findings suggests that it might be fruitful to include gender as an additional variable in the research topic, so if the research topic was "the relationship X and Y among children," the topic might become "a comparison of the relationship between X and Y for girls with the relationship between X and Y for boys."

---

[1] For class projects that will be conducted within short time frames, proposals might be informal and contain only a brief, preliminary review of literature. Writing a preliminary research proposal is covered in Chapter 11.

Table 3.1
Table that Summarizes Key Features of the Literature on a Topic

Identifier	Type of sample	Number of participants	Measurement approach	Overall results[1]	Notable features
Doe (2012)	College students	94	Questionnaire	X strongly related to Y	None
Jones (2013)	Adults	51	Questionnaire	X moderately related to Y	National sample
Black (2010)	College students	34	Questionnaire	X strongly related to Y	Based on attribution theory
Smith (2011)	Adults	16	Questionnaire	X weakly related to Y	None
Solis (2013)	Adults	42	Questionnaire	X weakly related to Y among women; no relationship for men	Examined gender as a moderator variable
Brooks (2013)	College students	523	Questionnaire	X strongly related to Y	None
Lynch (2013)	Adults	36	Questionnaire	No relationship between X and Y	None
Brice (2013)	College students	59	Direct observation of behavior	X moderately related to Y	Participants aware they were being observed
Henry (2012)	College students	56	Questionnaire	X strongly related to Y	Based on social learning theory
Billings (2013)	Adults	39	Questionnaire	X moderately related to Y	None
McGannon (2013)	College students	55	Questionnaire	X strongly related to Y among freshmen; weakly related among seniors	Examined class level as a moderator variable
Bruce (2012)	College students	22	Interviews	X moderately related to Y	None
Lu (2012)	College students	31	Questionnaire	X strongly related to Y among high achievers; weakly related among low achievers	Examined achievement level as a moderator variable

[1]Specific statistics may be recorded in this column. Because statistical methods are not discussed until later in this book, this example shows only general statements regarding the statistical results.

A table such as Table 3.1 will sometimes reveal weaknesses that a researcher might want to avoid in his or her research. For instance, in the table, the only study with a large sample (Brooks, 2013) had college students as participants. Thus, conducting a study with a large sample of adults might make a unique contribution. Second, all but two studies employed questionnaires, and all studies of adults in particular, employed questionnaires. Hence, a study in which some other method of collecting information from adults (such as interviews) might contribute to a better understanding of the topic.

Writing an Essay About the Literature

A literature review should be an essay that synthesizes information about a topic. The first step in writing such an essay is to prepare a topic outline. In it, include the articles' identifiers (such as authors' last names and years of publication) at appropriate points. Note that a particular article might be cited at various points in the outline and that more than one article might be cited to support a particular point. Example 3.1 shows a brief outline that illustrates these principles. For instance, Doe (2012) is cited at three different points in the outline, including Point III B, in which six other studies are cited.

Example 3.1
Partial topic outline for a literature review
I. Importance of X and Y established by citing statistics on the number of individuals affected by X and the number affected by Y
II. Definitions of X and Y
    A. Early definitions (Oliver, 2011) (Hastings, 2012)
    B. Criticisms of early definitions (Doe, 2012)
    C. Contemporary definitions (Doe, 2012) (Black, 2010)
III. Studies of college students
    A. Strong relationship in the study with largest number of participants (Brooks, 2013)
    B. Results of other studies vary from weakly related to strongly related (Doe, 2012) (Black, 2010) (Brice, 2013) (Henry, 2012) (McGannon, 2013) (Bruce, 2012) (Lu, 2013)
    C. Moderator variables: achievement level (Lu, 2012), gender (Solis, 2012), and class level (McGannon, 2013)
IV. Studies of adults
And so on.

As demonstrated, following a topic outline when writing a literature review will help prevent the common mistake of writing a string of summaries of one study after another.

Naming a Specific Topic Near the Beginning of a Review

Example 3.2 shows the beginning of a literature review on the possible association between attendance in Head Start and nutrition. The authors of the example did not start their review with statements about the nature of poverty and the federal government's attempts to reduce the incidence of poverty with educational programs. Such a beginning would be too broad for introducing a specific aspect of Head Start.

Example 3.2
Beginning of a literature review that introduces the specific research topic (nutritional outcomes of Head Start)

Head Start has served children from birth to age 5, providing a comprehensive program for low-income children including health services. As a comprehensive preschool program, nutrition is a major part of Head Start's mission and objectives. According to Head Start program performance standards, there are a number of mandates each Head Start program must follow to ensure proper nutrition. The purpose of the current study is to examine whether the enrollment duration of Head Start is associated with children's nutritional outcomes. (p. 73)[2]

Using Statistics to Establish the Importance of the Topic
Near the Beginning of a Review

Researchers frequently cite statistics that indicate the importance of a problem. The authors of Example 3.3 did this at the beginning of their literature review for their article on how children navigate intersections with continuous cross traffic.

Example 3.3
Beginning of a literature review that incorporates statistics to establish the importance of a specific research topic

Misjudging whether it is safe to proceed across a busy intersection can carry significant negative consequences, particularly for pedestrians and bicyclists. Motor vehicles are involved in **approximately one third of all bicycle-related brain injuries and in 90% of all fatalities** [emphasis added] resulting from bicycle crashes (Rivara & Aitken, 1998; Acton et al., 1995). Many of these collisions occur at intersections (Ashbaugh, Macknin, & VanderBrug Medendorp, 1995; Wachtel & Lewiston, 1994). Children and adolescents between the ages of 5 and 15 are overrepresented in the bicycle crash data, having the highest rate of injury per million cycling trips (Rivara & Aitken, 1998). Past research on children's road-crossing behavior has shown that. . . . (p. 23)[3]

Providing Conceptual Definitions Near the Beginning of a Review

Providing conceptual definitions is especially important when related concepts might be confused with the topic of the research. In Example 3.4, for instance, *premature discontinuation in therapy* is defined at the beginning of the example. The definition of a related concept *rejecting therapy* is given at the end of the example. Without these defini-

---

[2] Lee, A. & O' Laoire, S. O. (2013). Head Start impact on children's obesity: Moderation effects of family risk factors. *Research on Social Work Practice, 23*, 73–80. doi: 10.1177/1049731512459965
[3] Grechkin, T. Y., Chihak, B. J., Cremer, J. F., Kearney, J. K., & Plumert, J. M. (2013). Perceiving and acting on complex affordances: How children and adults bicycle across two lanes of opposing traffic. *Journal of Experimental Psychology: Human Perception and Performance, 39*(1), 23–36. doi:10.1037/a0029716

tions, the two terms might be mistakenly taken to mean the same thing.

Example 3.4

Definitions provided near the beginning of a literature review

Premature discontinuation in therapy can be defined as occurring when a client starts an intervention but discontinues prior to recovering from the problems (symptoms, functional impairment, distress, etc.) that led him or her to seek treatment (Garfield, 1994; Hatchett & Park, 2003; Swift et al., 2009). Implicit in this definition is the idea that the client has stopped the intervention without meeting the therapeutic goals or without gaining the full benefits that would have been available if the client had continued to attend and been fully invested in the sessions. Also implicit is the idea that the client has discontinued therapy prior to completing the full course of the intervention. Premature discontinuation occurs unilaterally by the client, rather than through a mutual agreement between the therapist and client to end treatment. Dropping out of therapy can be contrasted to both completing and rejecting therapy (Garfield, 1994). While dropping out implies that therapy has been started and then discontinued early, completing therapy implies a resolution of the activity, and rejecting therapy occurs when a client fails to start or show up for the initial therapy appointment. (p. 547–548)[4]

Providing a Brief History of the Topic Near the Beginning of a Review

Providing a brief history of the research on a topic can help set the stage for the study that is being proposed. Example 3.5 illustrates how this can be done briefly.

Example 3.5

Brief history of a topic presented near the beginning of a literature review

The first study to test mobile (cell) phones was carried out in one hospital and focused on the identification of multidrug-resistant . . . [bacterial] contamination of the devices (Borer et al., 2005). Interest in the inflation risks associated with telephony grows significantly from 2006 as mobile phone use became widespread. There was a similar increase in the number of studies undertaken in clinical settings, despite prohibitions on use due to concerns about interference with hospital equipment (Klein & Djaiani, 2003). This restriction was finally relaxed in the UK in 2009 (Department of Health, 2009). (p. 583)[5]

Writing a Critical Literature Review

In an uncritical review, all studies are treated as though they are equal in quality. This does a disservice to the readers, especially when there are contradictions in the literature. For instance, the original statement in Example 3.6 gives equal weight to both

---

[4] Swift, J. K. & Greenberg R. P. (2012). Premature discontinuation in adult psychotherapy: A Meta-analysis. *Journal of Consulting and Clinical Psychology, 80*(4), 547–559. doi: 10.1037/a0028226547

[5] White, S., Topping, A., Humphreys, P., Rout, S., & Williamson, H. (2012) The cross-contamination potential of mobile telephones. *Journal of Research in Nursing, 17,* 582–595. doi: 10.1177/1744987112458670

studies. In the improved statements, the fact that one study had a much larger sample (and presumably had more reliable results) is made clear by the writer.

Example 3.6
Original statement, giving equal weight to both studies
Doe (2013) reported a strong relationship between A and B among undergraduates, while Smith (2011) reported a weak relationship among graduate students.

Improved statement (critical)
In the study with the largest number of participants ($n = 679$), Doe (2013) found a strong relationship between A and B among undergraduates. In contrast, a study with only 16 graduate students found a weak relationship (Smith, 2011).

It is not necessary to indicate the quality of every study cited. However, in the absence of such indications, readers are likely to assume that the studies cited are of reasonable quality. Thus, it is important to provide information that indicates that a weak study is being cited. For instance, suppose a college professor named Sanchez provided immediate feedback on weekly quizzes to the 15 students in one of her classes and provided delayed feedback to another class of 15 students. Such a study could hardly be called definitive because of the small sample size and the lack of a randomized control group. Nevertheless, it was published as a pilot study. Note that in the original statement in Example 3.7, there is no hint that the study was a seriously flawed pilot study. The improved critical statements warn readers to be cautious.

Example 3.7
Original statement, failing to point out weaknesses in a study being cited
In one study, college students who received immediate feedback on weekly quizzes achieved significantly more and reported significantly greater satisfaction with the instructional process than students who received delayed feedback (Sanchez, 2012).

Sample improved critical statement (number of participants noted)
In a study of **30 college students** [emphasis added], the 15 students who received immediate feedback on weekly quizzes achieved significantly more and reported significantly greater satisfaction with the instructional process than the 15 who received delayed feedback (Sanchez, 2012).

Sample improved critical statement (number of participants noted and mention of "pilot study")
In a **pilot study using 30 college students** [emphasis added], the students who received immediate feedback on weekly quizzes achieved significantly more and reported significantly greater satisfaction with the instructional process than students who received delayed feedback (Sanchez, 2012).

Sample improved critical statement (number of participants noted, preliminary nature of study indicated, and a design flaw noted)
In a **preliminary experiment using 30 college students** [emphasis added], the students who received immediate feedback on weekly quizzes achieved significantly

more and reported significantly greater satisfaction with the instructional process than students who received delayed feedback (Sanchez, 2012). **Although Sanchez's experiment was flawed by the failure to assign students to treatment conditions at random** [emphasis added], it is suggestive and supports the theory that....

How much emphasis to put on the flaws of the individual studies that are cited is a subjective decision. However, some indicators should be provided to warn readers when a study is seriously flawed by a weak sample or by serious design flaws.

Sometimes, it is sufficient (and more efficient) to critique groups of studies that have common flaws. This is illustrated in Example 3.8.

Example 3.8
Critical statement regarding a group of studies (recommended)

Although all five studies just cited strongly suggest that immediate feedback is superior to delayed feedback on achievement variables, as well as students' satisfaction with the instructional process, it is important to note that all the studies were conducted with college students. This limits the generalizability of the results to other types of students. In addition, all the researchers used small samples of intact groups, failing to randomly assign students to the immediate and delayed feedback conditions. Thus, caution must be exercised in interpreting the results until more definitive studies are conducted.

An alternative (or supplement) to describing specific methodological weaknesses in studies is to use statements that indicate the degree of confidence that should be placed in them. This possibility is discussed under the next topic.

Indicating the Level of Confidence in a Research Finding

Because no measure is perfectly valid and reliable and because "perfect" samples of participants are rarely available, all empirical research may safely be assumed to be subject to error. As a result, when writing about the research findings of others, it is important to use wording that does not imply that the research has revealed some universal fact or truth. Instead, wording should be used to indicate the level of confidence that the writer has in the results. In Example 3.9, the author expresses a high level of confidence.

Example 3.9
Statement indicating a high level of confidence

Given the care with which the survey was conducted and the large, representative sample, Doe's conclusion is in all likelihood correct (2012, p. 115).

When citing the results of studies in which a high degree of confidence is warranted, consider using terms such as "overwhelming evidence," "strong evidence," "results of a definitive study," "seldom disputed," and "seems very likely that."

When citing the results of studies in which only a low degree of confidence is warranted, consider using terms such as "preliminary findings suggest," "based on a pilot study," "weak evidence hints at," "it appears that," and "suggests the possibility that."

It is not always necessary to use terms to indicate the degree of confidence. However, when the degree is not indicated, readers are likely to assume that the evidence is reasonably strong.

Pointing Out Consistent Findings in the Literature

For instance, in Example 3.10, the writers state that a finding has "a great deal of support," implying that they have much confidence in it. On the other hand, mentioning a tendency (as in *tend to* in the example below) implies less confidence in the finding as well as implying that it is not universal (i.e., does not occur in all cases).

Example 3.10
Results of previous studies yield

Furthermore, **it is commonly found** [emphasis added] that adolescents report higher levels of family conflict and lower levels of intimacy than parents (Noller, Seth-Smith, Bouma, & Schweitzer, 1992), that they are generally less satisfied with the family, and believe the family to be more conflictual and less cohesive compared with their parents (Noller et al., 1992; Oaikoff, Carlton-Ford, & Brooks-Gunn, 1993; Smetana, 1989) (p. 858).[6]

Pointing Out Gaps in the Literature

A literature review should point out not only what has been studied and what the findings are, but also note important gaps in what is known about a topic. It is especially important to point out gaps if the research proposal is designed to help fill in some of them. For instance, the authors of Example 3.11 point out a gap that their study was designed to fill.

Example 3.11
Statement pointing out an important gap in the literature regarding Asian Americans

We explore the quality and availability of support, secret fantasies of victims, and intergenerational impact on these diverse individuals, many of whom are of Asian descent. The current study **fills a gap in the literature** [emphasis added] by bringing forth the voices of Asian Americans, one of the fastest growing racial minority groups in the nation and yet one that continues to be stereotyped as a model minority who escapes racial aggression. Synthesizing the powerful stories of all of our participants, we offer an empowering message about what we can do to provide support, mitigate the adverse impact of racism, and help foster resiliency.[7] (Lowe, Susana Ming; Okubo, Yuki; Reilly, Michael F., p. 190)

---

[6] McDaniel, B. T., & Teti, D. M. (2012). The influence of discrepancies between adolescent and parent ratings of family dynamics on the well-being of adolescents. *Journal of Family Psychology, 26,* 858–868.

[7] Lowe, S. M., Okubo, Y., Reilly, M. F. (2012). A qualitative inquiry into racism, trauma, and coping: Implications for supporting victims of racism. *Professional Psychology: Research and Practice, 43*(3). 190–198. doi: 10.1037/a0026501

Using Subheadings in a Long Review

Using subheadings helps readers follow the transitions from one subtopic to another within a review. Usually, the major subheadings in the topic outline for the review (such as those identified by Roman numerals in Example 3.1 near the beginning of this chapter) will be effective subheadings. See the sample literature reviews near the end of this book for additional examples of the use of subheadings in the literature reviews.

Describing Relevant Theories

The desirability of selecting a topic with theoretical underpinnings was discussed in Chapter 1. If you have selected such a topic, be sure to discuss the theory and its relationship to the topic in enough detail that a reader with no knowledge of the theory will be able to understand its relevance to the research that will follow. Also, discuss relevant research that lends support to (or contradicts) the theory.

Noting the Relationship Between the Review and the Research Questions, Purposes, or Hypotheses

Having read the literature review, a reader should see the logical connection between what is known about the topic and the research questions, purposes, or hypotheses underlying the research that will be conducted. Consequently, research questions, purposes, or hypotheses are usually stated near the end of a literature review. Chapter 5 covers how to write these elements.

Using the Sample Literature Reviews at the End of This Book

The best way to learn how to write effective literature reviews is to read a number of high-quality reviews while paying attention to the techniques used by the writers to summarize and synthesize the literature they are citing. Four sample literature reviews are presented near the end of this book. For instructional purposes, only brief reviews are included.

The first three sample literature reviews are literature reviews that appear at the beginning of original research articles. The purpose of such reviews is to (1) introduce the topic of the research, (2) establish the importance of the topic, (3) provide an overview of what is known about the topic and its relationship to theories, if any, and (4) establish the need for the research study that follows the review.

The fourth literature review is a *stand-alone* review. It is not designed to introduce a new research report. Rather, it is a status report on the literature on a certain topic.

In the *Questions for Discussion*, you are asked to describe your reactions to the sample reviews. When commenting on them, keep in mind that all are from journal articles, in which relatively short reviews are typical. For a thesis, dissertation, or class project, your instructor may ask you to write a longer and more detailed review for instructional purposes.

Exercise for Chapter 3

Factual Questions

1. According to this chapter, preparing a table showing the key features of each article helps to overcome what problem?

2. What is the first step in writing an essay that synthesizes what studies report about a topic?

3. Suppose someone was writing a review on physical barriers faced in elementary schools by students with impaired vision. According to this chapter, which of the following would be a good approach for beginning the written literature review? Explain your answer.

   A. Write several paragraphs about the importance of education to all students in terms of self-development as well as finding employment. Then, point out the importance of education to society as a whole. Third, note that failure to accommodate students with physical and mental disabilities harms not only the students but also members of society at large.

   B. Begin by citing government estimates of the number of elementary school students who have impaired vision. Describe the types of physical barriers such students often face in schools, as well as recent attempts to remove or mitigate the effects of these barriers. Also, cite laws that relate to the removal of physical barriers for students with impaired vision and the effectiveness of these laws.

4. In an uncritical literature review, all studies are treated as though they are what?

5. Name several phrases that might be used when citing the results of studies in which you have a high degree of confidence.

Questions for Discussion

6. Have you prepared a table that shows the key features of each article? If yes, how effective was it in helping you get an overview of the available literature?

7. Have you prepared a topic outline as the basis for your literature review? If yes, bring it to class for discussion.

8. Answer the following questions for Sample Literature Review 1 ("Associations Between Marital Happiness, Problems, and Health"), which appears near the end of this book.

   A. What are the strengths of the review?

   B. In your opinion, are there any weaknesses? Explain.

C. In your opinion, did the review lead logically to the research hypotheses stated near the end of the review? Explain.

D. Did you notice any particular techniques that you might use in your literature review? Explain.

9. Answer the following questions for Sample Literature Review 2 ("Effects of Random Student Drug Testing in High Schools"), which appears near the end of this book.

A. What are the strengths of the review?

B. In your opinion, are there any weaknesses? Explain.

C. In your opinion, did the review lead logically to the research hypotheses stated near the end of the review? Explain.

D. Did you notice any particular techniques that you might use in your literature review? Explain.

10. Answer the following questions for Sample Literature Review 3 ("College Students' Perceptions of Their Grandparents and Communication Technology Use"), which appears near the end of this book.

A. What are the strengths of the review?

B. In your opinion, are there any weaknesses? Explain.

C. In your opinion, did the review lead logically to the research questions stated near the end of the review? Explain.

D. Did you notice any particular techniques that you might use in your literature review? Explain.

11. Answer the following questions for Sample Literature Review 4 ("A Review of Interventions for Substance Use Among Homeless Youth"), which appears near the end of this book.

A. What are the strengths of the review?

B. In your opinion, are there any weaknesses? Explain.

C. In your opinion, did the review lead logically to the research questions stated near the end of the review? Explain.

D. Did you notice any particular techniques that you might use in your literature review? Explain.

Notes:

Chapter 4
Citing References in APA and ASA Styles

Citations identify the sources of ideas and quotations used by a writer. Typically, a citation consists of two parts. The first part is a symbol, such as an asterisk, letter of the alphabet, word, number, or combination of these elements, that is used to mark the part of the text for which a source is being referenced in a footnote. The second part is a full bibliographic reference that identifies the source.

This chapter describes the basic styles (i.e., formats) for citing sources recommended in the *Publication Manual of the American Psychological Association* and in the American Sociological Association's *ASA Style Guide*.[1] These two publications are referred to in this chapter as the *APA Manual*, which describes APA style, and the *ASA Guide*, which describes ASA style.

In-Text Citations

The first part of a citation, which is embedded in the text, is called an *in-text citation*. In Example 4.1, the in-text citation is (Doe, 2013), which is in APA style. In ASA style, the in-text citation would also be in parentheses but not include a comma: (Doe 2013).

In both styles, the second part of the citation is the full bibliographic reference in an alphabetical list at the end of the manuscript. The basics of reference list preparation are described later in this chapter.

In-Text Citations in APA Style (For ASA Style, see pages 37–41.)

APA style uses a version of the "author–date" method for in-text citations. This method can be parenthetical or non-parenthetical, as described in the following examples. For each in-text citation, there will be a full bibliographic reference in the reference lists at the end of the manuscript.

Parenthetical In-Text Citations in APA Style

An in-text citation can be made parenthetical by putting the author's last name and the source's year of publication in parentheses, as illustrated in Example 4.1.

Example 4.1
APA style parenthetical in-text citation, ONE author
New data suggest that the influence of the mass media on social norms and customs is growing rapidly (Doe, 2013).

---

[1] This chapter describes some of the basics of each of the two for comparison. Students should refer to the *APA Manual* and the *ASA Guide* for details on how to cite sources and prepare reference lists. The *ASA Guide* is based primarily on *The Chicago Manual of Style*, published by the University of Chicago Press.

Example 4.2 illustrates APA style for a parenthetical in-text citation for a source with two authors. Note the use of the ampersand (&) between the last names of the two authors. In ASA style, the word *and* would be used instead of an ampersand, which illustrates the importance of paying attention to details when using a style guide.

Example 4.2
APA style parenthetical in-text citation, TWO authors
The influence of peer group pressure on bullying behavior by girls needs more investigation (Edwards & Jones, 2012).

If a source with one or two authors is cited more than once in a given manuscript, it should be cited the same way each time. However, when there are three to five authors of a given source, all names are used the first time the source is cited. Then, in subsequent citations, only the first author's last name followed by *et al.* is used, as illustrated in Example 4.3.

Example 4.3
APA style parenthetical in-text citation, THREE TO FIVE authors
First time the source is cited: More research is needed on the origins of gender-role socialization (Washington, Yu, & Galvan, 2013).

Second and all subsequent times the source is cited: More research is needed on the origins of gender-role socialization (Washington et al., 2013).

When a source being cited has six or more authors, use *et al.* the first and all subsequent times, as illustrated in Example 4.4.

Example 4.4
APA style parenthetical in-text citation, SIX OR MORE authors
First and all subsequent times the source is cited: Experiments on the effects of teachers' expectations on achievement have produced mixed results (Adams et al., 2012).

Often, two or more sources are in substantial agreement. For instance, there might be three sources with data indicating that the XYZ Program is strongly supported by most parents. These three sources may be cited within a single set of parentheses, as illustrated in Example 4.5. Note that semicolons are used to separate sources and that the sources are listed in alphabetical order.

Example 4.5
APA style parenthetical in-text citation, TWO OR MORE sources
In three recent surveys, a majority of parents expressed strong support for the XYZ Program (Black, 2012; Brown et al., 2011; White & Bright, 2010).

When the source is a group, such as a professional organization, government agency, corporation, or similar entity, cite its authorship using the whole name of the group, as shown in Example 4.6.[2]

Example 4.6
APA style parenthetical in-text citation, WHEN A GROUP IS A SOURCE
The origins of the Modified Exchange Program have been traced as far back as the 1920s (Association for Hypothetical Studies, 2010).

When an author wants to call attention to a specific passage within a source and quotes directly from a source, the author should include the page number(s) in the in-text citation, as illustrated in Example 4.7 where *pp.* is the abbreviation for *pages*. If only one page is concerned, use *p.* as the abbreviation.

Example 4.7
APA style parenthetical in-text citation, PAGE NUMBERS INDICATED
The strong correlation between the two variables was previously reported (Lincoln & White, 2012, pp. 6–9).

Non-Parenthetical In-Text Citations in APA Style

An in-text citation can be non-parenthetical, as illustrated in Example 4.8. In this example, the author's last name is the subject of the sentence, while the year of publication remains parenthetical as recommended by APA. Note the use of the word *and* instead of an ampersand (&). In APA style, an ampersand is used in parenthetical in-text citations, while *and* is used in non-parenthetical in-text citations.

Example 4.8
APA style non-parenthetical in-text citation
In a newly published book, Bush and Clinton (2013) stress the importance of reducing tensions among nations in the Middle East.

In-text citations are best used when a writer wants to emphasize the authorship of the source material. For instance, the writer of Example 4.8 might want to emphasize that the statement is based on the opinions of two former presidents by making them the subject of the sentence.

Reference Lists in APA Style

For each in-text citation there should be a full bibliographic reference in the reference list at the end of the manuscript. Example 4.9 shows how references are formatted in APA style for some common types of source materials. For other types of materials, consult the *APA Manual.*

Pay close attention to the punctuation throughout each reference. For instance, a missing period after the word "adolescence" in the first reference in Example 4.9 would be a flaw that might cost a student points if APA style is required.

---

[2] Under certain circumstances, the group's name may be abbreviated in the second and subsequent citations in the same manuscript. Consult the *APA Manual* for details.

Example 4.9

*Reference list in APA style for selected types of **printed sources***

Type of material	Reference
Journal article, one author:	Buhs, E. S. (2013). Review of friendships in childhood adolescence. *Journal of Applied Developmental Psychology, 34,* 119–121. doi: 10.1016/j.appdev. 2012.11.001

Comments:

In APA style, the capitalization rules for titles of articles are basically the same as the standard capitalization rules for sentences, including capitalization of the first word.

Note that "*34*" is the volume number. There is usually one volume per year, with four to 12 issues per volume. Page numbering throughout a volume is almost always continuous. However, in the rare case in which each issue begins on page 1, APA style requires the placement of the issue number in parentheses immediately after the volume number.

The page numbers are placed immediately after the volume number.

DOIs are identification numbers. Originally developed to identify documents on the Internet, they are now being widely used to identify journal articles in print. If a journal article has a DOI, it should be included in the reference in APA style. In the reference, use a lowercase "doi."

Type of material	Reference
Journal article, two authors:	Bettencourt, A. F., & Farrell, A. D. (2013). Individual and contextual factors associated with patterns of aggression and peer victimization during middle school. *Journal of Youth and Adolescence, 42,* 285–302. doi: 10.1007/s10964-012-9854-8285-302.

Comments:

Use the same method for journal articles with three to six authors. In APA style, the names of the authors are joined by an ampersand (&) and not joined by the word *and*.

Type of material	Reference
Journal article, seven or more authors:	Rhodes, S. D., Martinez, O., Song, E., Daniel, J., Alonzo, J., Eng, E., . . . Reboussin, B. (2013). Depressive symptoms among immigrant Latino sexual minorities. *American Journal of Health Behavior, 37,* 404–413. doi: 10.5993/AJHB.37.3.13

Comments:

When there are seven or more authors, include the first six followed by "…" and then followed by the name of the last author.

Type of material	Reference
Entire book, print version:	James, W. (1890). *The Principles of Psychology, Vol.1.* New York, NY: Cosimo, Inc.
Book chapter, print version:	James, W. (1890). The scope of psychology. *The Principles of Psychology, Vol.1.* New York, NY: Cosimo, Inc.

Example 4.10

*Sample reference list in APA style for selected types of **electronic sources***

Type of material	Reference
Online-only journal article:	Quin, J. (2012) Teachers changing worlds. *Power and Education*, *4*(1), 20–32. Retrieved from http://dx.doi.org/10.2304/power.2012.4.1.20
Electronic version of print book:	James, W. (1890). *The Principles of Psychology*. [The University of Adelaide eBook version]. Retrieved from http://ebooks.adelaide.edu.au/j/james/william/principles/index.html
Electronic-only book:	TenDam, H. (n.d.). *Politics, Civilization, & Humanity*. Retrieved from http://onlineoriginals.com/showitem.asp?itemID=201
Book chapter, electronic-only book:	TenDam, Hans (n.d.). "The atlas syndrome." In *Politics, Civilization, & Humanity*. Retrieved from http://onlineoriginals.com/showitem.asp?itemID=201

Each of the references in Examples 4.9 and 4.10 is a paragraph that is formatted with what is called a "hanging indent." A paragraph with a hanging indent has its second and subsequent lines indented. To create a hanging indent in Microsoft Word, click on Format, Paragraph, Special, and finally, Hanging.

Print and electronic references should be combined into a single list with the heading of **References**, which should be centered and in bold.

In-Text Citations in ASA Style (For APA Style, see pages 33–37.)

Like APA style, ASA style uses a version of the "author–date" method for in-text citations. This method can also be parenthetical or non-parenthetical, as described below. The two styles differ primarily in details. However, failure to pay attention to the details of a particular style may reflect poorly on the author of a manuscript and may result in a lower grade for student papers.

Parenthetical In-Text Citations in ASA Style

An in-text citation can be made parenthetical by putting the author's last name and year of publication in parentheses, as illustrated in Example 4.11.

Example 4.11

ASA style parenthetical in-text citation, ONE author

New data suggest that the influence of the mass media on social norms and customs is growing rapidly (Doe 2013).

Example 4.12 illustrates ASA style for an in-text citation to a source with two authors. Note the use of the word *and* between the last names of the two authors. In APA style, an ampersand (&) would be used instead of the word *and*. This illustrates the importance of paying attention to details when using a style guide.

Example 4.12
ASA style parenthetical in-text citation, TWO authors
The influence of peer group pressure on bullying behavior by girls needs more investigation (Edwards and Jones 2012).

If a source with one or two authors is cited more than once in a given manuscript, it should be cited in the same way each time. However, when there are three authors of a given source, the first time the authors are cited, all names are used. Then, in subsequent citations, only the first author's last name followed by *et al.* is used, as illustrated in Example 4.13.

Example 4.13
ASA style parenthetical in-text citation, THREE authors
First time the source is cited: More research is needed on the origins of gender-role socialization (Washington, Yu, and Galvan 2013).

The second and subsequent times the source is cited: More research is needed on the origins of gender-role socialization (Washington et al. 2013).

When a source being cited has four or more authors, use *et al.* the first and all subsequent times, as illustrated in Example 4.14.

Example 4.14
ASA style parenthetical in-text citation, FOUR OR MORE authors
Experiments on the effects of teachers' expectations on achievement have produced mixed results (Adams et al. 2012).

Often, two or more sources are in substantial agreement. For instance, there might be three sources with data indicating that the XYZ Program is strongly supported by most parents. These three sources may be cited within a single set of parentheses, as illustrated in Example 4.15. Note that semicolons are used to separate sources and that the sources are listed in alphabetical order.

Example 4.15
ASA style parenthetical in-text citation, TWO OR MORE sources
In three recent surveys, a majority of parents expressed strong support for the XYZ program (Black 2012; Brown et al. 2011; White and Bright 2010).

When the source is a group, such as a professional organization, government agency, corporation, or similar entity, cite its authorship using the sole name of the group, as shown in Example 4.16.

Example 4.16
ASA style parenthetical in-text citation, WHEN A GROUP IS A SOURCE
The origin of the Blue Moon technique has been traced as far back as the 1920s (Association for Hypothetical Studies 2010).

When an author wants to call attention to a specific passage within a source and quotes directly from a source, the author should include the page number(s) in the in-text citation. In Example 4.17, the page numbers appear immediately after the colon without a space and without an abbreviation for the word *page*.

Example 4.17

ASA style parenthetical in-text citation, PAGE NUMBERS INDICATED

The strong correlation between the two variables was previously reported (Lincoln and White 2012:6–9).

Non-Parenthetical In-Text Citations in ASA Style

An in-text citation can be non-parenthetical as illustrated in Example 4.18. In this example, the author's last name is the subject of the sentence, while the year of publication remains parenthetical as recommended by ASA.

Example 4.18

ASA style non-parenthetical in-text citation

In a newly published book, Bush and Clinton (2013) stress the importance of reducing tensions among nations in the Middle East.

Non-parenthetical in-text citations are best used when a writer wants to emphasize the authorship of the source material. For instance, the writer of Example 4.18 might have wanted to emphasize that the statement is based on the opinions of two former presidents, which may be why the writer made them the subject of the sentence.

Reference Lists in ASA Style

For each in-text citation, there should be a full bibliographic reference in the reference list at the end of the manuscript. Examples 4.19 and 4.20 show how references are formatted in ASA style for some common types of source materials. For other types of materials, consult the *ASA Guide*.

Example 4.19

*Sample reference list in ASA style for selected types of **printed sources***

Type of material	Reference
Journal article, one author:	Buhs, Eric. S. 2013. "Review of Friendships in Childhood Adolescence." *Journal of Applied Developmental Psychology* 34(2):119–21.

Comments:

The volume number is 34. The issue number is 2, which is in parentheses. Unlike APA, ASA requires inclusion of the issue number in all references to Journal articles. The last five numbers, 119–21, are the page numbers. The "21," which is elided, stands for "121."

Continued →

Example 4.19 continued.

Journal article, two authors:	Bettencourt, Amie F. and Albert D. Farrell. 2013. "Individual and Contextual Factors Associated with Patterns of Aggression and Peer Victimization During Middle School." *Journal of Youth and Adolescence* 42(2): 285–302.

Comments:

Only the name of the first author is inverted with the surname first. Also, ASA does not permit the use of "et al." in reference lists, but permits it in in-text citations.

Entire book, print version:	James, William. 1890. *The Principles of Psychology.* New York: Cosimo, Inc.

Comments:

When citing a book with two or more authors, only the name of the first author is inverted with the surname first.

In books that have more than one edition, include the edition number after the title of the book. For example, if the above example was in the 3rd edition, add "3rd ed." after *The Principles of Psychology.*

Book chapter, print version:	James, William. 1890. "The Scope of Psychology." Pp. 1–11 in *The Principles of Psychology.* New York: Cosimo, Inc.

Example 4.20

*Sample reference list in ASA style for selected types of **electronic sources***

Type of material	Reference
Online-only journal article:	Quin, Jane. 2011. "Teachers Changing Worlds." *Power and Education.* 4(1): 20–32. Retrieved March 5, 2013 (http://dx.doi.org/10.2304/power.2012.4.1.20)
Electronic version of print book:	James, William. 1890. *The Principles of Psychology.* New York: Cosimo, Inc. Retrieved March 7, 2013 (http://ebooks.adelaide.edu.au/j/james/william/principles/index.html).
Electronic-only book:	*See* Electronic version of print book *above.*
Book chapter, electronic-only book:	TenDam, Hans. n.d. "The Atlas Syndrome." In *Politics, Civilization, & Humanity.* Retrieved March 5, 2013 (http://onlineoriginals.com/showitem.asp?itemID=%20201).

Each of the references in Examples 4.19 and 4.20 is a paragraph that is formatted with what is called "hanging indent." Such a paragraph has its second and subsequent lines indented. To create a hanging indent in Microsoft Word, click on Format, Paragraph, Special, and finally, Hanging.

Reference Management Software

If you are undertaking a large research project and need help managing and organizing many references, there is a variety of reference management software available. The cost of such software ranges from free to hundreds of dollars, so anyone seriously considering a purchase should research the differences and capabilities of each.

Reference management software offers a variety of features for researchers, including the ability to bookmark web pages, tag, annotate, and highlight PDFs, and ultimately create a reference list based on hundreds of different reference styles. Some software is available only through the web, while others allow you to download the software directly to your computer. Many software options offer an add-on to your Internet browser to allow you to tag and bookmark pages as you surf the web.

Some examples of free software available include Zotero, Qiqqa, and Docear. Other software that normally has to be purchased, such as EndNote, often allows students to sign up for free accounts through their university.

Concluding Comments

APA style and ASA style differ primarily in details regarding punctuation and placement of various types of information. While these are details, they are important details in scientific writing, where consistency in style is important in order to avoid misunderstandings and errors.

Exercise for Chapter 4

Factual Questions

1. Which one of the following in-text citations is consistent with APA style?

    A. The field of psychology . . . dramatic turn (Smith, 2012).
    B. The field of psychology . . . dramatic turn (Smith 2012).
    C. The field of psychology . . . dramatic turn (Smith: 2012).

2. Which one of the following in-text citations is consistent with APA style?

    A. The results of recent research on the . . . consistent (Jones and Solis, 2012).
    B. The results of recent research on the . . . consistent (Jones and Solis 2012).
    C. The results of recent research on the . . . consistent (Jones & Solis, 2012).

3. Which one of the following in-text citations for a source with seven co-authors is consistent with ASA style?

    A. Teachers in the survey were the most . . . involvement (Chin et al., 2010).
    B. Teachers in the survey were the most . . . involvement (Chin et al. 2010).
    C. Teachers in the survey were the most . . . involvement (Chin e.g., 2010).

4. Which one of the following in-text citations is consistent with ASA style?

    A. The results of recent research on the . . . consistent (Jones and Solis, 2012).
    B. The results of recent research on the . . . consistent (Jones and Solis 2012).
    C. The results of recent research on the . . . consistent (Jones & Solis, 2012).

5. A student formatted the following reference to a journal article using APA style. There is one error in the reference. What is the error?

    Kirk, D. S., and Sampson, R. J. (2013). Juvenile arrests and collateral educational damage in the transition to adulthood. *Sociology of Education, 86,* 36–62. doi: 10.1177/0038040712448862

6. In the formatted reference in Question 5, what is the volume number?

7. In the formatted reference in Question 5, what is the name of the journal?

8. Suppose you were using the information in the formatted reference in Question 5 to write a reference formatted in ASA style. What information is missing that you would have to look up elsewhere in order to complete the reformatting?

9. A student formatted the following reference to a journal article using ASA style. There is one error in the reference. What is the error?

    Shriver, Lenka, Nancy M. Betts, and Gina Wollenberg. 2013. "Dietary Intakes and Eating Habits of College Athletes: Are Female College Athletes Following the Current Sports Nutrition Standards?" *Journal of American College Health* (1)61:10–16.

10. In the formatted reference in Question 9, what is the issue number?

11. In the formatted reference in Question 9, what are the page numbers?

Questions for Discussion

12. Will you be using the *APA Manual* in the future? Will you be using the *ASA Guide* in the future? Will you be using some other style guide in the future? Explain.

13. In addition to journal articles and books, what other types of sources do you expect to use in the near future in your writing?

14. Have you used software to format references? If so, describe your experience in terms of ease of use and cost.

Chapter 5
Writing Research Hypotheses, Purposes, and Questions

Research is conducted in order to test a research hypothesis, achieve a purpose, or answer a question.

Writing Research Hypotheses

A research hypothesis predicts the outcome of a research study. The prediction may be based on theory, the results of previous research, or a combination of both. Because relevant theories and results of previous research are described in a literature review, hypotheses are usually stated near the end of a literature review.[1]

To be an effective guide for research, a hypothesis should refer to specific variables. A *variable* is a trait or characteristic on which individuals differ from each other. A hypothesis must have at least two variables. For instance, in Example 5.1, there are two variables. The first is "interest in reading," on which individuals can vary from "little or no interest" to a "great deal of interest." The second is "number of minutes parents spend reading aloud to their children each week," which can vary from "zero minutes" to "1,443 minutes per week," which is the total number of minutes in a week.

Example 5.1
A hypothesis with TWO variables

It is hypothesized that children's interest in reading is directly related to the number of minutes parents spend reading aloud to their children each week.

A hypothesis can also contain more than two variables, as illustrated in Example 5.2.

Example 5.2
A hypothesis with THREE variables

It is hypothesized that children's interest in reading is directly related to the number of minutes parents spend reading aloud to their children and is inversely related to the number of minutes children are allowed to watch television each week.

Some hypotheses refer to treatments that will be administered to participants, which is the case in Example 5.3. In the example, "group therapy versus individual therapy" is known as the *independent variable* (i.e., the treatment variable). The outcome, "social anxiety," is known as the *dependent variable* (i.e., the outcome variable).

Example 5.3

---

[1] In a thesis or dissertation, research hypotheses may be stated in Chapter 1 (the Introduction) and restated at the end of Chapter 2 (the Literature Review). In a journal article or short report, the introductory statements are usually integrated into the literature review and the hypotheses are usually stated only once. This also is true for research purposes and questions, which are discussed later in this chapter.

A hypothesis that refers to treatments

It is hypothesized that clients who receive group therapy will report less social anxiety than those who receive individual therapy.

Under most circumstances, a hypothesis should *not* refer to a specific statistical outcome. To understand why, consider Example 5.4. For the hypothesis to be confirmed, the result must be exactly 50%. Even if a result is as close as 49% or 51%, the researcher will have to report that the hypothesis was not confirmed. An improved version shown in Example 5.5 does not name a specific statistical outcome but instead points out the direction of the predicted outcome, which is recommended.

Example 5.4
A hypothesis that refers to a specific statistical outcome (not recommended)

It is hypothesized that students will report that peer-related stress is 50% more important than family-related stress.

Example 5.5
An improved version of the hypothesis in Example 5.4

It is hypothesized that students will report that peer-related stress is more important than family-related stress.

A hypothesis should *not* state a value judgment because such judgments are not observable. For instance, consider Example 5.6. Because "goodness" is not directly observable, it cannot be tested with empirical methods (i.e., tested through observation). The improved version refers to a scale from 0 to 10 for measuring satisfaction, as responses to such a scale can be observed.

Example 5.6
A hypothesis that is a statement of a value judgment (not recommended)
It is hypothesized that democracy is good for the world's citizens.

Example 5.7
Improved version of the hypothesis in Example 5.6
It is hypothesized that citizens of democratic societies will report more satisfaction on a scale from 0 (no satisfaction) to 10 (complete satisfaction) with the laws that govern them than citizens of nondemocratic societies will report.

If there are a number of hypotheses to be investigated in a study, consider presenting them in a numbered list. This will make it easier to write the results section of the research report by permitting reference to the hypotheses by number. For instance, a researcher can present the results for the first hypothesis, then present the results for the second one, and so on while using the hypotheses' numbers.

Writing Research Purposes

When researchers believe they can predict the results of the research they are planning, they should state research hypotheses, as described above. However, frequently, researchers want to explore a particular topic but believe they are unable to predict the results. In this case, research purposes should be stated instead of research hypotheses.

Like a hypothesis, a research purpose should refer to specific observable behaviors. Consider the purpose in Example 5.8, which is inadequate because it lacks specificity. The purpose refers only to "effectiveness" without mentioning the specific observable behaviors that will be taken as signs of effectiveness. The improved version in Example 5.9 names specific, observable outcomes (i.e., identification of suitable career options).

Example 5.8
A research purpose that lacks specificity
The research purpose is to explore the effectiveness of the ABC Career Planning Program for students.

Example 5.9
Improved version of the research purpose in Example 5.8
The research purpose is to determine how effective the ABC Career Planning Program is in helping students identify career options that are consistent with their interests and talents.

Writing Research Questions

An alternative to writing a research purpose is to write a research question. Example 5.10 is the same as Example 5.9 except that a question is stated instead of a purpose.

Example 5.10
The purpose in Example 5.9 restated as a research question
The research question is: How effective is the ABC Career Planning Program in helping students identify career options that are consistent with their interests and talents?

Either form (purpose or question) is acceptable. However, when the question form is used, it should be stated in a way that it cannot be answered with a simple "yes" or "no" because the results of research are usually mixed. For instance, consider Example 5.11, which is worded as a "yes–no" question. In all likelihood, there will be *some degree* of social influence, which could not be described accurately with a simple "yes" or "no." The improved version in Example 5.12 does not have this problem.

Example 5.11
A research question phrased as a "yes–no" question (not recommended)
Are girls subject to social influences that encourage illicit drug use?

Example 5.12
Improved version of the research question in Example 5.11
To what extent are girls subject to social influences that encourage illicit drug use?

Identifying Populations in Research Hypotheses, Purposes, and Questions

Sometimes, researchers are interested in studying how variables operate in specific types of populations. When this is the case, the populations should be identified in research hypotheses, purposes, and questions. Example 5.13 is a hypothesis that refers to a population of interest (i.e., young adults).

Example 5.13
A research hypothesis that identifies a population of interest (young adults)

It is hypothesized that in a sample of young adults, those who report more involvement in religious activities will report lower levels of loneliness.

Example 5.14 is also a research purpose that identifies a population of interest.

Example 5.14
A research purpose that identifies a population of interest (young, never-married mothers)

The purpose is to determine what types of assistance young, never-married mothers receive with childrearing from close relatives.

Referring to Measurement Methods in Research Hypotheses, Purposes, and Questions

It is usually not necessary to name specific measures in research hypotheses, purposes, or questions. How variables will be measured is discussed in detail later in a research proposal or report. Hence, mention of the Doe Anxiety Inventory in Example 5.15 is not necessary. The research purpose could be improved by deleting the phrase "as measured by the Doe Anxiety Inventory."

Example 5.15
A research purpose that unnecessarily refers to a specific measurement tool (not recommended)

The purpose is to explore the relationship between social support and anxiety among older adolescents as measured by the Doe Anxiety Inventory.

The main exception to this guideline is when a specific measure is the subject of the research, which is the case in Example 5.16.

Example 5.16
A research purpose that refers to a specific measure that will be the subject of the investigation (recommended)

The purpose is to estimate the validity of the Workplace Safety Questionnaire in terms of congruence with ratings of safety practices provided by supervisors.

Concluding Comments

Consider writing several research hypotheses, purposes, or questions and asking for feedback on them from instructors and other students. Having several to compare and contrast will facilitate a discussion of each as the basis for a research project.

The next chapter describes the distinctions between quantitative and qualitative research, including how the two approaches differ when stating hypotheses, purposes, and questions.

Exercise for Chapter 5

Factual Questions

1. According to this chapter, what does a hypothesis predict?

2. What are the two variables in the following hypothesis?

    "It is hypothesized that there is a direct relationship between depression and anxiety."

3. What are the three variables in the following hypothesis?

    "It is hypothesized that quality-of-life ratings will be directly related to income and will be inversely related to social isolation."

4. In research, a treatment variable is known as
    A. A dependent variable.   B. An independent variable.

5. What is the deficiency in the following hypothesis?

    "It is hypothesized that nurses will report 25% more occupational stress than physicians will report."

6. What is the deficiency in the following research purpose?

    "The research purpose is to explore the effectiveness of therapy."

7. What is the deficiency in the following research question?

    "Do student nurses have favorable impressions of alternative medicine?"

Questions for Discussion

8. Write one research hypothesis, purpose, or question. If possible, state one you plan to investigate by conducting research.

9. How many variables does the hypothesis, purpose, or question you wrote in response to Question 8 contain?

10. Does the research hypothesis, purpose, or question you wrote in response to Question 8 refer to a specific type of population? If yes, what is the type of population?

11. Does the research hypothesis, purpose, or question you wrote in response to Question 8 mention a specific measurement tool? If yes, is it necessary to mention it?

Notes:

Chapter 6
Selecting a Research Approach

After selecting a research topic, reviewing the literature on it, and formulating research hypotheses, purposes, or questions, the next step is to select a research approach. The basics of the major approaches are discussed in this chapter, with more details on each provided in later chapters in this book.

Experimental Versus Nonexperimental Research

The purpose of experimentation is to explore a cause-and-effect relationship. Example 6.1 shows a research hypothesis, a purpose, and a question that concern such relationships.

Example 6.1
A research hypothesis, a purpose, and a question that concern cause-and-effect

Hypothesis: It is hypothesized that students who receive daily feedback on their performance on math worksheets will perform better on standardized math tests than students who receive only weekly feedback.

Purpose: The purpose is to determine whether student nurses who receive training in hospice care will report lower scores on a fear-of-death scale than student nurses who do not receive the training.

Question: To what extent do Drugs A and B differ in their ability to reduce pain associated with chemotherapy?

Researchers often conduct experiments in order to investigate cause-and-effect relationships. An *experiment* is defined as a study in which treatments are given in order to estimate their effects on some outcome variable(s).

The treatments (such as providing daily versus weekly feedback) constitute the *independent variable*. This is the variable that is under the control of the experimenter (i.e., is administered by the researcher or by research assistants). The outcome variable (such as performance on math tests) is called the *dependent variable*. By definition, all experiments have at least one independent variable and one dependent variable.

A classic design for an experiment is to form two groups: an experimental group that receives a new or alternative treatment and a control group that receives either no treatment or a conventional treatment. Example 6.2 describes such an experiment in which the type of information sheet is the independent variable, and wearing seat belts is the dependent variable.

Note that in Example 6.2, the participants were assigned at random to the two groups (in this case, by drawing names out of a hat), which guarantees that there is no bias in assigning participants to the groups. This permits us to say that at the beginning of the experiment, "the two groups are equal, except for random differences."

Example 6.2
An example of a two-group experiment with random assignment

A researcher pulled individuals' names out of a hat to form two groups of participants. The experimental group received an information sheet that described the safety benefits of wearing seat belts. The control group received a sheet that described the legal requirements regarding seat belt use. Subsequently, the researcher observed the participants as they left the parking lot where the experiment took place and determined the percentage of participants in each group that was wearing seat belts.

If the goal is to investigate a cause-and-effect relationship and two groups can be formed at random, select an experiment as your research approach. If you cannot form groups at random but still want to explore cause-and-effect, read Chapters 24–25 on experimentation to identify other suitable experimental designs that do not require random assignment.

Often, researchers want to explore causality but cannot administer the treatments of interest for practical reasons or for legal or ethical reasons. For instance, to study the effects of scolding on young children's social development, a researcher would not want to ask parents to scold their children for the purposes of an experiment. In this case, the best that can be done would be to identify children who had been scolded frequently for a comparison with children who had not been scolded frequently. Note that such a study is nonexperimental because no treatments were administered for the study. Instead, it is a type of nonexperimental study known as a causal-comparative study (also known as an ex post facto study), which is discussed next.

Major Types of Nonexperimental Research

Causal-Comparative Research

Nonexperimental research can be used to explore causality, but is typically used for this purpose only when it is not possible to conduct an experiment by administering treatments to participants. The primary type of quantitative nonexperimental research for exploring causality is *causal-comparative research* (also known as ex post facto research). Its name explains the basic approach: Existing groups are *compared* to identify a causal *sequence* in their histories. Example 6.3 describes a causal–comparative study.

Example 6.3
An example of a causal-comparative study (no treatments given by researchers)

A team of researchers wanted to identify the major reasons why some students with physical disabilities drop out of high school. First, the researchers identified a group of students with physical disabilities who had dropped out of high school. Then, they identified a group of students with the same types of physical disabilities (as well as being in the same age group and coming from the same socioeconomic backgrounds) who had not dropped out. Next, they administered a questionnaire that asked about variables that might have affected students' decisions to remain in high school or drop out, such as the presence or absence of barriers to physical mobility, having or not having teachers who were trained in assisting students with physical disabilities, and so on. A comparison of the responses of the two groups to such questions provided information on possible causes of dropping out.

A researcher should choose the causal-comparative method if three conditions are met: (1) the goal is to investigate a cause-and-effect relationship, (2) treatments cannot be given (for instance, it would be unethical to assign some students with disabilities to be taught by untrained teachers for the purposes of an experiment), and (3) two similar groups that differ in some outcome (such as dropping-out behavior) can be identified and questioned.

Surveys

Not all research is concerned with cause-and-effect relationships. Often, a research hypothesis, purpose, or question only calls for a description of what currently exists, not to determine what caused its existence. A *survey*, which is a type of nonexperimental study, is the most popular type of study for doing this. In a *population survey* (such as surveying all employees of a corporation), all members of the population are questioned. In a *sample survey*, only a subset of the population is questioned with the intention of researchers making inferences of how the population would have responded based on the responses of the sample.

The most popular method for collecting information in a survey is by using a questionnaire.[1] Questionnaires that are sent through the mail usually have very low response rates.

Face-to-face interviews are also widely used in surveys. Obviously, using interviews is more labor-intensive and expensive than using questionnaires. However, the interview method has certain advantages. Principally, they are (1) the ability to obtain additional information by probing participants' responses with follow-up questions (2) the ability to judge the extent to which respondents understand the questions and to clarify the questions, if necessary and (3) the ability to personalize the research process, which can help improve the quality of the information obtained when studying sensitive issues that participants might not want to reveal on a questionnaire for an unknown researcher to read.

While surveys are widely used to measure attitudes and opinions in most of the social and behavioral sciences, in educational research, *achievement surveys* are also popular. Frequently, all students at certain grade levels are administered achievement tests, the results of which are summarized with statistics. Less frequently, researchers in other fields conduct achievement surveys. Example 6.4 shows an example of an achievement survey conducted in a nonschool setting.

Example 6.4
An example of an achievement survey in a nonschool setting
Ten percent of the clients in a social welfare agency were selected at random to take a test on their knowledge of HIV transmission. The data were being collected in or-

---

[1] Principles for writing objective items that measure attitudes are discussed in Chapter 14.

der to determine the need for additional efforts to transmit such information to the clients.

If an achievement survey is the research approach selected, consult Chapter 14 for guidelines on writing multiple-choice items that measure achievement.

Surveys are often used to explore noncausal relationships between two or more variables. For instance, a survey might be conducted to determine how men and women differ in their opinions on gun control. Such a survey has two variables: (1) gender and (2) opinions on gun control. Based on such a survey, for instance, the researcher could report the percentage of men and the percentage of women who favor additional limits on the possession of handguns.

Correlational Studies

A correlational study is designed to examine the relationship between two or more sets of scores. For instance, in educational research, it is common to correlate pairs of achievement test variables with each other. As an example, one might hypothesize that scores on math word problems would be directly correlated with reading test scores (because word problems have a large reading component) as well as with math computational scores (because computations are needed to get the answers to word problems). Determining the degree of such relationships would provide insights into the nature of word-problem solving ability.

Variables other than achievement variables can also be correlated. For instance, the number of times adolescent male offenders have been arrested[2] can be correlated with scores on a self-report measure of respect for authority. For this relationship, the hypothesis might be that there will be an inverse correlation, such that those who score high on number of times arrested will score low on respect for authority *and* that those who score low on number of times arrested will score high on respect for authority.

The term *correlational research* is almost always reserved as a label for studies in which a particular statistic is employed: the correlation coefficient, which can be computed only when there are two sets of scores. (Note that nonquantitative variables, such as gender with the nonquantitative categories of "male" and "female," instead of scores do not lend themselves to the computation of correlation coefficients.)

A correlation coefficient is a statistic that can vary from 0.00 to 1.00 for direct relationships. A value of 0.00 indicates the complete absence of a relationship while a 1.00 indicates a perfect, direct relationship. A value around 0.70 might be described as relatively strong, a value of around 0.50 might be described as moderate, and a value of 0.30 might be described as relatively weak.

A correlation coefficient also can vary from 0.00 to –1.00 for inverse relationships (such as an inverse relationship between number of arrests and scores on a respect for authority scale). A value of 0.00 indicates the complete absence of a relationship while a –1.00 indicates a perfect inverse relationship. A value around –0.70 might be described as

---

[2] In research, the term *scores* refers to numerical values that indicate the amount of something that exists. It does not necessarily refer to the results of administering paper-and-pencil tests. Thus, for instance, "number of times arrested" is a score.

a relatively strong inverse relationship, a value of around –0.50 might be described as moderate, and a value of –0.30 might be described as relatively weak.

If a correlational study is the research approach selected, Chapter 17 and Appendix A should be consulted for more information on correlation coefficients.

Document/Content-Analysis Research

Sometimes, human behavior is explored by examining the contents of the documents, such as mass-market publications, school board records, and themes and characterizations in television programs and movies, as well as popular music. Example 6.5 is an example of such a study.

Example 6.5
An example of a document/content-analysis study
The purpose of the research was to explore changes in attitudes toward women's participation in the workforce through a content analysis of a sample of best-selling novels from the 1930s to the present. For each decade, counts were made of the number of references to main female characters being in the workforce, the types of occupations they held, and the social status of the occupations. Based on the assumption that novels reflect, in part, beliefs held by members of the general population, trends across the decades will reveal the timing and speed of attitudinal change.

An advantage of document/content-analysis research is that good samples can often be obtained. For instance, it might be relatively easy to obtain a random sample of the front-page stories published in *The New York Times* for the past decade in order to study coverage of an issue, such as emphasis on crime reporting in comparison with other types of stories. In contrast, consider the difficulty in using the authors of the stories as the sources of information for research. Some of the authors might not still be alive, others might not be available for some reason, and others may simply not want to take part in the research. Even if all authors could be located and persuaded to participate, the study would have to rely on the authors' recollections over a period of time that is so long ago that many details may have been forgotten and attitudes and beliefs may have become more or less intense.

A disadvantage of document/content-analysis research is that an assumption must be made that the contents of documents accurately reflect the attitudes and beliefs of those who wrote them as well as those who read them. For instance, suppose an increase was found in reporting crime over a decade in a major newspaper. Such an increase would be important only if it reflected an increased interest by the reading public. However, it is possible that increased coverage was a function of some other factor (such as a change in the editorial board of the newspaper) and not the public's hunger for information on crime.

While document/content-analysis research can provide informative results, conducting such research is greatly simplified by not having to deal directly with research participants. Consequently, conducting this type of research does not provide beginning researchers with the full research experience, and many instructors may want their students to select some other approach to a research topic.

Program Evaluation: A Hybrid

The evaluation of social and educational programs has become a major focus of researchers since the Great Society programs of the Lyndon Johnson administration in the 1960s. Program evaluation is called a "hybrid" here because some evaluation efforts have similarities to experimental research while others have similarities to nonexperimental research.

First, the programs that are administered can be viewed as treatments given to participants. (As you will recall from the beginning of this chapter, treatments are given to participants in experimental research.) Unlike researchers who conduct experiments, however, program evaluators seldom have control over the decision on who will receive the treatment and who will not. For instance, all students who qualify for the free school-lunch program in a district automatically receive it. An evaluator of such a program must then attempt to determine the effects of the program without a control group or by using a less-than-satisfactory control group, such as students in a school district that did not seek funds for the program.

Second, some elements of program evaluation do not deal with the effects or outcomes of the programs but rather, with factors affecting their implementation. For instance, an evaluator might examine the types and quality of the food provided by the program to see if it meets federal guidelines. Such an evaluation activity is not concerned with causation but instead, with the appropriateness with which the program is implemented. This aspect of program evaluation resembles nonexperimental research.

If program evaluation is selected as the research approach, Appendix C will be of special interest.

Quantitative Versus Qualitative Research

A major distinction in research is whether it is quantitative or qualitative. The terms themselves indicate much about the distinction. In quantitative research, the results are reduced to numbers, typically scores or frequency counts that can be analyzed with statistical methods. In order to make such an analysis meaningful, the procedures used to obtain the scores must be standardized so that they are the same for each participant. For instance, it would not be meaningful to compute an average score when some of the participants took the Brooks Algebra Achievement Test while others took the Smith Algebra Achievement Test. While this may seem obvious, the following implications may not. First, quantitative studies should be carefully and fully planned in advance to enhance the collection of data in a standardized way. Second, once a quantitative study is started, deviations from the plans should not be permitted because they may interfere with the standardization. In a way, then, quantitative research might be characterized as being rigid. Third, personalized interactions with participants should not be permitted because these might disrupt the standardization, causing different kinds of interactions with different participants. Hence, quantitative research might be also characterized as being distant and impersonal.

Contrast the characteristics of quantitative research just described with qualitative research. Because there is no need to standardize the data collection in order to obtain scores and frequency counts that can be summarized with statistics, qualitative research does not need to be as fully planned in advance and deviations in the plans cannot only be tolerated but might be welcomed. For instance, semi-structured interviews might be used to gather qualitative data. The interviewers might be encouraged to probe in different directions with different participants, depending on their initial responses. In addition, the responses of early respondents might lead to modifications in the questions asked of later participants due to insights gained from the early ones. Finally, close interpersonal interactions are permitted in qualitative research. This is not only true when interviewing participants but also when observing them. For instance, a widely cited method in qualitative research is *participant observation*, in which a researcher might join a group and directly participate in its activities while collecting research information on the group.

Note that some topics clearly lend themselves more to quantitative methods than qualitative methods. Example 6.6 shows a sample of such research topics.

Example 6.6
Sample topics that clearly lend themselves to the quantitative approach

1. Studies of the relationships among test scores, such as the extent to which college admissions test scores are valid predictors of college GPAs. (*Note*: GPAs are considered scores because they are quantities that indicate *how much* someone possesses. Specifically, they are an indicator of how much achievement students possess.)

2. Studies of rudimentary behaviors that are fully described by frequency counts, such as the number of times rats press levers in order to receive intermittent food rewards.

3. Studies involving economics, such as the cost-effectiveness of intervention programs like Big Brothers Big Sisters.

4. Studies of basic demographic characteristics of populations, such as percentages of various national origin groups that have completed high school.

Some topics lend themselves to either the quantitative or qualitative approach. For instance, consider the topic of adjustment of new immigrants to the United States. A quantitative researcher could draw up a list of possible adjustment problems and ask immigrants to indicate how serious each one has been on a scale from "strongly agree" to "strongly disagree." The percentage that marks each choice could be summarized with statistics, which is characteristic of quantitative research. On the other hand, a qualitatively-oriented researcher could conduct loosely structured interviews to uncover adjustment problems. As the respondents mention various problems, the qualitatively-oriented researcher could probe to obtain a better understanding of the origins and nature of the adjustment problems mentioned. The verbal responses would then be reviewed and analyzed for major and minor themes, as well as trends that can be described in words without numbers or statistics.

Each approach to studying the adjustment of immigrants to live in the United States has advantages. For instance, the quantitative researcher has a standardized data-collection method that potentially could be administered in a short amount of time to large numbers of respondents. On the other hand, the qualitative researcher has the advantage of not having to specify the potential adjustment problems in advance (as must be done in quantitative research using a printed questionnaire) and is free to pursue a line of questioning that can add depth to the understanding of this topic. As a result, the qualitative researcher is in a better position to identify unanticipated responses that might be overlooked by a quantitative researcher.

Put in general terms, quantitative researchers have the potential for more *breadth* in understanding a problem while qualitative researchers have the potential for more *depth* of understanding. A corollary to this is that quantitative researchers tend to emphasize drawing generalizations from samples to populations (i.e., inferring that what they found in their samples is true in the populations) while qualitative researchers tend to emphasize depth of understanding of purposively selected, small groups of individuals without regard to the appropriateness of generalizing the results to a population.

Because qualitative researchers do not need to standardize their data collection methods, their approach is often superior for tackling new and emerging topics. For instance, shortly after the attacks of 9/11, a qualitative study of the impact on the emotional lives of children in the New York City area would probably be preferable to a quantitative study because so little was known about trauma inflicted on children in the United States by an event of such magnitude. Selecting or constructing appropriate standardized measures for use in quantitative research on this topic would be difficult, at best.

Following are three implications of the above discussion for selecting between the quantitative and qualitative approaches:

1. Some topics are inherently quantitative. When studying variables that are naturally expressed as scores (such as counts of how many times a behavior occurs or economic data in relation to behaviors), the quantitative approach is usually superior to the qualitative one.

2. Other topics can be studied with either approach. Using the quantitative approach may provide more breadth and generality of results, while using the qualitative approach may provide more depth and is more capable of identifying unanticipated results.

3. Emerging new topics are often best studied with a qualitative approach because it can be difficult to construct in advance the standardized data-collection measures that would be needed for quantitative research.

The previous chapter covered writing research hypotheses, purposes, and questions. Note that because hypotheses require structured studies in order to test very specific predictions, hypotheses are almost exclusively used in quantitative research. In contrast, in qualitative research, rather broad statements of research purposes or research questions are used, such as "The purpose is to explore the contributions of grandparents to child-rearing by their unmarried grandchildren." In contrast, a purpose for a quantitative study would tend to be more specific, such as "The purpose is to compare the amount of financial and babysitting support grandparents provide to their unmarried granddaughters who have children with the support grandparents provide to their unmarried grandsons who have children."

While it might be argued that a researcher should pick a topic and then use the most appropriate methods (whether quantitative or qualitative) to study it, in reality, some researchers are more comfortable working with quantities while others are more skilled in working with a less structured approach. Thus, those with a strong orientation one way or the other should consider it when selecting a topic because, as noted above, some topics naturally lend themselves more to a quantitative approach while others lend themselves more to a qualitative approach. Although it is not very common, some researchers use both approaches when studying a topic in order to obtain the advantages of both.

Both quantitative and qualitative approaches are covered in detail in the remaining chapters of this book. In the discussions of qualitative research in the body of this book, it is assumed that most beginning researchers will conduct face-to-face interviews to obtain their qualitative data. Other methods of collecting qualitative data are briefly described in Appendix B.

Exercise for Chapter 6

Factual Questions

1. What is the purpose of an experiment?

2. Treatments are given in which type of research?
    A. Experimental research.   B. Nonexperimental research.

3. What type of nonexperimental research can be used to explore causality?

4. What is the most popular way of collecting information in a survey?

5. A correlational study is designed to explore the relationship between what?

6. What is an advantage of document/content-analysis research?

7. Why is program evaluation called a "hybrid" in this chapter?

8. Which type of research is more standardized?
    A. Qualitative research.   B. Quantitative research.

9. According to this chapter, which type of research has more potential for depth in understanding a problem?

   A. Qualitative research.   B. Quantitative research.

10. Which type of research is more likely to be based on research hypotheses?

    A. Qualitative research.   B. Quantitative research.

Questions for Discussion

11. Write a research hypothesis, purpose, or question. If possible, state one you plan to investigate by conducting research.

12. Does the hypothesis, purpose, or question you wrote in response to Question 11 lend itself to being investigated with "experimental" *or* "nonexperimental" research? Explain.

13. If your answer to Question 12 is "nonexperimental," which type of nonexperimental research would be best for the investigation?

14. Do you anticipate conducting a program evaluation? If yes, name the program.

15. Could qualitative research be used effectively to investigate the research hypothesis, purpose, or question you named in Question 11? Explain.

Chapter 7
Looking Ahead to Participant Selection

Having selected a research approach based on the material in the previous chapter, the next step is to look ahead to how the participants will be selected and how many are needed. This chapter provides an overview of some of the basic issues. Additional details can be found in later chapters in this book, especially Chapters 12 and 13.

Determining the Number of Participants

Usually lacking access to large numbers of participants, beginning researchers are understandably eager for an answer to the question, "How many participants will I need?" Unfortunately, the answer is, "It depends." The following are some of the variables on which it hinges.

First, if the research is being conducted for a term project, small numbers of participants might be acceptable, depending on the requirements of the instructor.

Second, for a thesis or dissertation, numbers larger than those required for a term project probably will be expected and, once again, the advice of instructors is needed to make a final determination of the appropriate sample size.

Third, there are varying norms for different types of research. For instance, well-designed and executed experiments with as few as 30 participants are often published in top-flight journals, especially when the results of the experiments have important implications for practicing professionals or for theory development.[1] In addition, because qualitatively oriented researchers focus on in-depth data collection through extensive interviews and/or observations, qualitative research is usually characterized by having relatively small numbers of participants, sometimes as few as a dozen or less. In contrast, in surveys of large, readily accessible populations, hundreds of participants might be expected for a survey to be judged reliable.

Fourth, some types of participants are especially difficult to locate or work with as participants. For instance, for a sociological study of criminals who are no longer being tracked by the justice system, locating and getting cooperation from a large sample might be exceptionally difficult, resulting in lowered standards for sample size by instructors or editors of journals.

Fifth, how the participants are selected is usually much more important than how many are selected. As a general rule, it is usually better to select a smaller sample that reflects the diversity of the population of interest than it is to select a larger sample of only a narrow segment of the population. For instance, for a study of adults in a community, using a large sample of adults who are readily available in an education program in one adult school will provide a sample that, in all likelihood, lacks the educational and socioeconomic diversity of the adult population at large. A smaller, more diverse sample

---

[1] As you will recall from the previous chapter, an *experiment* is a study in which treatments are administered to participants. A classic model is to have two groups: an experimental and a control group.

(drawn from various segments of the adult population, such as those obtained from door-to-door interviews in various neighborhoods) would be superior. As a corollary, if resources permit only a small, well-drawn sample, it should be preferred over a larger, poorly drawn one.

Examining the literature is one of the most fruitful ways to identify norms for the numbers of participants used in various types of studies on various topics. When researchers need to justify their plans for a particular number of participants in a term project, thesis, or dissertation, being able to cite the numbers used in reports of similar research published in journals can be quite helpful. Also, note that being able to show that a larger number of participants will be used in a proposed study than has been used in previous studies can be an important strength of a research proposal.

Chapters 12 and 13 explore issues in determining sample size in more detail.

Random Sampling for Quantitative Research

In quantitative research, the gold standard for selecting a sample from a population is *random sampling*. In this type of sampling, all members of a population must be identified, and each member of the population must be given an equal chance of being selected. A conceptually simple way to do this is to put the names of all members of a population on slips of paper, mix them together, and draw out the number needed for the study. The slips-of-paper method can be simulated with a computer program or by manually using a table of random numbers, which is illustrated in Chapter 12. By definition, a random sample is an *unbiased sample*.

One reason why random sampling is sometimes not used, even though it is desirable, is that it is frequently difficult to identify all members of a population. For instance, for a study of the population of homeless adults in a city, identification of all the homeless adults would not be possible. Thus, not all can be given an equal chance, resulting in a bias. The results of the study will apply only to the types of homeless individuals who can be identified, and the results might have little application to those homeless individuals who are more invisible.

Another common reason why random sampling is sometimes not used is because some potential participants whose names are selected by random sampling refuse to participate. Thus, even if a random sample of names is drawn, the refusal of some of those selected to participate makes the actual resulting sample nonrandom and therefore biased. Note that refusal rates are notoriously high for mailed questionnaires, where obtaining a return rate of more than 50% is often considered quite good, although the resulting data must be interpreted with extreme caution.

Additional details and variations on random sampling are covered in Chapter 12.

Stratified Sampling for Quantitative Research

In *stratified sampling*, a sample that is representative of its population in terms of key variables is drawn. For instance, if college census data show that 52% of freshmen are women and 48% are men, a sample might be drawn that has the same percentages of men and women. It is important to note that the purpose of seeking the appropriate percentages of men and women in stratified sampling is *not* to make a comparison of men and women in the research. Rather, the purpose is to obtain a sample that is representative in terms of gender, which will help in getting valid results to the extent that gender is related to the variable(s) being studied. For instance, there is a slight tendency for women to hold more liberal political beliefs than men. Thus, for surveys designed to predict the results of an election, it pays to have the correct percentages of men and women in the sample. Otherwise, a sample that has a disproportionately large number of men might lead to an incorrect prediction of a more conservative outcome than would be obtained with a gender-appropriate sample.

In *stratified random sampling*, the same percentage of individuals is drawn at random from each subgroup. For instance, if a population has 400 men and 500 women, drawing 10% of the men at random and then separately drawing 10% of the women will result in a sample consisting of 40 men and 50 women, which will correctly reflect the gender composition of the population.

Stratification is not always conducted with random sampling. Using stratification without random sampling, however, is not as useful as it might seem at first. For instance, calling for volunteers (instead of selecting at random) and accepting individuals into the study until 40 men and 50 women are obtained would bias the sample in favor of the types of individuals who tend to volunteer. This would be undesirable because the type of men who volunteer to be participants might not be representative of all men in the population.

Convenience Sampling for Quantitative and Qualitative Research

The use of volunteers is an example of the type of sampling called *convenience sampling* (also known as *accidental sampling*). As its name suggests, it refers to using individuals who happen to be convenient as participants in research. Often, convenience samples consist of college students because they are readily available to professors and students who are conducting research.

Even though convenience samples must be presumed to be biased samples (being biased in favor of the types of individuals who are convenient to study), they have a legitimate role in both quantitative and qualitative research. First, they allow researchers who do not have access to better samples an opportunity to make preliminary explorations related to their research hypotheses, purposes, or questions. Second, they allow researchers to pilot-test their measurement techniques (e.g., to try out a new questionnaire) as well as to determine the feasibility of administering particular treatments in an experiment. Third, promising research with convenience samples may inspire researchers with access to better samples to replicate the research. Despite these uses, results obtained with convenience samples must be interpreted with considerable caution.

Purposive Sampling for Qualitative Research

As you may recall from the discussion of qualitative research in Chapter 6, qualitative researchers tend to emphasize depth of understanding of purposively selected, small groups of individuals without regard to the appropriateness of generalizing from them to a population.

In *purposive sampling*, individuals are handpicked to be participants because they have certain characteristics that are believed to make them especially good sources of information. For instance, for a study with the purpose of identifying paths to high achievement among women in the corporate world, a researcher might purposively (i.e., deliberately) select only women who are officers in large corporations as an especially good source because there is much competition for such positions in corporations of this size. Thus, the researcher will be working with women who have achieved high positions in highly competitive environments, which might be an especially rich source of information on the topic.

The distinction between a purposive sample and a sample of convenience (see the previous topic in this chapter) is important because selecting a purposive sample is regarded as highly appropriate for a qualitative study, while using a sample of convenience should be avoided whenever possible in both qualitative and quantitative research. To qualify as a purposive sample, a researcher must (1) establish criteria for the selection of certain types of individuals (i.e., being a chief executive officer), (2) have a reason for establishing the criteria, and (3) make a planned and systematic effort to contact such individuals. If, on the other hand, for a study of high-achieving women, a researcher happens to be acquainted with several high-achieving women and uses these individuals as the participants only because they are readily available, a sample of convenience is being employed.

If only a sample of convenience is available, which is often the case because beginning researchers usually have limited resources, a study should not necessarily be abandoned. Conducting the research in spite of this weakness in sampling will allow a beginning researcher to gain experience that will be useful in later research projects. In addition, a pilot qualitative study with a sample of convenience will help to determine whether additional research with better samples is likely to be fruitful.

Using Literature When Making Plans for Participant Selection

Beginning researchers who will be conducting research as a term project in the near future should, at this point, make preliminary plans based on (1) the information in this chapter and (2) the descriptions of participant selection found in the literature on their topics. From the second source, note how many participants were used in various studies as well as how they were selected. Consider whether improvements can be made in either the numbers or method of selection.

Often, authors of published research discuss limitations in participant selection in the Discussion section near the end of research reports. They sometimes provide ideas as to how the same types of research topics can be pursued with other types of samples. Example 7.1 illustrates this. As it makes clear, a new study could contribute to an understanding of the topic.

Example 7.1
Discussion of limitation in participant selection; useful in planning additional studies

. . . there are several noteworthy limitations. The findings were based on the expressions of racial issues on one campus; it is unclear if these findings extend to other college settings. Future researchers should collect data from multiple sites and explore racial beliefs that are unique to the context of the specific campus such as the mascot or recent incidents. (p. 247)[2]

Put the preliminary plan for selecting participants in writing, and be prepared to modify it after reading Chapters 11 and 12, in which this topic is described in more detail.

Exercise for Chapter 7

Factual Questions

1. According to this chapter, which one of the following types of research would typically be expected to have a larger number of participants?
    A. Experimental research.   B. Qualitative research.   C. Survey research.

2. Which one of the following is usually more important?
    A. Selecting a large sample.
    B. Selecting a sample that reflects the diversity of the population.

3. According to this chapter, what is one of the most fruitful ways to identify norms for the numbers of participants used for various types of studies on various topics?

4. What is "the gold standard" for selecting a sample from a population in quantitative research?

5. What two reasons are given for why random sampling is sometimes not used?

6. Suppose that 10% of the names of students were drawn separately at random from each grade level in a high school. What is the name of this type of sampling?

7. Is the following a description of a purposive sample? Explain.
    "From the students who were enrolled in her sociology class, a professor selected the six students with the lowest test scores for a qualitative study on low-achieving undergraduates. The reason for their selection was that they were readily available to be interviewed by the professor."

---

[2] Neville, H. A., Yeung, J. G., Todd, N. R., Sanierman, L. B., & Reed, T. D. (2011). Color-blind racial ideology and beliefs about a racialized university mascot. *Journal of Diversity in Higher Education*, *4*(4), 236–249. doi: 10.1037/a0024334

8. According to this chapter, if only a sample of convenience can be obtained for a qualitative study on a given research topic, should a beginning researcher abandon the topic? Explain.

9. Where do authors of published research often discuss weaknesses in their participant selection?

Questions for Discussion

10. If you will be conducting quantitative research, do you plan to use random sampling? Stratified random sampling? Convenience sampling? Explain the reason for your choice.

11. If you will be conducting qualitative research, do you plan to use convenience sampling? Purposive sampling? Explain the reason for your choice.

12. How many individuals do you plan to use as participants in the study? Is the number based on the number readily available to you? Is it based on the numbers used by researchers who have published research on your topic? Did you use some other basis for determining the number of participants? Explain.

Chapter 8
Looking Ahead to Measurement

After making preliminary plans for participant selection based on the material in the previous chapter, the next step is to make preliminary plans for measurement (i.e., materials such as tests, questionnaires, interview schedules, or other measures that will be used).

The purpose of this chapter is to provide some practical guidance on the selection of measures for research. Technical aspects of measures are discussed in detail later in this book, especially in Chapters 14 through 16.

Using Measures Employed in Previous Research

When investigating a topic, researchers often use the same measures previously employed by other researchers who investigated the topic. Using the same measures has two potential advantages. First, much is often known about the validity of measures used in previous research, especially if they have been widely used. In their research reports, researchers usually briefly summarize what is known about the measures they used and quite often provide references where additional information can be found.

In Example 8.1, the researchers assert that the measure is valid and cite a number of studies in which the measure has been used. The frequency of prior use suggests that other researchers have judged the measure to be valid.

Example 8.1
Description indicating the validity of an existing measure used in previous research
The Functional Disability Inventory (FDI), Self- and Caregiver-report versions, is a 15-item inventory assessing the extent to which a child/adolescent has had physical difficulty performing typical daily activities over the past 2-week period. It has well-established validity . . . and has been used in numerous studies of pediatric pain and disability (Claar, Guite, Kaczynski, & Logan, 2010; Claar & Walker, 2006; Kaczynski, Claar, & Logan, 2009; Walker & Greene, 1991; Wicksell, Lennart, Lekander, & Olsson, 2009).[1]

The second advantage to using the same measures as were used in previous studies is that doing this helps in building a consistent body of research. Consider, for instance, a study being planned on the prevalence of loneliness among members of Ethnic Group X, which has not been studied as a separate group in the past (i.e., studied only as members of larger ethnically diverse groups). One possibility would be to use the UCLA Loneliness Scale, which has been very widely used in published studies. By using the same measure that was used in previous studies, the results of the study of Group X would be

---

[1] Carter, B. D., Kronenberger, W. G., Threlkeld, B., Townsend, A., & Pruitt, A. (2013). The Children's Health & Illness Recovery Program (CHIRP): Feasibility and preliminary efficacy in a clinical sample of adolescents with chronic pain and fatigue. *Clinical Practice in Pediatric Psychology*. Advance online publication. doi: 10.1037/cpp0000012

comparable to the results of previous studies. In other words, when the same measure is used, any differences between the results of the study of Group X and the results of previous studies of other groups cannot be attributed to differences in the measures. On the other hand, if a new measure is used, a difference might be because (1) Group X truly differs from other groups or (2) the different measures define and assess loneliness in different ways, causing an illusion of a difference between groups.

Certain research problems may require a modification of measures used in previous research. For instance, the UCLA Loneliness Scale contains questions about loneliness in general. For a study of loneliness among college freshmen who live in dormitories, the questions might be modified to refer to this particular context. Of course, any existing information on reliability and validity of the scale will not strictly apply to a modified measure.

A disadvantage of using a measure widely used in previous studies on a topic is that whatever flaws the measure has will affect the results of all the studies. Thus, there may be times where a justification for conducting another study on the same topic is to determine if similar results can be obtained using a different measure or even a different type of measure (e.g., observation of behavior instead of self-reports of behavior on a questionnaire).

Locating Existing Measures

Existing measures are frequently identified by reviewing the literature on a topic. Often, a reference is given before leading to a copy of the full measure. Less often, a measure is reproduced in full in a journal article. When researchers have difficulty in locating a particular measure, they can consult the Educational Testing Service's ETS Test Collection Database, which contains descriptions of over 25,000 measures, including research and unpublished measures, which may be of interest to researchers.[2] For each measure, the database includes information on the availabilty such as the name, address, and phone number of the author or publisher. When a measure has been reproduced in full in a journal article, the complete reference to the article is given. In addition, more than 1,000 of the measures are downloadable directly from ETS.

The ETS Test Collection Database is also useful for locating measures on specialized topics. Note that the database is not restricted to educational tests. Example 8.2 shows a small sample of measures with their descriptions that are provided in the database. The example illustrates the diversity of measures that can be found in the database.

Example 8.2
Sample of three of the 25,000 measures described in the ETS Test Collection Database
Nature and Function of Social Work Questionnaire. Designed to assess the attitudes of social workers and others who are well oriented to social work toward the profession. It encompasses five professional orientations: psychodynamic-mindedness,

---

[2] Any individual can access the database at http://www.ets.org/testcoll/ at no charge.

social action, social-environment-mindedness, title-protection and training, and private practice. The measure is recommended for group rather than individual analysis.

Edington Attitude Scale for High School Freshman Boys. Developed to determine favorable and unfavorable attitudes of high school freshman boys toward physical education. Participants are asked to respond to attitude statements on a six-point Likert scale.

The Social Phobia and Anxiety Inventory for Children (SPAI-C). A 26-item assessment used to assess the frequency and range of social fears and anxiety in childhood and early adolescence. It is for use with children between the ages of 8 and 14 years. Some of the questions require multiple responses and use a Likert-type scale. The inventory can be used to screen for social anxiety and phobias in various settings, including schools, residential treatment centers, juvenile detention facilities, outpatient clinics, inpatient units, and other clinical facilities.

Issues in Devising New Measures

Sometimes, new measures need to be devised to suit a particular research project. For instance, when evaluating a new program, new interview questions specifically tailored to the program might be more relevant and informative than using questions developed and used in evaluations of similar but not identical programs. The general rule is that if a match between the research goal and the measures can be improved greatly by devising a new measure, a new one should be devised.

Beginning researchers should note, however, that when they devise new measures, especially for thesis or dissertation research, they may be asked to defend the measures' validity and reliability (in quantitative research) or dependability and credibility (in qualitative research). These issues are discussed briefly later in this chapter and in more detail in Chapters 14 and 16.

Validity of Measures in Quantitative Research

In quantitative research, the *validity* of measures is of great concern. *Validity* refers to the extent to which the measures are measuring what they are supposed to be measuring. One of the major approaches to studying the validity of measures is to conduct statistical studies in which the results from administering a measure are correlated with other results. For instance, widely accepted theories say that "anxiety" and "depression" are moderately correlated. Thus, if the results from using a new measure of anxiety fail to correlate with an established measure of depression, the validity of the new measure might be called into question.

The other major approach to studying validity is to have experts make judgments regarding the contents of a measure. For instance, experts might classify each item in a geography test as to the types of skills required (e.g., interpretation versus memorization of facts) as well as the types of content (e.g., social geography versus physical geography). These judgments can then be used as a basis for determining whether the test is valid for a particular purpose (e.g., valid in light of the instructional objectives for a particular grade level).

These and other approaches to studying the validity of tests are described in more detail in Chapter 14. At this point, be aware that the validity of measures should be addressed in a research report, so attention should be paid to any available validity information on measures being considered for use in a research project.

Reliability of Measures in Quantitative Research

Reliability deals with the extent to which results are *consistent*. Consistency in measurement is desirable whenever a relatively stable trait is being measured. For instance, aptitude to learn algebra (i.e., the underlying skills needed for success in algebra) is believed to be rather stable. For example, those who are identified by an algebra aptitude test as having a high aptitude one week should, if retested a week later with the same test, again be identified as such. Likewise, those who are low one week should be identified as being low the next. Such patterns would indicate that the test yields results that are consistent from time to time.

One of the most important factors influencing the reliability of objective tests and scales is the number of items they contain. This is easy to see at the extreme. Consider an algebra aptitude test with only three multiple-choice test items. One week, an examinee might take three lucky guesses and get them all right. The next week, the examinee might guess on all three and get them all wrong. However, with a larger number of items (about 20 or more), the odds of such inconsistent results become exceedingly small.

Reliability is an especially important concern when the measure requires subjective judgments because these judgments can be quite unreliable if they are highly subjective. For this reason, quantitative researchers prefer measures that de-emphasize subjectivity. For instance, a quantitative researcher who wanted to study disruptive behaviors in a classroom would provide the observers with definitions, examples, and specific criteria for classifying a behavior as disruptive in order to reduce the subjectivity. Without taking such measures, what one observer records as disruptive, another observer might not, leading to an inadequacy in what researchers call poor "interobserver reliability."

Reliability is usually described using correlation coefficients, which are described in detail in Chapter 18 and Appendix A. If a new measure is being constructed for a study, the researcher might be expected to collect and report data on its reliability using one or more of the techniques described in Chapter 14.

Credibility of Measures in Qualitative Research

In qualitative research, the *credibility* of the measure is roughly equivalent to the concept of *validity* of measure in quantitative research. However, qualitative researchers attempt to establish credibility with different approaches from those described above for validity. For instance, employing "member checks" helps to do this. It consists of sharing the interpretations of results with the participants (or a sample of the participants) in order to get feedback on how well the interpretations reflect the meanings intended by the participants during the study. To the extent that the member checks are positive (i.e., the participants agree with the interpretations), the results can be said to be credible. In addition, researchers can increase credibility by modifying interpretations in light of the member checks.

Employing prolonged engagement in the field is also a method for assuring credibility. For instance, spending a month observing interactions between employees and supervisors in an employment setting would have more credibility than a one-shot observation.

When resources do not permit prolonged engagement, credibility can be enhanced by time sampling. For instance, making four two-hour observations on different days of the week during a month (for a total of eight hours) should provide more credible data than a single observation of eight hours on only one day.

Qualitative researchers also use what they call "triangulation of data sources," which means using more than one type of source for data. For instance, in a study of students, a researcher might interview not only the students but also two other types of sources: the students' teachers and their parents. To the extent that different types of data sources yield similar results, the overall results from all three sources have greater credibility.

These and other methods are discussed in Chapter 16. At this point, students who are planning qualitative research should make some preliminary decisions on what steps they might take to enhance the credibility of their measures.

Dependability of Measures in Qualitative Research

Traditionally, qualitative researchers are much more tolerant of subjectivity in their measures than quantitative researchers. Nevertheless, they do concern themselves with whether subjectivity (such as interpretations of responses to open-ended interview questions) is sufficiently controlled so that the results reflect on the participants without undue influence of those making the subjective judgments. However, instead of using the term "reliability," which is strongly associated with objective testing, they tend to use other terms (in particular, "dependability").

One way to examine dependability in qualitative research is to have more than one individual code and interpret the data (such as the responses to open-ended questions) and note the extent to which they both agree. When areas of disagreement among the individuals emerge, they can be resolved through discussions designed to lead to a consensus on the best interpretations. A consensus is usually taken to be more dependable than a single individual's judgment.

Dependability in qualitative research can also be improved through the use of "triangulation of measure." Unlike triangulation of data sources discussed above in which various types of sources are employed, triangulation of measure uses only one source (such as one group of students) but uses more than one type of measure. For instance, triangulation of measures could consist of open-ended interviews with a group of students along with direct observations of the same group's overt behavior. To the extent that different types of measures yield similar results, the results can be said to be dependable.

More information on these and other techniques will be discussed in Chapter 16. At this point, be aware that a discussion of dependability of the measures in qualitative research might be expected in a research proposal and report.

Exercise for Chapter 8

Factual Questions

1. This chapter mentions two potential advantages of using measures employed in previous research. What is the second one that is mentioned?

2. What is a disadvantage of using a measure widely used in previous studies on a topic?

3. "A limitation of the Educational Testing Service's ETS Test Collection Database is that it is restricted to educational tests." Is the preceding statement true *or* false?
    A. True.   B. False.

4. According to this chapter, is there any circumstance under which beginning researchers should devise new measures? Explain.

5. Which of the following deals with the extent to which the results are consistent?
    A. Validity.   B. Reliability.

6. Having experts make judgments regarding the contents of a measure is an approach to studying which of the following?
    A. Validity.   B. Reliability.

7. Using "member checks" is a technique in qualitative research that helps to establish which one of the following?
    A. Credibility of measures.   B. Dependability of measures.

8. Having more than one individual code and interpret the data and noting the extent to which they agree is a technique in qualitative research that helps to establish which one of the following?
    A. Credibility of measures.   B. Dependability of measures.

Questions for Discussion

9. Have you identified any measure(s) that have been widely used in research on the topic on which you will be conducting research? If yes, name the measure(s).

10. If you answered "yes" to Question 9, do you plan to use the measure(s) in your research? Why? Why not?

11. If you answered "yes" to Question 10, does the literature provide a summary of what is known about the measure(s)? Explain.

12. If you have consulted the ETS Test Collection Database online, did you find any measure(s) that might be useful in your research? Explain.

13. If you will be devising one or more new measures for use in your research, very briefly describe them and indicate why you decided to devise new ones.

Notes:

Chapter 9
Looking Ahead to Data Analysis for Quantitative Research

The measures discussed in the previous chapter will generate data that will need to be analyzed. The purpose of this chapter is to describe several frequently used models for analyzing quantitative data. Many readers will find one or more of them suitable as models for writing a data analysis section in a preliminary proposal for their research. The data analysis section can be evaluated and possibly modified after reading Chapters 17 through 19.

The descriptions of many of the statistics in this chapter are quite concise. For students who have taken a course in statistics, this chapter will serve as a review. Students who have not taken such a course will want to study the more detailed descriptions in Chapters 17 through 19, where the statistics mentioned here are defined and illustrated in more detail.

Analysis of Nominal Data

Many variables in research yield what is called *nominal data*. Nominal data have words (instead of numbers) that describe their categories. For instance, for the variable called gender, the two categories are "male" and "female." This is nominal because we naturally use words to describe a participant's gender, not a number.

Another example of a variable that yields nominal data is political affiliation. Once again, the categories use the words such as "Democrat," "Republican," "Green," and "Other," not numbers. Note that nominal data do not have a natural order on which we could all agree. For instance, we would not all agree on whether "Democrat" is a higher or lower category than "Republican."

Percentages

Percentages are widely used to analyze nominal data. A percentage indicates the number of cases per 100 that have some characteristic. For instance, if a researcher states that 55% of a sample consists of women, the researcher is saying that 55 out of every 100 participants are women.

Sometimes, researchers are interested in the relationship between two nominal variables. When this is the case, a two-way table (called a "contingency table") can help in determining whether a relationship exists. For instance, Example 9.1 shows a contingency table for the relationship between geographical area and opinions on newly proposed legislation. The relationship is such that those who live in the Southeast are more in favor of it than those who live in the Northeast. In more general terms, the data indicate that knowing which region an individual lives in is predictive of his or her opinion on the new legislation. Thus, for instance, if an individual lives in the Northeast, the best bet based on the data is that he or she will be opposed to the new legislation.

Notice that in Example 9.1, the numbers of cases, which are indicated by the italicized letter *n*, are provided along with the percentages. This is a desirable reporting technique because percentages, by themselves, can sometimes be misleading. For instance, if you were told that 33% of the students majoring in Russian had dropped out last semester, knowing that there were only *three* students majoring in Russian and *one* (33%) dropped out is important to know.

Example 9.1

A contingency table for the relationship between two nominal variables

	Favor new legislation	Oppose new legislation
Northeast United States	40% ($n = 80$)	60% ($n = 120$)
Southeast United States	60% ($n = 120$)	40% ($n = 80$)

Chi-Square

While the relationship in Example 9.1 seems clear, it is based on a rather small sample, with a total *n* of only 400 participants. Assuming that the sample was drawn at random, perhaps selecting names at random from lists of registered voters (see Chapter 7 on participant selection), there is a possibility that the pattern of differences was created by the process of random selection. In other words, perhaps the populations of voters in the two geographical areas are actually the same in their opinions but, by the luck of the draw (i.e., random sampling errors), samples that provide unrepresentative data were obtained.

The possibility that random samples differ from each other only because of random sampling has a technical name in statistics: the *null hypothesis*. Two equally acceptable ways of expressing this hypothesis are

1. random sampling has created a difference between the samples that does not exist between the populations, or

2. there is no true difference between the populations.[1]

For the relationship between two nominal variables, the null hypothesis can be tested (i.e., evaluated in order to reject or accept it) using a *chi-square test*. Performing calculations that are beyond the scope of this book,[2] a chi-square value can be obtained. Based on it, the probability of the null hypothesis being true can be determined. As it turns out for the statistics in Example 9.1, the value of *p* is less than .001 (i.e., less than 1 in 1,000). This is a very low probability, which would lead almost all researchers to reject the null hypothesis. Having rejected it, they would declare the relationship in the example

---

[1] The null hypothesis is discussed in more detail in Chapter 19 of this book. It is important to distinguish between a research hypothesis, which is a prediction that a researcher makes before beginning a study, and the null hypothesis, which is a statistical hypothesis that exists when samples have been studied.

[2] In this book, none of the calculations for testing null hypotheses are described. The calculations (either with a calculator or computer) of the ones mentioned in this chapter are universally covered in introductory statistics textbooks and courses.

to be *statistically significant*. In other words, the relationship is sufficiently reliable that it is unlikely that it was created by random sampling errors.

While one chance in 1,000 is quite low, allowing a highly confident rejection of the null hypothesis, most researchers would reject a null hypothesis with a probability only as low as .05 (five in 100). This probability level is mentioned in Example 9.2.

For those whose research will produce two sets of nominal data in order to examine the relationship between them, Example 9.2 provides a model for proposing the data analysis.

It is important to note that the last sentence in Example 9.2 should be deleted if an entire population instead of a sample is used because the null hypothesis refers to sampling error, which cannot exist when there is no sampling. In other words, tests of statistical significance (such as the chi-square test) are *not* required when populations are studied.

Example 9.2

Plans for analyzing the relationship between two nominal variables for the statistics in Example 9.1

A two-way contingency table showing the percentages and underlying numbers of cases will be prepared and examined for regional differences of opinion on the proposed new legislation. The null hypothesis states that there is no true relationship between the two variables. This hypothesis will be tested with a chi-square test using the .05 significance level.[3]

Analysis of Group Differences on Interval Variables

As you know from the above discussion, a nominal variable has categories that are described in words. In contrast, an *interval variable* has numbers that represent "how much" of something exists.[4] Interval data in the social and behavioral sciences are often generated by tests and scales that have objective-type items that yield overall scores. However, not all scores are generated by paper-and-pencil tests. A score could be "income," expressed in dollars, or "height," expressed in inches. Both of these are described with numbers and indicate "how much" of something a participant has.

Means and Standard Deviations for One Group

The central tendency for interval data can be described with an average. In statistics, there are three averages. By far, the *mean* is the most widely used. It is the average that is obtained by summing all the scores and dividing by the number of scores.[5]

---

[3]The degree of relationship between the two variables could be examined using other statistics, such as a type of correlation coefficient known as the phi coefficient. Also note that stating that the .05 level will be used implies that .05 *or any lower level* will trigger a declaration of statistical significance.

[4]Distances among the numbers on an interval scale are equal. Also, the four types of variables that affect plans for analysis are nominal (naming), ordinal (rank ordering), interval, and ratio. Only the two most common types (nominal and interval) are discussed in this chapter. More information on all four types of variables can be found in Chapter 17.

[5]The mean is not always the appropriate average. It is especially inappropriate when a distribution is highly skewed, in which case the average (called the "median") is usually preferred. See Chapter 17 for more.

While knowing the average of a set of scores is very informative, an average does not indicate how spread out the scores are. For instance, a group might have an average of 40 correct on a test. Knowing this does not indicate whether all individuals in the group are clustered tightly around the score of 40 or are spread out, with some individuals scoring very high and others scoring very low.

The technical term for the "amount of spread" in a set of scores is *variability*. One way to describe variability is to report the range of scores, as in "the scores range from 2 to 80." For reasons discussed in Chapter 17, however, a much more common way to describe variability is to use the *standard deviation*, which was designed to indicate the variability of the middle two-thirds of a group. For instance, suppose the mean of a group is 40 and the standard deviation is 10. This indicates that about two-thirds of the group have scores between 30 (the mean of 40 minus the standard deviation of 10) and 50 (the mean of 40 plus the standard deviation of 10).[6]

Example 9.3 shows a research purpose that indicates that interval data will be collected using one group of participants. Example 9.4 shows a proposed model for data analysis.

Example 9.3

A research purpose that identifies two variables at the interval level for one group

The purpose is to use objective scales to describe the levels of optimism and self-efficacy of newly arrived immigrants from Southeast Asia.

Example 9.4

Plans for analyzing the data for the hypothesis in Example 9.3

The means and standard deviations of the optimism and self-efficacy scores will be reported.

Means and Standard Deviations for Two or More Groups

Consider the hypothesis in Example 9.5. In it, two groups are named: "boys" and "girls." The interval variable is vocabulary knowledge, with each score being a category (e.g., 0 right is a category, 1 right is another category, and so on).

Example 9.5

A hypothesis that identifies a variable at the interval level for two groups

It is hypothesized that the fifth-grade girls attending Franklin School will score higher than the fifth-grade boys on a standardized vocabulary test.

Assume that for the hypothesis in Example 9.5, the entire population (i.e., not a sample) of the girls and boys will be administered a vocabulary test. Example 9.6 shows how the plans for the analysis might be expressed.

Example 9.6

Plans for analyzing the data for the hypothesis in Example 9.5 (populations—not samples—will be tested)

---

[6] The two-thirds rule strictly applies only when a set of scores has a bell-shaped (i.e., normal) distribution. Otherwise, it should be treated as only a rough rule-of-thumb. See Chapter 17 for more information on the interpretation of the standard deviation.

The means and standard deviations of the vocabulary scores will be reported separately for girls and boys.

If there are more than two groups, the analysis would be similar, as shown in Example 9.7, where the populations of students at three grade levels will be tested with a mathematics test.

Example 9.7
Plans for analyzing interval data for more than one group (populations—not samples— tested)
The means and standard deviations of the mathematics scores will be reported separately for first-, second-, and third-graders.

t Test for Two Means

Suppose these two means were computed: 52.00 for girls and 50.00 for boys. If the entire populations of girls and boys had been tested (such as all fifth-grade girls and all fifth-grade boys in a school district), the conclusion would be that the girls are superior by two points. In contrast, if only random samples of girls and boys had been tested, the null hypothesis would become an issue because it would raise the possibility that there is no true difference between girls and boys in vocabulary knowledge (i.e., the two-point difference might be created by the random sampling; it is possible that the two-point difference is only a random deviation from a difference of zero points).

To test the null hypothesis between two means, a test called the *t* test can be used. Performing calculations that are beyond the scope of this book, a value of *t* can be computed and used to determine the probability that the null hypothesis is true. As with the chi-square test discussed above, if the probability is .05 or less (such as .01 or .001), the null hypothesis should be rejected.

Plans for the analysis for the circumstances described here are shown in Example 9.8.

Example 9.8
Plans for analyzing interval data for two groups when sampling has been used
The means and standard deviations of the vocabulary scores will be reported separately for girls and boys. The null hypothesis states that there is no true difference between the two means. This hypothesis will be tested with a *t* test using the .05 significance level.

Analysis of Variance (ANOVA) for More Than Two Means

Example 9.9 shows a hypothesis that will compare the means of more than two groups.

Example 9.9
A purpose that will generate interval data for more than two groups (freshmen, sophomores, juniors, and seniors)
The purpose of this study is to examine the differences in academic self-concept among freshmen, sophomores, juniors, and seniors.

Because the *t* test is used for comparing only two means, its use is not appropriate for the data generated for the purpose in Example 9.9. For more than two means, analysis of variance (known as ANOVA) can be used. This is proposed in Example 9.10.

Example 9.10
Plans for analyzing the relationship between a nominal and interval variable based on the hypothesis in Example 9.9

The means and standard deviations of the academic self-concept scores will be computed separately for the samples of freshmen, sophomores, juniors, and seniors. The null hypothesis that states that there is no true difference among the four means will be tested with ANOVA using the .05 significance level.[7]

Once again, if the entire populations of the groups are tested, there is no need to test the null hypothesis because it refers to sampling errors, which do not exist when there is no sampling.

Analysis of Change on Interval Variables

Researchers often administer pretests and posttests in order to measure the amount of change. A classic model is a two-group experiment in which an experimental group receives a pretest, followed by a treatment, followed by a posttest. In the meantime, a control group receives a pretest, followed by no special treatment, followed by a posttest. By subtracting each participant's posttest score from his or her pretest score, a *change score* is obtained. The usual analysis for such a setup is to calculate the means and standard deviations for the pretest, posttest, and change scores for each group. These statistics are shown for an experiment of this type in Example 9.11. Inspection of the means shows that, on average, the experimental group gained 4.00 points (i.e., changed 4.00 points in the positive direction) while the control group gained only 1.00 point.

Assuming that the 30 participants in Example 9.11 are random samples from a larger population, the null hypothesis states that the difference between the mean of 4.00 and the mean of 1.00 is the result of random sampling errors. To test the hypothesis, a *t* test could be used.

Example 9.11
Means, standard deviations, and numbers of cases for a two-group experiment, with mean change scores from pretest to posttest shown in bold

	Pretest	Posttest	Change
Experimental group ($n = 30$)	$m = 15.00$ $s = 2.00$	$m = 19.00$ $s = 2.00$	**$m = 4.00$** $s = 2.00$
Control group ($n = 30$)	$m = 14.00$ $s = 2.00$	$m = 15.00$ $s = 2.00$	**$m = 1.00$** $s = 2.00$

---

[7] Those who previously studied statistics may realize that ANOVA will only indicate whether the set of differences is statistically significant. For individual pairs of means, a multiple-comparisons test could be proposed. See Chapter 19.

Example 9.12 is the proposed analysis of the type of data represented in Example 9.11.

Example 9.12
Plans for analyzing change scores from pretest to posttest with two groups when sampling has been used

The means and standard deviations of the pretest scores, posttest scores, and change scores will be calculated. The null hypothesis states that there is no true difference between the two means of the change scores. This hypothesis will be tested with a *t* test using the .05 level to determine whether the difference between these two means is statistically significant.

Analysis for the Relationship Between Two Interval Variables

When examining the relationship between two interval variables, such as two sets of test scores, the most widely used statistic is the *correlation coefficient* (informally called the Pearson *r*).[8] A correlation coefficient describes the direction of a relationship. The direction of a relationship is either *direct* (also called *positive*) or *inverse* (also called *negative*). Example 9.13 shows a hypothesis for a direct relationship in which it is hypothesized that those with higher math computation scores will have higher math word problem scores.

Example 9.13
A hypothesis for a direct relationship; could be analyzed with a correlation coefficient

It is hypothesized that there will be a direct relationship between math computation scores and math word problem scores.

Example 9.14 shows a hypothesis for an inverse relationship in which it is hypothesized that those with higher self-esteem will have lower social anxiety.

Example 9.14
A hypothesis for an inverse relationship; could be analyzed with a correlation coefficient

It is hypothesized that there will be an inverse relationship between self-esteem and social anxiety.

As mentioned above, not all scores are derived from paper-and-pencil tests and personality scales. For instance, "years of education completed" are scores, which could be correlated with scores called "income." The relationship between these two variables could be described with a correlation coefficient.

Correlation coefficients are described in more detail in Chapter 18. At this point, note that coefficients for a direct relationship range from 0.00 to 1.00, with 0.00 indicating no relationship and 1.00 indicating a perfect direct relationship. For an inverse relationship, the range is from 0.00 (no relationship) to –1.00 for a perfect negative relation-

---

[8] Its formal name is the *Pearson product-moment correlation coefficient*. Its symbol is the italicized letter *r*. Computation of it is beyond the scope of this book.

ship. Hypotheses typically do not name a specific predicted value of a correlation coefficient but sometimes refer in general terms to its strength in a statement such as, "It is hypothesized that there will be a *moderate* inverse relationship between self-esteem and social anxiety," in which the word "moderate" indicates, in general terms, the strength of the relationship expected.

When correlation coefficients are reported, it is conventional to also report the mean and standard deviation. Also, if a sample was studied instead of the population, the statistical significance of the correlation coefficient should be tested, which is indicated in Example 9.15.

Example 9.15
Plans for analyzing the relationship between two interval variables based on the hypothesis in Example 9.14

The means and standard deviations of the academic self-esteem scores and the social anxiety scores will be computed. A correlation coefficient will be computed to examine the relationship between the two sets of scores. The null hypothesis that states that there is no true relationship between the two variables will be tested using the .05 significance level.[9]

Concluding Comments

At this point, many readers will be able to select a basic plan for analysis of quantitative data. Those who find that none of the models are suitable should consult Chapters 17 through 19, which discuss statistical analysis in more detail. In addition, even if one of the models in this chapter seems suitable, some modifications in the preliminary statement of the analysis plans may be made after reading the chapters. At the same time, examining the methods of analysis in the research reviewed in preparation of the literature review may help in developing a suitable plan for analysis.

Exercise for Chapter 9

Factual Questions

1. Data that have words instead of numbers to describe their categories are called what type of data?

2. For the relationship between two nominal variables, the null hypothesis can be tested using what test?

3. Rejecting the null hypothesis indicates that a result is
   A. Statistically significant.   B. Statistically insignificant.

---

[9] Those who previously studied statistics may know that a variation on the *t* test is used to determine the significance of a correlation coefficient. However, it is not customary to mention the *t* test when proposing an analysis to determine the significance of a correlation coefficient.

4. When using entire populations in a study, is it necessary to test the null hypothesis?

5. For which of the following is it appropriate to calculate means and standard deviations?
   A. Nominal data.   B. Interval data.

6. What is the technical term for the "amount of spread" in a set of scores?

7. Which of the following is used to describe variability?
   A. The mean.   B. The standard deviation.

8. The *t* test tests the null hypothesis for the difference
   A. Between two means.   B. Among more than two means.

9. Suppose you conducted an experiment in which both the experimental and control groups were given a pretest and a posttest in order to measure the amount of change for each group. How many *t* tests should be conducted? Explain.

10. Which statistic mentioned in this chapter is designed to describe the relationship between two interval variables?

Questions for Discussion

11. If you will be conducting quantitative research, state your research hypothesis (not the statistical hypothesis called the "null hypothesis"), purpose, or question.

12. Will any of the statistics mentioned in this chapter be useful for analyzing the data for the hypothesis, purpose, or question you stated in response to Question 11? If so, write a statement describing your preliminary plans for analysis.

Notes:

Chapter 10
Looking Ahead to Data Analysis for Qualitative Research

The purpose of this chapter is to describe basic methods for analyzing qualitative data, which can be used when writing the Analysis section in a preliminary research proposal. Preparation of a research proposal is the topic of the next chapter.

Because most beginning researchers who choose the qualitative approach to research collect and analyze interview data, this chapter is written on the assumption that responses to interview questions will be analyzed. The principles and guidelines presented here, however, also apply to other types of data such as that generated by focus groups, participant observation, and nonparticipant observation.

The Intermingling of Data Collection and Data Analysis

In quantitative research, it is traditional to collect all data from all participants before beginning the data analysis, which is almost always done with statistical methods. In contrast, preliminary, informal data analysis is usually performed during the process of collecting the data in qualitative research. This is illustrated by three practices commonly employed by qualitative researchers. First, while collecting data, qualitative researchers often engage in *memo writing*, in which the interviewers make notes of their own reactions and interpretations of the data as they are being collected.[1] These memos are then considered later during the more formal data analysis.

Second, as data are being collected, qualitative researchers reflect on it (a form of informal analysis) and use their reflections as a basis for modifying questions, formulating additional questions, and even changing the line of questioning in order to obtain more useful data.

Third, qualitative researchers often collect data from additional participants until they reach the point of *data saturation*. This refers to the failure of additional cases to add new information beyond what was collected from previous participants. The point of data saturation can be determined only by informal data analysis during the course of the interviews.

Selecting a General Approach to Data Analysis

To guide their data analysis, qualitative researchers usually select a general, overarching approach. Some approaches are well delineated with specific data-analytic techniques that guide the analysis. Others are more philosophical and provide only a general

---

[1] Memo writing is also widely used during subsequent, more formal data analysis sessions in which researchers also make notes on their own reactions to the data, their changing interpretations, and the basis for their interpretations.

orientation within which specific analytic techniques (described later in this chapter) are applied. Two general approaches are described next. These descriptions are necessarily brief. (Each approach would require an entire book to describe it fully, much like an entire book would be necessary to fully describe basic statistical methods employed by quantitative researchers.)

The Grounded Theory Approach

Perhaps the most frequently used approach is *grounded theory.*[2] At first, the term "theory" in "grounded theory" can be a bit misleading because it does not refer to a theory of human behavior. Instead, it refers to an *inductive method* of analysis that can lead to theories of behavior. In the inductive approach, which is characteristic of all qualitative research, the results (including "theories") emerge through consideration and analysis of the data. In other words, qualitative researchers start with the data and develop theories based on the data (i.e., grounded in the data).

Put another way, qualitative researchers start with the "pieces" (such as the things the participants say about being abused by their spouses) and make generalizations from them (such as a psychological theory that accounts for why some spouses are abusive and others are not).[3]

The first step in the grounded theory approach is called *open coding*. In this step, segments of the transcripts of the interviews are examined for distinct, separate segments (such as ideas or experiences of the participants) and are "coded" by identifying them and giving each type a name. For instance, in a study of adolescent delinquents, each statement referring to overt aggression by the participants might be coded with a certain color highlighter. Subcategories should also be developed, when possible. For instance, "overt aggression" might have two subcategories: "overt aggression toward peers" and "overt aggression toward adults, including parents and teachers."[4] Preliminary notes on any overarching themes noticed in the data should also be made at this point.

The second step in the grounded theory approach to data analysis is called *axial coding*. At this stage, the transcripts of the interviews and any other data sources, such as memos written during data collection, are reexamined with the purpose of identifying relationships between the categories and themes identified during open coding. Some important types of relationships that might be noted are (1) temporal [X usually precedes Y in time], (2) causal [X caused participants to do Y],[5] (3) associational [X and Y usually or always occur at about the same time but are not believed to be causally connected], (4)

---

[2] See the seminal work on this approach by Strauss & Corbin (1990) for more information.

[3] In contrast, many quantitative researchers start with an existing theory or deduce a new one from existing information and collect data to test the theory. They typically do not examine the data they collect in order to develop completely new theories. Thus, quantitative researchers use a *deductive method*. Put another way, quantitative researchers start with a theory and gather "pieces" of information to test the theory.

[4] In keeping with the inductive approach, categories and subcategories should be suggested by the data during data analysis, not developed prior to analyzing the data. Categories and subcategories developed at this stage should be regarded as preliminary and subject to change during the remainder of the analysis.

[5] Participants' claims that "X caused me to do Y" should be viewed with caution because participants sometimes are not sufficiently insightful into the causes of their behavior. Qualitative researchers need to look at the full context of the behavior and make judgments about the reasonableness of a causal connection.

valence [participants have stronger emotional reactions to X than to Y], and (5) spatial [X and Y occur in the same place *or* X and Y occur in different places].

In the final stages of the grounded theory approach to analysis, qualitative researchers develop a *core category*, which is the main overarching category under which the other categories and subcategories belong. They also attempt to describe the *process* that leads to the relationships identified in the previous stage of the analysis. A process description should describe how the categories work together (or in opposition to each other) in order to arrive at the conditions or behaviors contained in the core category. Such a process description can be illustrated with a diagram, a possibility illustrated later in this chapter.

Consensual Qualitative Approach

Hill's Consensual Qualitative Research approach (CQR), which emphasizes having several individuals participate in the analysis, has specific steps designed to lead to a consensus regarding the meaning and interpretation of the results.[6]

Example 10.1 shows a brief description of the consensual approach in a form that might be included in a brief preliminary proposal for research.

Example 10.1

A brief description of the Consensual Qualitative Research approach to data analysis for a brief, preliminary research proposal

Hill et al.'s (1997) Consensual Qualitative Research approach (CQR) specifies a series of procedures to code the data across participant responses. First, the primary research team will follow these two steps for each case: (a) assign chunks of data to domains (or themes) and (b) develop abstracts within domains based on core ideas (i.e., essence of participant responses). In each step, the primary team members will initially complete the tasks independently and work together to develop a consensus version of the product (i.e., one that is agreeable to everyone on the research team). Then, an auditor who will not be involved in the previous procedure will examine the domains and core ideas to ensure that the data were accurately represented. Any inaccuracies identified by the auditor will be reconsidered by the primary team for possible changes. Following the audit, the primary research team will follow these two steps: (a) identify categories (i.e., clusters of core ideas across cases) based on core ideas in each domain and (b) determine the frequency of categories across cases. Again, the primary research team initially will work independently and then work together to form consensus products in each of the two steps, and the auditor will examine the categories and their frequency to verify their accuracy.[7]

---

[6] For more information, see Hill, C. E. (Ed.). (2011). *Consensual qualitative research: A practical resource for investigating social science phenomena*. Washington, DC: American Psychological Association.
[7] Based on Noonan, B. M., Gallor, S. M., Hensler-McGinnis, N. F., Fassinger, R. E., Wang, S., & Goodman, J. (2004). Challenge and success: A qualitative study of the career development of highly achieving women with physical and sensory disabilities. *Journal of Counseling Psychology, 51,* 68–80.

Specific Techniques for Analysis of Qualitative Data

Below are some commonly used techniques for analyzing qualitative data.

Enumeration

Enumeration is counting how many respondents mentioned each important construct (such as a feeling, behavior, or incident). Some researchers use the information in writing up their results, as illustrated in Example 10.2. Using terms such as "many," "some," and "a few" based on enumeration data makes it possible to discuss the results without cluttering them with specific numbers and percentages for each type of response.[8]

Example 10.2
Sample use of enumeration to guide in the description of the results
Enumeration data were used in the results section that follows. Specifically, the word "many" indicates that more than 50% of the participants gave a particular type of response, the term "some" indicates that between 25% and 50% did so, while the term "a few" indicates that less than 25% did so.

Selecting Quotations

It is very common to present quotations from participants to illustrate points made in the results section of a qualitative research report. Preliminary decisions should be made on which quotations to use during data analysis. Perhaps the most common criterion for the selection of quotations is that they are somehow "representative," which might be indicated by enumeration data discussed above (e.g., the more frequently something is said, the more likely that it is representative). Another criterion is the degree to which a quotation articulates main ideas in the results. For instance, many participants might report the same thing, but one might state it more clearly and forcefully. A third criterion is intensity. Statements made with strong words or higher-than-normal volume might indicate an emotional intensity associated with the statements. These might be more important in helping readers understand the results than less emotional statements.

Intercoder Agreement

When possible, it is desirable to have two or more researchers code the data (as in *open coding* described above under grounded theory). It is customary to have them consult with each other to determine the general approach (e.g., grounded theory, as described above) as well as the specific techniques that will be employed (e.g., enumeration, as described above). Having made these determinations, the researchers typically begin by working independently (i.e., working without consulting with each other) in coding the data. Then, they consult with each other to determine the extent to which their

---

[8] Another approach to enumeration is to count how many times a particular response is given regardless of how many participants gave it. For example, one participant might give the response five times during the interview, another participant might give it three times, and another might give it zero times. The total count for this example is eight. Counting how many times something is said could be reported in the results section of a research report along with how many participants said it, which would provide consumers of research with two types of information.

codes and interpretations are in agreement. If the researchers largely agree, this is evidence of the dependability of the results. Large areas of disagreement indicate that the data are subject to more than one good interpretation. The researchers might then work together to strive to reach a consensus on the results, which is an important feature of Consensual Qualitative Research described earlier. In the Results section of a research report, the extent to which there was initial agreement and the extent to which the researchers were able to arrive at a consensus should be discussed.

Diagramming

Having performed the analysis, qualitative researchers often diagram the results. This is done by placing the *core concept* (an overarching concept identified in the data analysis) in a box at the top and showing the array of related categories below it. Figure 10.1 shows an example for a hypothetical study of misbehavior in a first-grade classroom.

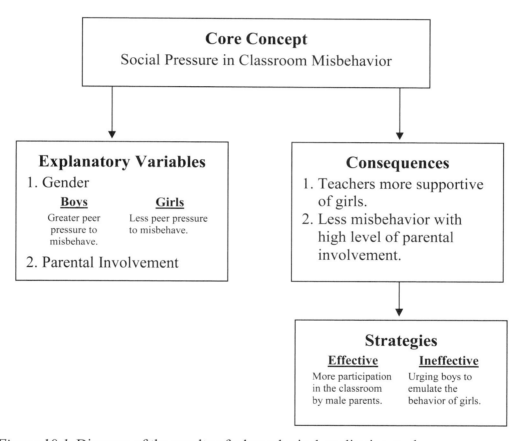

Figure 10.1. Diagram of the results of a hypothetical qualitative study.

For instructional purposes, the drawing in Figure 10.1 was deliberately kept simple. When diagramming real data, as many boxes should be used as are needed to show the complete results. In addition to the types of boxes shown above, others could include boxes for (1) Intervening Conditions (such as reasons why some parents are more involved than others), (2) Associational (such as times of day when misbehavior occurs most often), and (3) Implications (such as training to make teachers more aware of social influences on misbehavior).

Peer Debriefing

Peer debriefing consists of having a qualified researcher who is not directly involved in the data collection or the analysis of the results consult with the researcher. This outsider should consider whether the theory and hypotheses emerging from the data are reasonable in light of how the data were collected and the contents of the transcripts of the interviews as well as any other materials, such as the researchers' memos. For a thesis or dissertation, one or more of the committee members might help with this activity. For those conducting a term project, if the instructor has too many students in a class, using another student for peer debriefing might be useful even though the student is not an experienced researcher.

Auditing

To use auditing, a researcher must keep detailed accounts of how the data were collected and the thought processes used while analyzing the data. Some of these accounts might be in the form of memos resulting from the process of "memo writing," mentioned earlier in this chapter. In preparation for auditing, journals, which are more extensive records of the research process than memos, might also be kept. Keeping accurate records as well as preserving the original raw data is known as creating an *audit trail*.

Auditing is similar to peer debriefing in that a qualified outsider is used for the activity. However, in peer debriefing, the outsider acts more as a consultant who is assisting the researcher. In auditing, the auditor is more like an outside financial auditor for a corporation. The auditor's role is not to participate in the research but to examine it near the end in the hope that he or she will be able to certify the appropriateness of the research methods and interpretations of the results.

Note that the use of auditing is described in Example 10.1 near the beginning of this chapter.

Member Checks

In "member checks," the term "member" refers to participants. When conducting member checks, participants are asked to meet again with the researcher to review the data and results. For instance, they can be asked to verify the accuracy of the transcriptions of the interviews, and they can be asked to comment on the adequacy of the interpretations of the data. When participants disagree with certain interpretations, the researcher should explore how they might be reformulated to take into account the participants' views.

Conducting thorough member checks can be quite time-consuming. As a consequence, qualitative researchers sometimes ask only a sample of the original participants to participate in this activity.

Identifying the Range of Responses

Even when all or almost all respondents provide similar accounts in terms of content, their responses can range in emotional tone (e.g., from mild to strong) as well as in frequency (e.g., an incident that frequently happened to some participants but seldom happened to others). Noting the range of responses when analyzing the data can assist in writing up the results, as illustrated in Example 10.3.

Example 10.3
A sample statement noting the range of emotional responses
Among the subgroup that reported having cold, distant fathers, the emotional language used in describing their relationships with their fathers ranged from mild (such as "I was glad when he would spend a Sunday away from home") to very strong (such as "I felt so unloved that I hated to be near him").

Discrepant Case Analysis

During data analysis, it is important to note and consider discrepant cases. For instance, if almost all those who had cold, distant fathers report negative attitudes toward their fathers but a few are positive, those with the positive attitudes should be noted as discrepant cases. Researchers should consider whether there are other ways that might explain the discrepancy in which the minority differs from the majority. For instance, did the discrepant cases have fathers who were absent most of the time, did they have fathers who became more emotionally warm later in life, and so on. If the original data do not answer these types of questions, it might be useful to ask some of the discrepant cases to return for another interview.

Exercise for Chapter 10

Factual Questions

1. In qualitative research, preliminary, informal data analysis is usually performed when?

2. According to this chapter, what is "perhaps the most frequently used" approach to analysis of data in qualitative research?

3. When using grounded theory, which comes first?
   A. Open coding.   B. Axial coding.

4. "In open coding, categories and subcategories should be developed before beginning to analyze the data." Is the preceding statement true *or* false?
   A. True.   B. False.

5. Is auditing used in consensual qualitative research?

6. Three criteria are mentioned in this chapter for selecting quotations to use in a report of the results. What is the second one that is mentioned?

7. "Peer debriefing" consists of what?

8. In "member checks," the term "member" refers to whom?

9. When identifying the range of responses, this chapter suggests considering emotional tone as well as what else?

Questions for Discussion

10. If you will be conducting qualitative research, have you selected a general approach to the analysis? Explain.

11. If you will be conducting qualitative research, which specific techniques mentioned in this chapter, if any, do you plan to use?

Chapter 11
Preparing a Preliminary Research Proposal

A research proposal is a plan for conducting research. Putting the plan in writing facilitates getting constructive, specific feedback on its adequacy. In addition, approval of a written plan by an instructor or committee helps assure that the research activity will meet the minimum requirements for a satisfactory course grade or approval of a thesis or dissertation. The more specific and detailed a plan is, the more beneficial it is to all concerned.

This chapter is designed to assist in the preparation of a *preliminary* proposal. Readers should anticipate modifying and improving it on the basis of the information in the remaining chapters in this book.

The Title of a Proposal

Typically, the title of a proposal should be a brief statement that names the major variables in the research hypothesis, purpose, or question. In addition, if the research is specifically aimed at certain types of individuals (such as "fraternity members" in Example 11.1), the types of individuals should be mentioned. Finally, to distinguish a proposal from a report of completed research, researchers often give it this subtitle: "A Research Proposal." If this phrase is not included as a subtitle, it should be prominently placed on a cover page that contains the title.

Example 11.1 shows a research hypothesis and the associated title for the research proposal. Notice how the two elements mirror each other. Also notice that the title is not a sentence and does not end with a period, which are appropriate characteristics of titles.

Example 11.1
A research hypothesis and the corresponding title for a research proposal

The research hypothesis: It is hypothesized that small-group counseling intervention will be effective in reducing alcohol consumption among fraternity members.

The corresponding title: The Effectiveness of Small-Group Counseling in Reducing Alcohol Consumption Among Fraternity Members: A Research Proposal

Example 11.2 shows a research purpose and the corresponding title for a proposal. Once again, notice how closely the two mirror each other.

Example 11.2
A research purpose and the corresponding title for a research proposal

The research purpose: The research purpose is to identify practices implemented by elementary school principals to reduce bullying in their schools.

The corresponding title: Practices Implemented by Elementary School Principals to Reduce Bullying: A Research Proposal

Example 11.3 shows a research question and the corresponding title for a proposal. Note that questions are rarely used as titles of research proposals and reports. Hence, the title in the example is a statement and not a question.

Example 11.3

A research question and the corresponding title for a research proposal

The research question: To what extent are farm workers with limited English language skills aware of the risks of pesticide exposure?

The corresponding title: Awareness of the Risks of Pesticide Exposure Among Farm Workers with Limited English Language Skills: A Research Proposal

The Introduction and Literature Review

Student researchers should seek guidance on whether they are expected to begin their proposal with an introduction followed by a separate literature review *or* to begin with an essay that integrates the two elements (i.e., an integrated introduction and literature review).[1]

If the introduction is to be a separate essay, it should contain the following elements:

1. identification of the problem area;
2. conceptual definitions of key terms;
3. an indication of why the topic is worthy of investigation, including the types of implications the results might have;
4. a brief description of any relevant theories, which should be expanded on in the literature review; and
5. a statement of the specific research hypotheses, purposes, or questions the research is designed to explore.

When providing conceptual definitions of key terms, it is not only acceptable but often desirable to quote or paraphrase definitions that have been found in the literature on the topic. Using previously published definitions, assuming they are adequate, helps to build a body of consistent research on a topic, with various researchers using the same definitions. Also, published definitions typically have been developed by professionals who have extensive experience in the field, and their definitions have usually been reviewed and found acceptable by their peers. Example 11.4 shows a conceptual definition of "potentially traumatic events" (PTEs) from an authoritative source presented in a literature review.

Example 11.4

A conceptual definition of a key term in an introduction (quotation of a published definition is acceptable and often desirable)

---

[1] Frequently, the requirements for a thesis or dissertation, including the proposal for it, specify that the introduction is to be presented in the first chapter and a separate literature review is to be presented in the second chapter. The requirements for proposals and reports of research conducted as term projects will vary, depending on course objectives.

. . . most studies focus exclusively on events that meet the definition of a traumatic event (i.e., Criterion A1) in the *Diagnostic and Statistical Manual of Mental Disorders* (4th ed., text rev.; *DSM–IV–TR*; American Psychiatric Association, 2000): experiencing, witnessing, or being confronted with an event that involved actual or threatened death or serious injury or a threat to physical integrity. [2]

A *conceptual definition* is a dictionary-like definition that sets the general boundaries that establish the meaning of a construct. In contrast, *operational definitions* describe the physical process used to identify the construct and "see" it. For instance, to operationalize the conceptual definition in Example 11.4, the authors employed a "17-item self-report measure consisting of items that assess the symptom criteria for a PTSD . . . . Participants responded to items in terms of their self-nominated most distressing lifetime event. Items were rated on a 5-point scale ranging from 1 (*not at all*) to 5 (*extremely*) with regard to the previous 2 weeks." Having the participants respond to the scale is a physical process, which results in scores that represent the construct.

While conceptual definitions are presented in the introduction to a research proposal, operational definitions typically are presented in the Methods section of a proposal, which is covered later in this chapter.

In an introduction that is presented separately from the literature review, the number of supporting references should be limited because most of them should be reserved for use in the separate review. However, it is acceptable in a separate introduction to refer to important points that the literature supports without giving references, as illustrated in Example 11.5.

Example 11.5
A statement in a separate introduction that refers to the literature review that will be presented separately (common in theses and dissertations)
As the literature review in Chapter 2 will show, the XYZ model of change for interventions for alcohol abuse has been widely studied with adults and generally has been reported to be effective. However, there have been no studies of the effectiveness of the model with college students, which will be explored in the research proposed here.

Of course, any assertions that are made in the introduction based on the literature should be reiterated with appropriate in-text citations in the separate literature review that follows.

If an integrated introduction and literature review is expected, the same five introductory elements that were mentioned above for a separate introduction should be covered.

The Introduction and Literature Review in Qualitative Research

The material up to this point in this chapter applies equally to quantitative and qual-

---

[2] This example was adapted and modified from Anders, S. L., Frazier, P. A., & Shallcross, S. L. (2012). Prevalence and effects of life event exposure among undergraduate and community college students. *Journal of Counseling Psychology*, *59*, 449–457. doi: 10.1037/a0027753

itative research. However, in qualitative research, the personal perspectives and experiences of the researcher relating to the research topic might be addressed in the introduction (or combined introduction and literature review). Because qualitative research is inherently more subjective than quantitative research, qualitative researchers recognize that their personal perspectives and experiences may influence their collection and interpretation of data.[3] By acknowledging this in writing, qualitative researchers reinforce their own awareness of this possibility and provide a disclaimer. Usually, it is sufficient to discuss this matter briefly and in general terms. Example 11.6 shows such a statement.

Example 11.6
A statement regarding personal perspectives and experiences for inclusion in the introduction to a proposal for qualitative research

My interest in this research topic (spirituality of nurses and its effects on nursing practices) stems from my own deep religious beliefs as a Catholic who practiced nursing for a decade in a hospital affiliated with the church. My religious beliefs were a source of personal strength, especially when assisting terminally ill patients. In conducting this proposed research, my experiences will undoubtedly provide a filter through which I will view the emerging data. However, because this study will be conducted in a hospital that is not affiliated with a religious institution and has nurses with diverse religious backgrounds, I will be open to the possibility that my perceptions may not parallel the perceptions of the nurses selected to participate in this study.

Another distinction between proposals for quantitative and qualitative research is that proposals for qualitative research seldom contain hypotheses. This is because qualitative researchers emphasize "following the data," an inductive process discussed in the previous chapter. Thus, the introduction/literature review for a qualitative research proposal should end with general purposes or questions rather than predictions specified with hypotheses.

The Method Section of a Proposal

The Method section is given the major heading "Method," which is usually centered on the page. It almost always has at least two subsections: one on participant selection and one on measures, in that order. Typically, these two sections have subheadings that are flush left and in italics (i.e., *Participants* and *Measures*). These are sometimes followed by a subsection on procedures, as needed, which is discussed below.

Participants
Start this subsection of the proposal with a description of the population or the pool of potential participants from which the participants will be selected, and state the basis for the selection (e.g., random selection, convenience sampling). Second, indicate how many names will be drawn. Even if it is subject to change, name a specific number or

---

[3] In contrast, quantitative researchers strive to be objective and try to plan studies in such a way that their personal perspectives do not influence how the data are collected and interpreted.

range of numbers such as 20 to 30, which will allow for feedback from instructors on the adequacy of the sample size. Third, provide a best guess as to the rate of participation, allowing for the fact that some of those contacted may refuse to participate.[4] Fourth, describe the informed consent procedures used, if any. Typically, informed consent is in writing. Most colleges and universities as well as funding agencies have specific guidelines for obtaining such consent. Fifth, discuss any anticipated limitations in the selection of participants and, if possible, discuss how these might affect the results. Example 11.7 illustrates how these five elements might be presented in a proposal.

Example 11.7
Sample statement describing participants that covers the five elements mentioned above

The population consists of all 104 social workers employed at the main office of the state social work agency in a large Midwestern city. Fifty percent ($n = 52$) of the names will be drawn at random for the sample. Because the questionnaires will be distributed by the social workers' immediate supervisors, a high rate of participation, perhaps as high as 80%, is expected, which would yield a working sample of 42 social workers. An informed consent form that has been approved by the funding agency and that indicates that participation is fully voluntary will be distributed with the questionnaires along with a stamped, self-addressed envelope for return of the forms and questionnaires. In addition to items that measure attitudes, the questionnaire will contain several items that test for knowledge of laws regarding the topic of this research. Because of this, those social workers who are less knowledgeable might be less inclined to participate in the research. To the extent that this is true, the results of the proposed survey might overestimate social workers' knowledge of the laws relating to the research topic. A second limitation results from the fact that a sample of convenience consisting only of workers employed at the main office will serve as participants. Because those who work in the main office may differ from those who work in satellite offices, any generalizations to all social workers in the city will need to be made with considerable caution.

Note that if a sample of convenience (also known as an accidental sample) is used, it is a good idea to explicitly acknowledge this as a weakness, which is done near the end of Example 11.7 above. In this particular example, a random sample will be drawn (a strength), but it will be drawn only from a convenient group (a weakness). Note that a random sample from a convenient pool of potential participants is called a convenience sample despite the use of random selection.

---

[4] Rates of participation can vary greatly depending on the circumstances of sampling and the topic of the study. For instance, in an institutional setting such as a corporation, a high rate of participation might be expected (such as 95% or more) when the research is being conducted for corporate purposes. On the other hand, for a mailed survey to the general public, a response rate of 20% or less would not be surprising. Beginning researchers should consult the literature they reviewed to determine participation rates reported in published research on their topics and use this information as a basis for estimating possible participation rates in their proposals.

Measures

This subsection of a research proposal should describe the measures (e.g., questionnaires, interview questions, tests) that will be used in the research.

In qualitative research, demographic data (i.e., data on the background characteristics of the participants) are often collected with interview questions. In quantitative research, this type of information is usually collected with a questionnaire. In either case, the types of demographics that will be collected should be described in a proposal. Example 11.8 shows how one author did this.

Example 11.8
Sample description of demographic information that will be collected

Participants will complete a brief demographic form immediately before participating in their respective focus group. Information about participants' age, gender, race, year in school, and the number of diversity courses taken during the course of their entire university experience will be collected. The researchers will provide students with four broad categories of diversity courses to guide their reporting of how many such courses they plan to take, including ethnic studies, gender and women's studies, general diversity, and intergroup relations. Consistent with the study purpose, demographic data will provide a fuller description of our sample and served as a point of comparison across our two groups.[5]

To collect the data relating to their research purposes and questions (data that go beyond the collection of demographics), qualitative researchers frequently interview participants using semi-structured or loosely structured interviews. Even though they will not be highly structured, the Measures section of a proposal should indicate the types of information that will be collected with the interviews. This is illustrated in Example 11.9.

Example 11.9
Sample description of types of information to be collected via open-ended questions in a qualitative study

In the resulting semi-structured protocol, each participant will answer a standard set of questions (e.g., overall experiences as an international student; relationship with advisor; discussion with advisor of experiences as an international student; how being an international student affected advising relationship; advice for international students and their advisors), and researchers will pursue additional areas based on participant answers. The complete protocol appears in the Appendix. (p. 49)[6]

For studies that will employ interviews, other matters that should be addressed in a proposal are the anticipated length of the interviews, where they will take place, and whether they will be audiotaped. This is illustrated in Example 11.10.

---

[5] This example was adapted and modified from Kordesh, K. S., Spanierman, L. B., & Neville, H. A. (2012). White university students' racial affect: Understanding the antiracist type. *Journal of Diversity in Higher Education, 6,* 33–50. doi: 10.1037/a0030102

[6] This example was adapted and modified from Knox, S., Sokol, J. T., Inman, A. G., Schlosser, L. Z., Nilsson, J., & Wang, Y. (2013). International advisees' perspectives on the advising relationship in counseling psychology doctoral programs. *International Perspectives in Psychology: Research, Practice, Consultation, 2,* 45–61. doi: 10.1037/ipp0000001

Example 11.10

Description of key characteristics of data for interviews in a qualitative study

The interviews will last approximately two hours each and take place at a location of the participants' choosing. Participants will be asked for permission to audiotape the interviews. For those who do not grant permission, detailed notes will be taken. The information from the initial interviews will be examined for themes that will be explored in the follow-up interviews, which will last approximately 90 minutes each. (p. 155)[7]

Quantitative researchers usually use objective-type measures to collect the data relating to their research hypotheses, purposes, or questions. Their proposals should (1) name the measures that will be used, (2) briefly describe what they measure, (3) describe the possible range of scores, (4) provide references where more information can be obtained, (5) provide samples if their reproduction in a proposal will not violate test security or copyright law, and (6) summarize validity and reliability information. All six of these elements are present in Example 11.11.

Example 11.11

Description of an objective scale to be used in quantitative research

Social support will be measured using the Medical Outcomes Study Modified Social Support Survey (MSSS; Sherbourne & Stewart, 1991), an 18-item measure of perceived social support. This measure assesses four aspects of social support: (a) tangible (e.g., "help if you are confined in bed"), (b) emotion/information (e.g., "listen to you when you need to talk"), (c) affection (e.g., "show you love and affection"), and (d) positive social interaction (e.g., "do something enjoyable with"). Scores will range from 0 to 100 on all four subscales. The measure possesses good convergent and divergent validity, correlating strongly and positively with family and marital functioning, mental health, and social activity, and negatively with loneliness and role limitations. There is also good evidence of test-retest reliability and stability over a one-year interval with coefficients for the four subscales ranging from .72 to .78 (Sherbourne & Stewart, 1991). (p. 108)[8]

If new measures will be developed for use in the proposed research, the description of them should be as specific as possible, indicating what they will measure, how many and what types of items will be written (e.g., multiple-choice; Likert-type from strongly agree to strongly disagree), the possible range of scores, as well as sample items. In addition, the proposal should indicate whether the new measure will be pilot-tested and, if so, what types of information will be obtained in the pilot test. For a class project, a pilot test of a new measure could have as its goal only to determine whether the pilot study participants understand the questions and are responsive. For theses and dissertations, more

---

[7] This example was adapted and modified from Cabrera, N. L., & Padilla, A. M. (2004). Entering and succeeding in the "culture of college": The story of two Mexican heritage students. *Hispanic Journal of Behavioral Sciences, 26,* 152–170.

[8] This example was adapted and modified from Williams, R. M., Turner, A. P., Hatzakis, M., Chu, S., Rodriguez, A. A., Bowen, J. D., & Haselkorn, J. K. (2004). Social support among veterans with multiple sclerosis. *Rehabilitation Psychology, 49,* 106–113.

technical information (e.g., statistical evidence of validity and reliability of the scores) might be expected. As a consequence, if a suitable, previously published measure for which technical information already exists can be identified, it should be used instead of developing a new measure.

As noted near the beginning of this chapter, the introduction to a proposal should provide *conceptual definitions* of key variables. The specific measures that will measure the key variables provide the *operational definitions* (i.e., the definitions in terms of physical operations or steps that will be taken to "see" the variables). Readers of a research proposal will not be able to understand the operationalization without detailed descriptions of the measures, which makes having an adequate measures subsection of a research proposal essential to a good proposal.

Procedures

The subsection called "Procedures" is usually flush left in italics under the major heading of "Method." It usually follows the subsections on "Participants" and "Measures."

The subsection on procedures is needed whenever there are important physical steps that will be taken in order to conduct the research that were not duly described under "Participants" and "Measures." A common use for the "Procedures" subsection is to describe the steps that will be taken to administer the measures. This is illustrated in Example 11.12.

> **Example 11.12**
> *Description of procedures relating to informed consent*
> After Human Subjects Committee approval, prospective participants will be sent cover letters describing the survey study and will be offered $20 as an inducement to participate. After a 2-week period, telephone contact will be attempted with those who have not already returned signed consent letters. For those individuals who are not able to complete the survey independently, an anonymous call-in telephone response format will be made available. (p. 141)[9]

The proposed procedures for an experiment should also be described. Sometimes, this material is in the "Procedures" subsection. Sometimes, it is presented under its own subheading of "Experimental Procedures." This subsection should describe the experimental treatments in detail (e.g., who will administer them, how they will be administered, when they will be administered) as well as the number of groups that will be formed for the experiment and how the groups will be formed (e.g., through random assignment to treatment conditions).

The Analysis Section of a Proposal

The Analysis section is given the major heading "Analysis," which is usually centered on the page. For a quantitative proposal for basic research, this section can be rather

---

[9] This example was adapted and modified from Sherman, J. E., DeVinney, D. J., & Sperling, K. B. (2004). Social support and adjustment after spinal cord injury: Influence of past peer-mentoring experiences and current live-in partner. *Rehabilitation Psychology, 49,* 140–149.

brief, naming the statistics that will be computed. If there is more than one hypothesis, purpose, or question and different statistics will be used for each, then organize the description of the analysis accordingly (e.g., "For the first hypothesis, the following statistics will be computed…")."

The Analysis section of a qualitative proposal may be somewhat longer than that of a quantitative proposal if the general approach to the analysis as well as the specific analytic techniques are to be described in detail. For instance, a qualitative proposal that describes who will participate in the analysis and how they will participate (as recommended in the previous chapter) will require a longer narrative than simply stating in a quantitative proposal that standard statistical tools will be used, as in this statement: "Means and standard deviations will be computed."

For a quantitative proposal, it is usually not considered necessary to indicate whether a statistical computer program will be used nor is it necessary to name the particular program because it is assumed that all programs will yield the same values of standard statistics. On the other hand, if a computer program will be used in qualitative analysis, it should be named because the available programs differ greatly in their underlying assumptions and approaches to the more loosely structured data generated by qualitative studies.[10]

The preliminary plans for analysis based on the material in the previous two chapters will usually be sufficient as a starting point in a preliminary proposal. Feedback on it from instructors and others as well as material presented later in this book may lead to refinements and improvements in this section of a proposal.

The Discussion Section of a Proposal

The Discussion section is given the major heading "Discussion," which is usually centered on the page. Typically, this section begins with a brief summary of the proposal up to that point. The summary should briefly describe not only the mechanical aspects of the study that will be conducted but also restate the research hypotheses, purposes, or questions to be explored, as well as the context for the study (such as that provided by theory and previous research). Following this, the possible implications of the study results should be stated. Example 11.13 shows how this might be done.

Example 11.13
A statement of implications for a proposal
If the hypotheses are confirmed, there will be three major implications. First, preservice teachers should experience internships early in their teacher education programs. Second, the internship should be of at least an academic year's duration. Fi-

---

[10] Discussing the use of computer programs for the analysis of data is beyond the scope of this book. The most popular program for quantitative analysis is SPSS. More information on it can be obtained by visiting the publisher's website at www.spss.com. At www.content-analysis.de/qualitative.html, some popular programs for qualitative analysis are described.

nally, interns should have experiences working at more than one grade level. (pp. 154–155)[11]

Finally, an acknowledgment of the limitations (i.e., weakness of the proposed study, such as having to use a sample of convenience) and a description of the strengths of the proposed study (e.g., such as using a larger sample than previous researchers) should be included.

References at the End of a Proposal

The References section is given the major heading "References," which is usually centered on the page. Note that it should include only references that were cited in the proposal. It should *not* be a "suggested reading list" in which related sources that are not cited are included.

Chapter 4 describes how to format selected source material in American Psychological Association style and American Sociological Association style.

The Major Components of a Proposal

The following is an outline of the major components of a research proposal, all of which have been mentioned in this chapter. Note that the major headings are centered and in bold. The subheadings under the main heading "Method" (i.e., *Participants*, *Measures*, and *Procedures*) are in italics and are flush left. Additional subheadings may be added as needed. For instance, in a long literature review, there could be subheadings such as "*Early Studies*," "*Related Theories*," and "*Recent Findings*."[12] Also, in a long discussion, there might be subheadings such as "*Summary*," "*Limitations*," "*Implications*," and "*Directions for Future Research*."

Title: The Influence of X on Y Among Residents of
King County: A Research Proposal

Introduction[13]
Literature Review
Method

Participants

Measures

Procedures (or *Experimental Procedures*)

Analysis

---

[11] This example was adapted and modified from Pollard, R. R., & Pollard, C. J. (2003). Principals' perceptions of extended teacher internships. *Education, 124*, 151–156.

[12] These subheadings are only suggestive. They will vary greatly depending on the content of the literature review.

[13] As noted earlier in this chapter, the introduction is typically presented in Chapter 1 and the literature review is presented in Chapter 2 in a proposal for a thesis or dissertation. For a proposal for a term project, instructors may require that it begin with a literature review in which the introductory statements are integrated.

Discussion
References

Concluding Comments

It is important to put the preliminary plans for research in writing as a preliminary research proposal early in the research process. This will allow time for the writer to later review the proposal with a fresh mindset as well as to obtain feedback from others, which can be used in improving it. Waiting to begin writing until an "outstanding" proposal has been mentally conceptualized is almost always a mistake.

Note that much of the material in a research proposal can be used again in the preparation of the written research report, which is the last step in the research process that is covered in Chapter 27. Thus, efforts made to write a solid proposal will pay off not only in terms of providing concrete guidance for conducting research but also in terms of making the preparation of the final report easier.

Exercise for Chapter 11

Factual Questions

1. According to this chapter, the title of a research proposal should be a brief statement that names what?

2. According to this chapter, is it acceptable to quote definitions from the literature?

3. For which type of research is it usually more appropriate for the writer to describe personal perspectives and experiences that relate to the research topic?
    A. Qualitative research.   B. Quantitative research.

4. Which of the following subheadings usually appears first under the major heading of "Method"?
    A. Participants.   B. Measures.

5. "According to this chapter, because it is impossible to know how many of the individuals contacted will actually participate in a study, a proposal should not name a specific number." Is the preceding statement true *or* false?
    A. True.   B. False.

6. How many elements should be covered in the section of the proposal on participants?

7. "When qualitative researchers plan to interview participants using open-ended questions, they should indicate in the proposal the types of information that will be collected." Is the preceding statement true *or* false?

    A. True.   B. False.

8. Which type of definition is stated in terms of physical operations that will be taken to "see" the variables?

    A. Operational definitions.   B. Conceptual definitions.

Question for Discussion

9. At this point, you should be prepared to write a preliminary proposal for research. Which of the major components of it are you best prepared to write? Are there any parts you think will be difficult for you to write? Explain.

Part B

Issues in Participant Selection

An overview of issues in participant selection for qualitative and quantitative research was provided in Chapter 7 in Part A of this book. More detailed information is provided in this part of the book.

Students who wrote preliminary research proposals based on the material in Part A should reconsider the section on participant selection in light of the material in the next two chapters.

Notes:

Chapter 12
Participant Selection in Quantitative Research

The fundamentals of participant selection in both quantitative and qualitative research were covered in Chapter 7. In this chapter, methods for selecting participants in *quantitative* research are discussed in more detail. A more detailed discussion for *qualitative* research is presented in Chapter 13.

Populations and Bias in Sampling

A *population* is the group in which the researcher is ultimately interested. A population can be large, such as all credentialed teachers in California, or small, such as all teachers employed at a particular school. A *sample* is any subgroup drawn from a population.

It is useful to distinguish between a *population of interest* and an *accessible population.* For instance, a researcher might be interested in all criminals who have committed a certain type of crime. However, the accessible population consists only of those who have been arrested for the crime. Successful criminals who have never been apprehended are unknowable to the researcher and, therefore, cannot be included in the sample. Note that generalizations to the population of interest based on the results of studying a sample of the accessible population should be made cautiously because the two groups might differ in fundamental ways.

Biased sampling is any procedure for drawing a sample that gives some types of individuals a greater chance of being included in the sample than other types. For instance, calling for volunteers to participate in a study is a biased sampling procedure because the types of individuals who tend to volunteer to be participants have a greater chance than the types who tend not to volunteer. Likewise, using participants who happen to be readily available, such as the students in a professor's class (known as a convenience or "accidental" sample), is biased against the types of students who, for whatever reason, are not taking that particular class with that professor.

A bias in sampling can be subtle. For instance, one might look at an audience and try to select a representative sample from it, judging such things as the ethnic diversity, age, and gender makeup of the members of the audience. Still, there might be some subtle bias such as tending to select those who appear to be more agreeable, or tending to select those who are seated near the front of the auditorium, and so on. Such individuals might be different from the audience as a whole in ways that could affect the outcome of the study. To avoid both subtle and obvious biases, human judgment should be removed from the selection process. This can be achieved by using a neutral, nonjudgmental process called *random sampling.* Two types of random sampling are described next in this chapter.

Simple Random Sampling

The only way to preclude bias in sampling is to draw a *random sample* of names and to convince all those individuals whose names have been selected to participate in the study.[1] Conventional wisdom dictates that if a sample is not drawn at random, it should be presumed to be biased.

Simple random sampling consists of giving each member of a population an equal and independent chance of being selected. Conceptually, the simplest way to do this is to write the names of all members of a population on slips of paper, put them in a container, and draw the number needed for the sample. With this process, each individual has an equal chance of being selected. In addition, the selections are independent (i.e., who is selected first has no influence on who is selected second, and so on).

Another way to draw a simple random sample is to use a table of random numbers. To do this, begin by giving each member of a population a "number name." For a population consisting of hundreds of individuals (say 500), each number name should contain three digits. The first name would be 000, the next would be 001, the next would be 002, and so on. Because individuals are merely being renamed (and not selected) at this point, it does not matter who is given which name, as long as each individual is given a unique number and all number names contain the same number of digits. The next step is to consult a table of random numbers; a sample page from such a table is shown in Table 1 near the end of this book. Without looking at the numbers, the researcher should place his or her finger on the page. The number nearest to the finger is the starting point. Assume that the finger is closest to the first number in Row 18 in the table. This number is 2. Because three digits are needed for a population of 500, the two digits following the 2 are also needed, yielding the number 233. Thus, the individual with the number name of 233 is selected for the sample. The next three-digit number to the right in the row is 255, so individual number 255 is also selected. The next number is 769. Because the population has only 500 individuals, there is no one named 769, so this number is discarded. Proceeding across the row, the next number is 497, so individual number 497 is selected, and so on.

Tables of random numbers are constructed so that the numbers in them have no sequence or relation to each other. Conceptually, this is how a table is prepared: (1) write the digits from 0 through 9 on slips of paper, (2) mix them up in a container and draw one without looking, (3) write down whatever number is on the slip that was drawn. Then, put the slip that was drawn back into the container and repeat the three steps until a book of random numbers has been compiled.[2] Considering how a table of random numbers is constructed shows that there is no bias in the placement of the numbers because each number had an equal and independent chance of being placed in each position in the table. Thus, there is no bias when the table is used to select a sample.

---

[1] For ethical reasons, individuals frequently cannot be forced to participate in a study nor can they be penalized for refusing to participate. However, there are exceptions. For instance, researchers at a corporation doing research on an issue of corporate interest might be able to penalize nonparticipants. In addition, some types of data are available without the consent of individuals to whom they apply. For instance, under certain circumstances, institutional researchers can obtain grades from cumulative records for a random sample of students without the students' permission.

[2] In practice, computer programs are used to prepare tables of random numbers.

Consider Example 12.1, which shows how to use the table of random numbers for a population of 90.

Example 12.1

Using the table of random numbers near the end of this book to select a sample from a population of 90 individuals

Because the population size has two digits (i.e., 90), the researcher gave each member of the population a two-digit name. The first individual in the population list was given the name 00, the next person was given the name 01, the next 02, and so on. Then without looking at the page, the researcher placed a finger on the page in a table of random numbers (i.e., Table 1 near the end of this book) and happened to touch the first number in Row 10. The first two digits in this row are 8 and 5 so person number 85 was selected to be in the sample. The next two digits (ignoring the space between them) are 0 and 3, so individual number 03 was selected. The next two digits are 9 and 4, which form the number 94. Because the population contains only 90 individuals, this number does not select anyone. The next two digits are 3 and 4, so individual number 34 was selected. This process was continued until the researcher had drawn 50% of the names.

It is important to note that because a sample is random (and therefore unbiased), it is not necessarily free of errors. In fact, it is safe to presume that all random samples have been influenced by random errors (i.e., chance errors). This becomes clear with an extreme example. Suppose a population consists of 200 men and 200 women. Drawing a random sample of only six individuals might easily yield a sample with four men and two women even though 50% of the population consists of men. Thus, this random sample would be unrepresentative in terms of gender. Fortunately, because random sampling is unbiased (toward men or toward women), the larger the random sample is, the smaller are the chances of a large misrepresentation (of gender or any other characteristic). Sample size is discussed further near the end of this chapter.

A major advantage of random sampling is that a class of statistics known as *inferential statistics* allows researchers to estimate how likely it is that the results have been influenced by random sampling errors created by the random sampling. Perhaps the most well-known inferential statistic is a *margin of error*. In reports of political polls, for instance, a margin of error is often cited. If 54% of a random sample is in favor of a certain ballot proposition and the margin of error is 3 points, then about three percentage points on either side of 54% should be allowed because of the possible influence of random errors. Thus, the best estimate is that the true percentage in the population that favors the proposition is between 51% (i.e., 54% minus 3%) and 57% (i.e., 54% plus 3%). Various types of inferential statistics and their uses are described in Chapter 19. At this point, however, it is important to note that there are no general statistical methods to assist in the assessment of the errors created by a bias in sampling; inferential statistics evaluate only random errors—not errors created by a bias.

Stratified Random Sampling

Random selection can be improved by combining it with stratification on a relevant variable. When a researcher *stratifies*, he or she divides the population into subgroups, each of which has a common characteristic. For instance, populations are often stratified on the basis of gender. To do this, the names of men are put into a pool separate from the names of women (this is the stratification). Then, random samples are drawn separately from each of the two pools. Typically, a researcher will draw the same percentage—not the same number—from each pool. For instance, if a population of social workers has 100 women and 60 men, drawing 10% at random separately from the pool of women and the pool of men will yield a sample with 10 women and 6 men, which is representative of the gender composition of the population. This is an example of the processes called *stratified random sampling*.

It is possible to stratify on more than one variable. In Example 12.2, there are two stratification variables.

Example 12.2
Stratified random sampling with two stratification variables (gender and years of experience)

The population of 160 teachers employed by a school district was divided into four groups for the purposes of stratification: (1) 60 women with five or more years of experience, (2) 40 women with fewer than five years of experience, (3) 20 men with five or more years of experience, and (4) 40 men with fewer than five years of experience. Random sampling was used to select 20% separately from each of the four subgroups, yielding a random sample stratified on the basis of gender and years of experience.

Systematic Sampling

Selecting every other person on a list is an example of systematic sampling. In this instance, every 2nd individual is drawn. For a smaller sample, a larger interval might be used such as every 10th individual. Thus, the definition of *systematic sampling* can be stated in this way: Systematic sampling is drawing every nth individual from a list, where n is the interval size such as a small interval of 2 or a larger interval of 10.

A potential weakness of systematic sampling is that the population list might be ordered in such a way that a biased sample is selected. For instance, perhaps a teacher's list of students has a pairing of students such that every other student is above average and the alternating students are below average. Selecting every other student from such an ordered list would result in either a sample of all above-average or a sample of all below-average students. To avoid this type of problem, an alphabetical list should be used. Furthermore, selections should be made all the way through the list. For instance, it would be inappropriate to select every other student only through the letter "K" because different ethnic/national origin groups tend to be in different areas of the alphabet.

Even though systematic sampling is not random,[3] using an alphabetical list and drawing throughout the list until the end of the list is reached is considered, for all practical purposes, to be as good as random sampling.

Cluster Sampling

Cluster sampling can be used when all members of a population are already assembled into groups. Each group is called a cluster, and clusters instead of individuals are selected for a sample. For instance, all Girl Scouts in New York could be a population of interest. All the members belong to a group called a troop. By drawing 50% of the troops, a cluster sample of 50% would be obtained.

An advantage of cluster sampling is that it is often more convenient to draw clusters instead of individuals. For instance, for a study of attitudes of Girl Scouts toward some issue, it would be far easier to select a sample of troops and contact each group leader (to ask for cooperation in distributing and collecting attitude scales) than it would be to contact individual Girl Scouts. Also, note that the girls are more likely to cooperate and participate in such a study when asked to do so by their troop leaders than by a letter sent by a researcher that the Scouts do not know.

For cluster sampling to qualify as an excellent method of sampling, two conditions must be met. First, a reasonable number of clusters must be drawn, regardless of the number of individuals in them. For instance, suppose for a study of patient satisfaction with hospital services in Texas, two hospitals were drawn and the hospital administrators agree to help in getting responses from their patients. If both are large hospitals, the survey might have hundreds of respondents. However, with only two hospitals, it is likely that the sample does not contain the full range of diversity as the entire population of hospital patients in Texas. It could easily be, for instance, that both hospitals are privately owned (as opposed to public), it could be that both are located in suburban areas, and so on. To overcome this lack of diversity, a much larger number of hospitals would need to be drawn.

The second condition for cluster sampling to be regarded as excellent is that the clusters must be drawn at random. Otherwise, the process for selecting the clusters will be presumed to be biased, resulting in a biased sample.

Sample Size in Quantitative Research

As you know from Chapter 7, there is no easy answer to the question of what size a sample should be. Five considerations were described on pages 59 and 60. Briefly, they are: (1) the requirements of an instructor regarding sample size for a term project; (2) the requirements for a thesis or dissertation; (3) the norms for different types of research, which can often be determined by noting the sample sizes in published research of various types; (4) the difficulty of locating some types of participants; and (5) trading off a

---

[3] In random sampling (such as drawing names out of a hat), each selection of a participant is independent of all other selections. Systematic sampling does not have independence; once the first person is selected, all others who will be selected are immediately determined. For instance, if the first individual selected is number 02 and every other person is to be selected, then individuals 04, 06, 08, and so on are also selected.

smaller sample in favor of obtaining a more diverse sample. Additional considerations are discussed below.

Potential for Harm to Participants

If it is anticipated that potential harm might result from procedures used in a research study, then initial studies using very small numbers of participants should be conducted. This will allow researchers to determine the possible magnitude of the harm as well as the benefits. An example is a medical study in which an experimental type of surgery is to be used. Because of the potential for harm from surgery, initial studies might have only one participant each. If these indicate that the harm is manageable while creating a reasonable benefit, then subsequent studies with larger numbers of participants would be justified.[4]

The Need for Pilot Studies

A *pilot study* is an initial study that is conducted to determine feasibility. For instance, will participants fully cooperate, will there be a high rate of participation, and, do the measurement tools work as well as expected? To get preliminary answers to such questions, only a small number of participants are needed. Based on their reactions, decisions can be made on modifying research methods so that subsequent research with larger numbers of participants is more likely to be fruitful.

Pilot studies can contribute to knowledge on a topic and often are publishable in an academic journal when their results are especially promising and the rationale underlying the research is demanding (such as testing a tenet of an important theory). Publication of such studies sometimes stimulates other researchers to conduct more definitive studies on this topic.

Number of Subgroups to Be Examined

As a general rule, the more subgroups that will be examined in a study, the larger the total sample size should be. For instance, in a study of algebra readiness among freshmen in a high school, a sample of 100 might be deemed adequate, depending on the population size. If, however, the readiness is to be compared across four subgroups representing four different socioeconomic levels, then the 100 students will be divided into four groups of perhaps 25 each, which would be on the small side for a survey. Increasing the total sample size would yield subgroups with more participants, which would make the results for subgroups more reliable.

Importance of Precise Results

The larger the sample, the more *precise* the results are. If highly precise results are needed, then very large samples should be used. For instance, consider the surveys conducted by the United States Bureau of Labor to determine the unemployment rate. For political and economic reasons (such as stock prices), highly precise percentages are

---

[4] Note that participants should be informed in writing of potential harm. They also should be informed of potential benefits, which will assist them in making an informed decision on participation. As a rule, beginning researchers should avoid conducting studies with any obvious potential for harm.

needed. For instance, a shift of only a couple of tenths of a point could cause major changes in the stock market prices because unemployment is an important indicator of economic conditions. To get results that are precise to the level needed, the bureau interviews as many as 60,000 individuals regarding their employment status. In contrast, when it is not important if a result is off by several percentage points, as in a typical national political poll, researchers might use 1,500 or fewer participants.

Statistical Significance

Quantitative researchers are usually hoping to identify statistically significant differences. While this concept is covered in detail in Chapter 19, it is sufficient to say at this point that a statistically significant difference is one that is larger than one would expect on the basis of chance alone. One of the key factors in significance testing is sample size. The larger the sample, the more likely a given difference is statistically significant. Thus, failure to identify a difference as statistically significant can be largely the result of using a sample that is too small.

A Table of Suggested Sample Sizes

Table 2 near the end of this book provides suggested sample sizes for populations of various sizes. For instance, for a population of 1,000, a sample size of 278 is suggested. Of course, the other issues in determining sample size discussed in this chapter and Chapter 7 should be considered when using this table. For instance, if there is clear potential for harm to participants, a researcher might appropriately decide to use a sample with substantially fewer than 278 participants.

Exercise for Chapter 12

Factual Questions

1. Biased sampling is any procedure that does what?

2. The way to avoid both subtle and obvious biases is to remove what from the selection process?

3. What is described in this chapter as being a "neutral, nonjudgmental process"?

4. Suppose you pointed at Table 1 near the end of this book and your finger landed on the first number on line 24. If you were drawing a sample from a population of 80 individuals, what are the numbers of the first three individuals who would be selected?

5. "If a sample has been drawn at random, it is safe to assume that it is free of errors." Is the preceding statement true *or* false?
    A. True.   B. False.

6. What is the name of the type of sampling in which a population is first divided into subgroups and then individuals are drawn at random from each subgroup?

7. Selecting every third name from a list is an example of what type of sampling?

8. This chapter mentions how many conditions that must be met for cluster sampling to be regarded as excellent?

9. "Pilot studies with small samples are almost never publishable in academic journals." Is the preceding statement true *or* false?
   A. True.   B. False.

10. According to Table 2 near the end of this book, what is the recommended sample size for a population of 1,200?

Question for Discussion

11. Based on the information in this chapter, will you make any changes in your plans for participant selection in the research that you will be conducting? Explain.

Chapter 13
Participant Selection in Qualitative Research

The fundamentals of participant selection in both quantitative and qualitative research were covered in Chapter 7. In this chapter, methods for selecting participants in qualitative research are discussed in more detail.

Purposive Sampling

While quantitative researchers strive to use unbiased samples so they can generalize to populations, qualitative researchers strive for in-depth information about purposeful samples without special regard to the issue of generalization. As you may recall from Chapter 7, in *purposive sampling*, individuals are handpicked to be participants because they have characteristics that make them especially good sources of information. Various types of purposive sampling are discussed next.[1] While considering them, keep in mind that they can be used in combination, which will be discussed later in this chapter.

Criterion Sampling

Some researchers use the terms *purposive sampling* and *criterion sampling* synonymously. However, it is best to reserve the term *criterion sampling* for use when very clear-cut, specific criteria are established for identifying potential participants.

Example 13.1
A description of criterion sampling
All mothers were contacted during one of the meetings of their prenatal education classes at the hospital, in two towns in northern Italy. From the pool of primiparous mothers interested in our study (about 20% of mothers approached), mother–neonate dyads were selected on the basis of (a) absence of obstetrical and neurological complications (no particular medication during pregnancy and delivery; spontaneous full-term delivery; normal birth weight, i.e., above 2,500 g; 1- and 5-min Apgar scores of 8 or above), (b) absence of medical indications of physical or psychological diseases on the part of the mothers, (c) the mother's age being above 20 and under 40 years, and (d) both the mother and the father being Italian and living in the home. (p. 3)[2]

Notice in Example 13.1 that the researchers purchased a list of names of managers from which to draw the participants. "List brokers" who compile various types of lists can be a good source of contact information for possible participants. In addition to lists

---

[1] The technical terms for various types of purposive sampling described in this chapter are drawn from Patton (2001). They are widely used by qualitative researchers.
[2] Lavelli, M. & Fogel, A. (2013). Interdyad differences in early mother–infant face-to-face communication: Real-time dynamics and developmental pathways. *Developmental Psychology*. Advance online publication.

of individuals holding various occupations, lists can be purchased (or rented at a modest fee for one-time use) for a wide variety of characteristics, such as having new babies in the family, living in certain zip codes, filing for bankruptcy, as well as other specialized interests and memberships. In addition to list brokers, professional associations usually will rent their membership lists (or parts of the list such as those who belong to special interest groups within the association) for legitimate purposes.[3]

When planning participant selection, researchers often consider exclusion criteria as well as inclusion criteria. Example 13.2 illustrates this.

Example 13.2
A description of criterion sampling with exclusion criteria
To be included in the study, participants had to be enrolled on an Assertive Community Treatment team certified as meeting Indiana Division of Mental Health and Addiction ACT standards, and the parent of at least one biological, adopted, or stepchild. Exclusion criteria included the presence of a cognitive disability that would interfere with the ability to understand study questions, current inpatient hospitalization, active episode of acute psychiatric symptoms. (p. 23)

Random Purposive Sampling

When the potential purposive sample is too large, individuals can be selected at random using random selection, which is described in the previous chapter. Because the purchased list of potential participants mentioned in Example 13.1 near the beginning of this chapter contained too many names, the researchers used random purposive sampling as described in Example 13.3.

Example 13.3
A description of random purposive sampling
A research assistant randomly called listings from the database to describe the purpose of the study, made sure these individuals met the criteria for being participants, explained the tasks to each participant, and found out whether they were interested in being involved in the study. (p. 143)[4]

Note that in random purposive selection, potential participants are first selected purposively. If too many are identified, random selection is used as a means of objectively selecting from them.[5]

---

[3] For list brokers in a given area, refer to the Yellow Pages or search for them on the Internet. To rent lists from professional associations, contact their "mailing list" department.

[4] Modified and adapted from Levine, D. W., Kripke, D. F., Kaplan, R. M., Lewis, M. A., Naughton, M. J., Bowen, D. J., & Shumaker, S. A. (2003). Reliability and validity of the Women's Health Initiative Insomnia Rating Scale. *Psychological Assessment, 15,* 137–148.

[5] In quantitative research, random selection is used to draw a sample from a population so that generalizations to the population can be made. In random purposive sampling in qualitative research, random selection is used to select from a pool of those individuals already identified for a purposive sample. The purposive sample may or may not be a good one for generalizing to a population.

Typical Case Sampling

Sometimes, qualitative researchers purposively select participants who are, in some sense, typical or "normal." For instance, for a study of the influence of student–teacher interactions on achievement, schools that are known for having students who achieve at about average levels might be selected. Obviously, this is appropriate whenever a researcher is interested in learning more about typical cases.

Studying typical cases can be an advantage because it reduces the complexity of the data collected, making analysis easier. For beginning researchers, this can be important since the intensity of qualitative research produces large amounts of data, which can be overwhelming to novices. Studying typical cases can also be viewed as a disadvantage because sometimes, much can be learned by comparing typical cases with extreme or deviant cases, which is described next.

Extreme or Deviant Sampling

Some research topics concern extreme or deviant cases, such as "the social influences on marijuana use among adolescents who are extremely heavy users of marijuana." For a study of such cases, criteria should be established to identify what is meant by "extremely heavy users," and then individuals who meet the criteria should be purposively selected.

Oftentimes, it is useful to conduct an initial study on extreme or deviant cases even if the research topic is not restricted to such cases. For instance, suppose a research topic is "political influences on police–community relations." For an initial study on the topic, studying some exemplar cases, such as police departments that have received awards for fostering good community relations, might be an information-rich source that can provide insights into how to examine the same topic with typical cases in subsequent studies. This is true because the distinctive characteristics of extreme cases are often more obvious than in typical cases.

Extreme or deviant sampling can also be used to select participants from *both ends* of a continuum. For instance, one might select some students who have extremely positive attitudes toward school and some with extremely poor attitudes. Contrasting the two extremes in a qualitative study might provide insights into the dynamics of such attitudes.

Intensity Sampling

In *intensity sampling*, researchers purposively select individuals whom they believe are likely to have intense experiences or feelings relating to the topic of the research. For instance, to examine the unique psychosocial needs of bereaved African American older women, the author of Example 13.4 states that individuals who were likely to have an intense bereavement experience were purposively selected.

Example 13.4
A description of intensity sampling
It was my belief that grandmothers who identified themselves as women who had lost a child to AIDS and were parenting that child's children were women who had

experienced loss *intensely* and would need to tell the story of their grief experience. (p. 95)[6]

Although extreme (or deviant) sampling discussed above seems, at first, like intensity sampling, note that extreme sampling focuses on selecting individuals who are very different from most others, while intensity sampling focuses specifically on selecting individuals who have had more intense experiences than most others. For instance, a police department might be an exemplar department in some respect (making it extreme) but the members of the department might not feel any more intense about their experience than members of other police departments.

Maximum Variation Sampling

In *maximum variation sampling*, cases are selected so that the full range of characteristics of interest is present in the sample. Example 13.5 describes the variation sought by a team of researchers for a study of the career development of highly achieving women with physical and sensory disabilities.

Example 13.5
A description of maximum variation sampling
Following approval from a university behavioral research ethics board, five groups of older adult participants (65 years) were purposely selected from across geographical sectors within a Western Canadian province to reflect its urban but also highly rural landscape. **Sample selection sought to maximize variation** [bold added for emphasis] in the older adult demographic, important at this exploratory stage in broadly assessing an understanding of strength. Those persons who were unable to give informed consent or unable to speak English were excluded from the study. (p. 10)[7]

An advantage of this type of sampling is that it makes it possible to compare results across a wide spectrum of variables. It also makes it possible to determine whether research findings apply only to certain subgroups or apply equally across the spectrum.

Homogeneous Sampling

Homogeneous sampling is the opposite of maximum variation sampling previously discussed. In homogeneous sampling, individuals who are similar in important ways are purposively selected. In Example 13.6, the researchers deliberately selected a sample that was homogeneous in terms of the hospital where they were treated, age range, and years of employment.

Example 13.6
A description of homogeneous sampling

---

[6] Winston, C. A. (2003). African American grandmothers parenting AIDS orphans: Concomitant grief and loss. *American Journal of Orthopsychiatry, 73*, 91–100.
[7] Rush, K. L., Watts, W. E., & Janke, R. (2013). Rural and urban older adults' perspectives of strength in their daily lives. *Applied Nursing Research, 26*, 10–16.

All of the participants were treated at the same hospital and experienced an SCI [spinal cord injury]. The participants'...age [was deliberately restricted to be] from 30 to 49 ($M = 35$ years). All participants had been employed at least 2 years before their injury. (p. 403)[8]

Homogeneous sampling clearly narrows the scope of a study and allows one to concentrate on the main variables of interest (e.g., returning to employment after a spinal cord injury) without having to consider a host of other variables that might influence the results, such as age and previous employment history. In short, this type of sampling simplifies the research process and data interpretation, while maximum variation sampling makes them more complex. Neither is inherently better than the other; choosing between them is a matter of the researcher's interest.

Opportunistic Sampling

Opportunistic sampling is based on selecting participants for a study as the opportunity arises. For instance, a researcher may be interested in the working relationships between physicians and the nurses who work for them. While working in a hospital setting, the researcher may note that one physician seems to be highly admired by the nurses for the professionalism of his or her interactions with them. This provides an opportunity to select a physician to include in the study who might be especially information-rich.

The main distinction between this type of sampling and the others mentioned earlier in this chapter is that opportunistic sampling is not planned in advance. Instead, individuals who might provide insights are selected as the opportunity arises.

Note that this type of sampling is not the same as convenience sampling, in which cases are selected only because they happen to be convenient.[9] In opportunistic sampling, the individuals that are identified as the opportunity arises may not be at all convenient to study. For instance, during the conduct of a study, a researcher might learn of an especially interesting case. Pursuing the opportunity to use this case, the researcher might find that the individual resides in a distant city or is someone who cannot participate immediately, thereby delaying the completion of the study.

Stratified Purposive Sampling

To stratify, subgroups of interest in the population must first be identified. Then participants from each subgroup must be selected so that all subgroups are represented in the sample.[10] In other words, stratification is used to ensure that all important subgroups are included in the sample. In Example 13.7, ten subgroups (referred to as "cells") were formed. The researchers then selected three individuals from each subgroup.

---

[8] Chapin, M. H., & Kewman, D. G. (2001). Factors affecting employment following spinal cord injury: A qualitative study. *Rehabilitation Psychology, 46*, 400–416.

[9] As you know from Chapter 7, convenience sampling is avoided when possible by both qualitative and quantitative researchers. Convenience sampling is addressed again later in this chapter.

[10] This process is similar to *stratified random sampling* discussed in the previous chapter, except that random selection is not used here.

Example 13.7
A description of the use of stratified purposive sampling
…sampling was stratified to ensure representation of key subgroups (Weiss, 1994). The three variables employed in selection were parental education (high school or less vs. more than high school), number of parents in the household, and gender. In addition, for both men and women, we created an additional category of young people not living with a parent or a parental figure. This process resulted in 10 cells… (p. 433)[11]

Snowball Sampling

In *snowball sampling* (sometimes called *chain sampling* or *network sampling*) the initial participant(s) identifies additional participants for a study. This is especially useful when the research topic calls for studying hard-to-find types of individuals. For instance, for a study of food sources of the "invisible homeless" (i.e., those who do not beg in public and do not use public service agencies or welfare), a diligent researcher might be able to identify one or two such individuals to participate in the study. If each of these can identify several others and these others can each identify even more hard-to-find participants, the sample size will grow geometrically like a snowball rolled in the snow (hence, the name).

There are two keys to using this type of sampling to identify hard-to-find participants. First, at least one individual with at least one additional contact must be located by the researcher. Sometimes, a researcher is fortunate enough to happen to already know such an individual. Second, the researcher must build rapport with the initial participants; otherwise, they will be unlikely to refer the researcher to additional cases.

Snowball sampling can also be used to locate information-rich individuals who are not necessarily "hidden" or "hard to find." For instance, a researcher might be interested in the characteristics of "model elementary school teachers." He or she might identify a teacher who has received an award for excellence, which would indicate the teacher's suitability for the research. However, while it is not difficult to identify additional teachers in general, the researcher might have difficulty in knowing how to identify those who might be regarded as models. This problem can be overcome if the award-winning teacher is asked to identify several other teachers whom he or she regards as models. These can then be contacted and asked to identify additional ones.

Example 13.8 shows how one researcher described her use of snowball sampling in a study of African American grandmothers who had lost their children to AIDS.

Example 13.8
A description of the use of snowball sampling
The process of including in the study grandmothers who were referred to me by other participants is known as network, chain, or snowball sampling. The initial set of contacts passes the names of other possible subjects to the researcher, and they in turn refer others, and so on. To be selected for the study, the women had to have

---

[11] Dillon, C. O., Liem, J. H., & Gore, S. (2003). Navigating disrupted transitions: Getting back on track after dropping out of high school. *American Journal of Orthopsychiatry, 73,* 429–440.

lost an adult child to AIDS and be the surrogate parent to the child or children of the deceased at the time the study was undertaken. (p. 94)[12]

Combination Purposive Sampling

It is sometimes desirable to use a combination of various types of purposive sampling to obtain a single sample. For instance, one might combine snowball sampling (i.e., using referrals from some participants to identify additional participants) with homogeneous sampling (i.e., accepting referrals only if the new potential participants have similar characteristics as the previous ones, such as age and ethnicity).

In addition, in a given study, one might use two or more types of samples and analyze the results separately for each type. This permits the researcher to identify similarities and differences between types of samples. This makes the research process, and especially the data interpretation, much more complex than when employing a single type of sample in a research study.

Improving Convenience Sampling

As you know from Chapter 7, convenience sampling (also known as accidental sampling) is avoided by both quantitative and qualitative researchers. However, for many researchers, especially beginning ones or ones with limited resources for conducting research, this may be the only type of sampling available. When this is the case, researchers should consider trying to obtain convenience samples from diverse sources. For instance, a teacher who is conducting research on attitudes toward the physical sciences using the students who happen to be in his or her class might ask other teachers they know (perhaps even in other schools) if their students could participate. This would help convince those who read the research report that the results are not just a reflection of one type of student, which might be idiosyncratic and influenced by the instruction in the physical sciences provided to the students by the teacher. This example assumes, of course, that the teacher's research interest is broader than just learning about his or her particular students' attitudes.

The authors of Example 13.9 sought participants from diverse sources even though they used a convenience sample of volunteers from a limited geographical location. This type of convenience sampling might be called *diversity convenience sampling* to distinguish it from *simple convenience sampling* in which there is no attempt to use diverse sources for obtaining participants.

Example 13.9
A description of diversity convenience sampling
…in an attempt to achieve a broad sample of community-dwelling women, we recruited them from senior centers, health clinics, community housing agencies, and churches. (p. 201)[13]

---

[12] Winston, C. A. (2003). African American grandmothers parenting AIDS orphans: Concomitant grief and loss. *American Journal of Orthopsychiatry, 73*, 91–100.

When convenience samples are used, plans should be made to collect demographic information so that the convenience sample can be described in detail.[14] Example 13.10 shows such a description of a convenience sample. Such a description helps readers of the research "see" the participants, which makes convenience sampling less problematic for consumers of research.

Example 13.10
A description of a convenience sample (detailed description recommended)
Participants were 10 (7 male and 3 female) Asian American students at a large mid-Atlantic university; CQR method calls for a sample size between 8 and 12. They ranged in age from 18 to 23 years with a mean of 19.3 years ($SD = 1.6$). Participants immigrated to the United States between the ages of 4 and 9 years ($M = 6.8$, $SD = 1.6$), and, at the time of their participation, had spent between 9 to 18 years in the United States ($M = 12.5$, $SD = 2.7$). In terms of ethnic background, 5 were Koreans, 2 were Asian Indians, 1 was Chinese, 1 was Filipino, and 1 was Thai. There were 6 first-year students, 3 sophomores, and 1 junior. Four participants were majoring in computer, mathematical, or physical sciences; 3 were majoring in engineering; 1 was majoring in education; 1 was majoring in behavioral and social sciences; and 1 participant had not yet declared a major. All of the participants reported growing up in a mid-Atlantic state, and half of them reported living in a neighborhood whose Asian population was 10% or less. Four participants reported a family income between $70,001 and $110,000, 3 between $40,001 and $70,000, and 3 between $10,001 and $30,000. (pp. 158–159)[15]

Participant Recruitment in Qualitative Research

Qualitative researchers use a variety of means to recruit participants. When the population is divided into groups with a leader for each group, the leaders may help solicit participants. This is illustrated in Example 13.11 in which leaders of the Assertive Community Treatment (ACT) program for individuals with severe mental illness participate in participant recruitment.

Example 13.11
A description of participant recruitment by team leaders
To generate the sample, team leaders of five ACT teams were contacted, informed about the purpose of the study, and asked to help with recruitment by distributing recruitment flyers to potential participants. The five teams were selected from 16 ACT teams across Indiana to ensure inclusion of teams from different regions (e.g.,

---

[13] Borrayo, E. A., & Jenkins, S. R. (2003). Feeling frugal: Socioeconomic status, acculturation, and cultural health beliefs among women of Mexican descent. *Cultural Diversity and Ethnic Minority Psychology, 9*, 197–206.

[14] Regardless of the type of sampling, demographic information should be collected. When convenience sampling is used, it is especially important to provide a highly detailed description.

[15] Kim, B. S. K., Brenner, B. R., Liang, C. T. H., & Asay, P. A. (2003). A qualitative study of adaptation experiences of 1.5-generation Asian Americans. *Cultural Diversity and Ethnic Minority Psychology, 2*, 156–170.

northern vs. southern), settings (e.g., urban, rural, suburban), and consumer demographics (e.g., ethnicity, SES, gender). Three of the five team leaders agreed to aid in recruitment. Team leaders were asked to focus recruitment efforts on consumers judged to be psychiatrically stable and able to participate in the study. Recruitment materials instructed interested participants to contact the first author or inform the team leader of interest in the study. Interviews were scheduled either directly when participants contacted the first author or in coordination with the team leader. (p. 23)[16]

Other qualitative investigators use multiple methods of participant recruitment in a single study, as illustrated in Example 13.12.

Example 13.12
A description of multiple methods of participant recruitment
Participants from the cross-sectional study were recruited via flyers posted in community settings around Boston, MA, through word of mouth from other participants, and via online posting (boston.craigslist.org). Interested people were screened for eligibility criteria, which included male gender, age 18–40 years, and history of a gunshot or stab wound injury for which they sought medical care.[17]

In a research proposal, the proposed method of participant recruitment should be described in detail so that your instructor and others can give you feedback on the appropriateness of your plans for recruitment.

Sample Size in Qualitative Research

Samples used in qualitative research tend to be smaller—often much smaller—than samples used in quantitative research. As an illustration, sample sizes reported in a random sample of research articles recently published in *The Journal of Counseling Psychology* were examined. For the qualitative studies, the average (i.e., median) sample size was found to be 14. For the quantitative research, the average was 431.[18]

The use of relatively small samples in qualitative research is attributable to two factors. First, qualitative researchers strive to purposively select individuals who are "information-rich," (i.e., likely to be especially good sources of information). Therefore, they expend their resources in selecting the most promising types of individuals rather than in obtaining large samples. Second, qualitative methods, such as person-to-person interviews, can require large amounts of time to be spent with each participant, limiting the number of participants who can be accommodated with limited resources.

---

[16] White, L. M., McGrew, J. H., & Salvers, M. P. (2013). Parents served by assertive community treatment: Parenting needs, services, and attitudes. *Psychiatric Rehabilitation Journal, 36*, 22–27. doi: 10.1037/h0094743

[17] Schwartz, S., Hoyte, J., James, T., Conoscenti, L., Johnson, R., & Liebschutz, J. (2010). Challenges to engaging black male victims of community violence in healthcare research: Lessons learned from two studies. *Psychological Trauma: Theory, Research, Practice, and Policy, 2*, 54–62. doi: 10.1037/a0019020

[18] For qualitative research, the sample sizes ranged from 1 to 35 cases. For quantitative, they ranged from 158 to 5,472.

An important concept in determining sample size in qualitative research is *saturation*. This refers to adding additional participants to a sample until new participants fail to provide new insights and information. In other words, the point of saturation (also known as the *point of redundancy*) is the point at which a researcher judges that adding additional participants will not provide additional insights into the research topic. Despite qualitative researchers' willingness to be open-ended regarding sample size, beginning researchers should specify a *target number* in their research proposals. This will allow instructors to provide feedback on the suitability and feasibility of using the target number, allowing for the fact that the number might be modified during the course of the study.

Whether or not saturation is used as a criterion for determining sample size, it is a good idea to discuss in research proposals and reports any considerations or concerns that bear on the selection of a sample size for a qualitative study. This will help readers of your proposal understand why a particular number is being proposed. Example 13.13 shows one such discussion.

Example 13.13

A description of issues relevant to determining sample size (recommended)

The minimum sample size of 10 grandmothers was selected as a reasonable number of subjects to interview in depth over a limited period. Unlike quantitative inquiry, qualitative study does not seek representative sampling in order to generalize about a larger population. Although Lincoln and Guba (1985, p. 202) recommended sample selection to the point of redundancy, I believed that the minimum sample size would allow for the development of contextually rich narratives that would deepen our understanding of the grief response and coping strategies of the women in the study. A second consideration in limiting the sample size was the relative difficulty in locating grandmothers who met the study criteria and were willing to discuss very sensitive issues. (p. 95)[19]

Exercise for Chapter 13

Factual Questions

1. Are qualitative researchers especially concerned with drawing samples from which they can generalize to populations?

2. According to this chapter, it is best to reserve the term *criterion sampling* for use when what is done?

---

[19] Winston, C. A. (2003). African American grandmothers parenting AIDS orphans: Concomitant grief and loss. *American Journal of Orthopsychiatry*, *73*, 91–100.

3. "Extreme or deviant sampling is sometimes used to select participants from both ends of a continuum." Is the preceding statement true *or* false?
   A. True.   B. False.

4. Homogeneous sampling is the opposite of what other type of sampling?

5. "The term *opportunistic sampling* is synonymous with the term *convenience sampling.*" Is the preceding statement true *or* false?
   A. True.   B. False.

6. What type of sampling is especially recommended for identifying hard-to-find individuals?

7. For improving convenience samples, it is recommended that researchers use
   A. Homogeneous sampling.   B. Diverse sampling.

8. Do qualitative studies *or* quantitative studies tend to have larger samples?

9. The point of saturation (also known as *the point of redundancy*) is the point at which a researcher makes what judgment?

Question for Discussion

10. How do you plan to recruit participants for your study?

11. Based on the information in this chapter, will you make any changes in your plans for participant selection in the research that you will be conducting? Explain.

Notes:

Part C

Issues in Measurement

An overview of issues in measurement for qualitative and quantitative research was provided in Chapter 8 in Part A of this book. More detailed information is provided in this part of the book.

Students who wrote preliminary research proposals based on the material in Part A should reconsider the section on measurement in light of the material in the next three chapters.

Notes:

Chapter 14
Measurement in
Quantitative Research

The fundamentals of measurement for both quantitative and qualitative research were covered in Chapter 8. In this chapter, measures for quantitative research will be discussed in more detail.

Standardization and Objectivity of Measurement

Quantitative researchers value *standardization*, which refers to using the same (standard) measurement methods for each participant, such as the same directions, the same questions, and the same time limits. They also value *objectivity*. An *objective test* or *scale* is one that can be scored without subjective judgment. For instance, given an answer key for a measure such as a key for a multiple-choice test, two or more clerks who are conscientious can arrive at the same score for each participant with almost no exceptions.

Social Desirability

The term *social desirability* refers to the tendency of participants to provide responses that they believe are desirable from a social point of view (i.e., desirable in the eyes of others). For instance, parents may overreport on a questionnaire the amount of time they spend helping their children with homework because providing this type of help is socially desirable.

Researchers can reduce the influence of social desirability by assuring participants that the information they provide is for research purposes only and that only group statistics such as averages and percentages will be reported. The influence of social desirability can also be reduced by asking for anonymous responses to sensitive questions.

Reliability and Internal Consistency

The Concept of Reliability in Measurement

Quantitative researchers favor measures (i.e., tests and scales) that yield consistent scores. In this context, *consistency* is synonymous with the more technical term: *reliability*. A physical example makes clear the need for consistency in measurement. Consider a carpenter who has constructed a doorframe for a new house in an area where the building code specifies that all doorways must be at least 30 inches wide. Suppose further that a building inspector finds that the doorway opening is only 29 inches wide and requires the carpenter to widen it. Then, on the next inspection after it is widened, the inspector declares that it is now only 28 inches wide. These discrepancies indicate a lack of reliability in the measurement of the width of the doorway. The lack of reliability can be attributable to the measure itself (perhaps the tape measure is made of rubber) or attributable to the person using the yardstick (perhaps the inspector is careless in using the tape measure).

Test-Retest Reliability

Test-retest reliability is determined by administering a test or other measure twice to a sample of examinees. Typically, the two administrations are one or more weeks apart. If a test has good test-retest reliability, those who score high one week will score high the next week when they take the same test again. Likewise, those who score low one week will score low the next week. In responses to even the best measures, there will be at least some fluctuation from one administration to the next, which will reduce test–retest reliability. This is because of the influence of three factors:

1. Guessing on a test *or* making random marks in response to questions. For instance, some examinees will score higher on one administration of a test than on the other administration due to guessing.

2. Changes in the physical and mental status of the examinees. For instance, on the first administration of a test, an examinee might be ill and score lower than on the second administration when the examinee feels better.

3. Changes in how the test was administered and testing conditions. For instance, on one administration of a test, there might be noises that some examinees find distracting that are not present on the second administration.

Reliability is measured with a statistic called a *reliability coefficient*.[1] While it is theoretically possible for reliability coefficients to be negative, in practice they range from 0.00 (indicating no consistency from one administration of the test to the next) to 1.00 (indicating perfect consistency). Tests and scales published by major publishers usually have very high reliabilities, with coefficients typically ranging from 0.85 upward. The consensus among quantitative researchers is that tests and scales with reliability coefficients below 0.75 should be avoided or, if used, the results of the research should be viewed with considerable caution.

In Example 14.1, the test-retest reliability of the Women's Health Initiative Insomnia Rating Scale is described.

Example 14.1
A description of test-retest reliability
Two hundred forty-three women were administered the Insomnia Rating Scale (IRS). The interval between the two administrations varied from 8 days for some of the women to 14 days for others. For the total group of 243 women, the test–retest reliability coefficient was .84. Thus, the IRS scores were acceptably stable over

---

[1] Mathematically, a *reliability coefficient* is a *correlation coefficient*. Correlation coefficients are discussed in more detail in Chapter 18 and Appendix A.

time. (p. 139)[2]

In Example 14.2, the test-retest reliability of the SMUIS measures online social media use. The total scale consists of two subscales. If the scores from each subscale will be considered separately in the research report, the reliability of each subscale should be reported.

Example 14.2
A description of test-retest reliability

Test–retest over a 3-week period suggested that SMUIS responses remained stable, with reliability correlations of $r = .803$ for total scale, $r = .804$ for subscale 1, and $r = .676$ for subscale 2.[3]

Internal Consistency

Internal consistency (sometimes called *internal consistency reliability*) refers to the consistency of results from one part of a test or scale to another. The meaning of this can be seen by considering an example. Suppose a teacher administered a 40-item history test. For the purposes of studying internal consistency, the teacher scored the odd-numbered items (1, 3, 5, and so on) separately from the even-numbered items (i.e., 2, 4, 6, and so on). Even though only one test was administered, the teacher has two scores for each examinee. Correlating the two sets of scores, the teacher can determine the extent to which those who scored high on the odd-numbered items scored high on the even-numbered items, and vice versa. The result of correlating would be called a *split-half re-liability coefficient*. Like a *test-retest reliability coefficient*, it has a possible range of 0.00 to 1.00, with 0.75 being the lowest generally acceptable level.

In practice, the split-half technique has been replaced by a more sophisticated form called *Cronbach's alpha* (α). It is mathematically equivalent to splitting a test over and over in as many ways possible (not just odd- and even-numbered items), computing a co-efficient for each possible split, and then averaging the split. Thus, alpha can be defined as a measure of internal consistency based on the average of the coefficients for all possible splits. This is interpreted in the same way as a split-half reliability coefficient, with 0.75 being the lowest generally acceptable level.

What does it mean if an internal consistency coefficient is low? It could mean one of two things. First, the scores may have been influenced by guessing or by examinees making random marks. Second, it could be that the scale or test measures more than one skill or trait. For example, consider two mathematics tests for first-graders. The first one contains only one-digit addition and subtraction problems. The second one contains both the one-digit problems and word problems. Other things being equal, a researcher should expect more internal consistency (and a higher alpha) for the first test because its content

---

[2] This example was adapted and modified from Levine, D. W., Kripke, D. F., Kaplan, R. M., Lewis, M. A., Naughton, M. J., Bowen, D. J., & Shumaker, S. A. (2003). Reliability and validity of the Women's Health Initiative Insomnia Rating Scale. *Psychological Assessment, 15*, 137–148.

[3] Jenkins-Guarnieri, M. A., Wright, S. L., & Johnson, B. (2012). Development and validation of a social media use integration scale. *Psychology of Popular Media Culture, 2*, 38–50. doi: 10.1037/a0030277

is more homogeneous. If the test-makers' goal is to measure a homogeneous trait, a low alpha would indicate that the test is deficient in this respect.

Another example will help illustrate why internal consistency is of concern. Consider the Insomnia Rating Scale mentioned in Example 14.1. It is designed to measure a single construct: insomnia symptoms. Because all items are designed to measure this one single construct, there should be high internal consistency. However, if alpha is low, this indicates that the set of items are measuring more than one construct, perhaps because some items were poorly worded, were ambiguous, or did not clearly relate to insomnia. This would call into question the adequacy of the measure. As it turned out, however, the alpha for the measure was .84, indicating an adequate degree of internal consistency.

It is common for researchers to find that published instruments have high levels of internal consistency, such as in Example 14.3.

Example 14.3
Excerpt with typical levels of Cronbach's alpha (bold added for emphasis)
The 36-item Bulimia Test Revised (BULIT-R; Thelen, Mintz, & Vander Wal, 1996) assesses bulimic symptoms based on *DSM–IV* criteria (APA, 2000), though only 28 items are included in the total score. Athletes rated items such as "I eat a lot of food even when I am not hungry," on a 5-point scale that ranged from 1, *absence of a disturbance*, to 5, *extreme disturbance*. Total score is the sum and can range from 28, *no symptoms*, to 140, *high level of symptoms*. Cronbach's alpha have ranged from **.88** (male undergraduates; McFarland & Petrie, 2012) to **.95** (men in community; Russell & Keel, 2002); Cronbach's alpha for the current sample was **.89**.[4]

Comparison of Test–Retest and Internal Consistency Methods

Both test-retest and internal consistency techniques provide information that helps in understanding how well a test or scale works. When possible, information on both types should be reported.

Note that test-retest reliability is a measure of consistency across a period of time, while alpha is a measure of consistency among test or scale items at one point in time. Thus, they provide two different types of information. The authors of Example 14.4 report both types of coefficients. Note that while the values of alpha are at an acceptable level, the test–retest reliability is somewhat low.

Example 14.4
A description of internal consistency (alpha) and test-retest reliability
Internal consistency (coefficient alphas) for the Impression Management subscale scores ranged from .75 to .86 in the previous studies. The test–retest reliability correlation for the Impression Management subscale was found to be .65…. (p. 224)[5]

---

[4] Galli, N., Petrie, T. A., Reel, J. J., Chatterton, J. M., & Baghurst, T. M. (2013). Assessing the validity of the weight pressures in sport scale for male athletes. *Psychology of Men & Masculinity*. doi:10.1037/a0031762

[5] Wang, Y.-W., Davidson, M. M., Yakushko, O. F., Savoy, H. B., Tan, J. A., & Bleier, J. K. (2003). The scale of ethnocultural empathy, development, validation, and reliability. *Journal of Counseling Psychology*, *50*, 221–234.

Interobserver Reliability

Interobserver reliability refers to the extent to which two or more observers arrive at the same scores when they observe the behavior of the same participants. This becomes an important issue whenever the observational process is not completely objective. For instance, to study prejudice against individuals who are overweight, two observers might watch as customers enter a store and count the number of seconds that it takes for a salesperson to greet each customer. If each uses a stopwatch, a high degree of consistency would be expected. However, if the observers also are asked to classify each customer as being either overweight or not overweight, the observers will have to use some degree of subjectivity in making these decisions. To determine the consistency of these judgments, a researcher could calculate the percentage of customers on which the two observers agreed. Typically, if the rate of agreement on whether the customers are overweight or not is 75% or more, the interobserver reliability would be judged to be sufficient for most research purposes.

What does it mean if interobserver reliability is low? First, it could mean that the characteristic being observed is inherently difficult to judge. For instance, it would be very difficult to judge the intelligence of customers by observing them while entering a store. It would be less difficult to judge whether or not each one was overweight. Second, it could be that one or more of the observers were careless or not properly trained in how to make the observations. Thus, low interobserver reliability would call into question the results of a study based on observations.

Validity and Its Relationship to Reliability

Validity refers to the extent to which a measure assesses what it is designed to measure.

It is important to note that a test or scale can be highly reliable yet be invalid. For instance, suppose a researcher measures mathematical problem-solving ability using a test written in English with a group in which some examinees have very limited English language skills. Test–retest reliability might be quite high, with those whose English is very limited scoring low both times. However, for these examinees, the test results would not be a valid measure of mathematical problem-solving ability because the math problems were not presented in a language they could comprehend.

Judgmental Validity

Two types of validity are based almost exclusively on human judgment.

Content Validity

Content validity is based on experts' judgments of the appropriateness of the contents of a scale or test for a particular purpose. For achievement tests, content validity is determined by having experts compare the contents of a test with the instructional objectives contained in a curriculum guide. To the extent that the two are consistent with each other (the test items measure the stated objectives), the test can be said to have content validity.

Content validity can also be used to provide information on the validity of other types of measures such as personality scales. For instance, the authors of Example 14.5 validated their measure of emotion regulation for 8- to 12-year-old children using experts' judgments.

Example 14.5
A description of the content validation of the How I Feel (HIF) scale
Ten experts in the area of emotional development provided data for the study. Experts were volunteers from among faculty participants in the 2003 Emotional Development Pre-Conference of the Society for Research in Child Development (April, Tampa, FL) and included individuals widely known and cited in the area of emotional development. Each expert was provided with a written copy of the HIF. He or she was asked (a) to sort the items into those reflecting positive emotional arousal, negative emotional arousal, and control over positive or negative emotional arousal, and (b) to suggest item additions, deletions, or wording changes. (p. 401)[6]

Face Validity

Face validity is an assessment of validity based on nonexpert judgments of what a test appears to measure on the surface (i.e., on the face of it). For instance, an outsider might examine a nursing test and challenge its validity because it contains math calculation problems. This would indicate that the examination has low face validity. An expert, however, might examine the same test and recognize that the calculation problems are the type nurses use for dose calculations (calculating the dosage of medications to give to patients). Thus, while the nonexpert's judgments indicate that the test has low face validity, the expert's judgment indicates that it has high content validity.

Researchers are mainly concerned with content validity—not face validity. However, face validity becomes a concern if examinees do not think that a test is valid and therefore refuse to take the test or fail to try their best. For instance, applicants to a nursing program might be administered the calculation test described above. Because the items lack face validity for nursing school, some applicants might believe the test is unfair and arbitrary in content and become unmotivated to do well on the test.

In short, face validity is more of a public relations concern than a scientific one. Nevertheless, failure of a measure to have face validity might affect the performance of examinees.

Criterion-Related Validity

Criterion-related validity is based on the extent to which scores on a test or scale correlate with scores on a criterion. A *criterion* is a standard by which something can be judged. For instance, for a new reading test, a criterion might be teachers' judgments of their students' reading abilities. To the extent to which scores on the test correlate with

---

[6] Walden, T. A., Harris, V. S., & Catron, T. F. (2003). How I feel: A self-report measure of emotional arousal and regulation for children. *Psychological Assessment, 15*, 399–412.

teachers' judgments, the test is said to be valid. Put another way, if the assumption that teachers are reasonably good judges of students' abilities is accepted, a failure of test scores to correlate substantially with teachers' judgments would cast doubt on the validity of the new reading test.

There are two types of criterion-related validity. First, when the test that is being validated is administered at about the same time as the criterion scores are gathered (such as administering a reading test and getting teachers' ratings of students' reading ability at about the same time), the results indicate the tests' *concurrent validity*.

The second type of criterion-related validity is predictive validity. This is the type of validity that should be determined for all tests and scales that are designed to predict some future behavior. For instance, algebra readiness tests are designed to measure basic mathematical skills that are needed when learning algebra. The authors of such tests claim that they are of value in predicting the extent to which examinees will be successful in algebra classes. The validity of such a test should be determined by administering it to students who have not taken algebra yet, then collecting a measure of achievement in algebra (such as algebra grades) after they have taken a course in correlating. To the extent that those who score high on the test earned high algebra grades and those who scored low on the test earned low algebra grades, the test can be said to have predictive validity.

Criterion-related validity (both concurrent and predictive) is usually expressed with a *validity coefficient*. Mathematically, it is calculated in the same way as a reliability coefficient. Like reliability coefficients, in practice, they range from 0.00 to 1.00 in criterion-related validity studies.[7] Unfortunately, test makers are typically much less successful in getting high validity coefficients than in getting high reliability coefficients. Although there are no generally accepted standards, these very rough guidelines should be useful to beginning researchers:

Coefficients below .20 = poor validity
Coefficients between .20 and .39 = modest validity
Coefficients between .40 and .60 = good validity
Coefficients above .61 = excellent validity

Examples 14.6 and 14.7 show how concurrent validity was explored in two studies. Note that *r* is the general symbol for correlation coefficients. Because these coefficients are being used to describe validity, they should be called validity coefficients.

Example 14.6
A description of the concurrent validity of a psychopathy checklist
Youth Version Scores on the Youth Version of the Psychopathy Checklist correlated with the number of different kinds of criminal activity in which individuals

---

[7] Reliability coefficients and validity coefficients are *correlation coefficients*, which are discussed in more detail in Chapter 18 and Appendix A. At this point, note that when a correlation coefficient is used to express the degree of reliability, it is called a *reliability coefficient*. When it is used to express the degree of validity, it is called a *validity coefficient*. Negative values of validity coefficients are possible and will be discussed later in this chapter.

participated ($r = .45$) and the number of different kinds of weapons that adolescents acknowledged using ($r = .37$). (p. 104)[8]

Example 14.7

A description of the concurrent validity of an interview measure of gambling behavior

As part of an interview method for measuring self-reported gambling behavior, gamblers were asked to report the amount of money they spent on gambling over a six-month period. At about the same time, the researchers asked the gamblers' spouses how much they thought was spent on gambling during the same six-month period. These estimates provided by the spouses of gamblers constituted the criterion for judging the validity of the gamblers' self-reports. In other words, to the extent that the gamblers' self-reports correlated with the spouses' estimates, the self-reports would be judged to be valid. The criterion-related validity coefficient was .57, indicating a good degree of concurrent validity. (p. 247)[9]

Example 14.8 describes a predictive validity study.

Example 14.8

A description of the predictive validity of the Graduate Record Examination (GRE)

To determine the validity of the GRE General Test for predicting first-year grade point averages (GPAs) in veterinary medical schools, GRE scores were correlated with GPAs earned by students in 16 veterinary medical colleges, resulting in a validity coefficient of .59, indicating adequate predictive validity. (p. 208)[10]

Construct Validity

A *construct* is a label for a cohesive set of related behaviors. For example, "depression" is a construct that is evidenced by behaviors such as inappropriate crying, sleep disturbance, appetite change, and verbalization of suicidal behavior. Researchers cannot directly see depression; they can only see the behaviors that are its indicators. The behaviors that indicate a construct are "cohesive" because they logically belong together.

Construct validity refers to the extent to which a measure yields scores that are consistent with what is known (or generally believed to be true) about the construct it is designed to measure. For instance, it is logical to assume that various types of task performance will be hindered by the behaviors that define the construct called "depression." One of the most important types of task performances is job performance in the workplace as indicated by job performance ratings. By correlating scores on a new measure of depres-

---

[8] This example was adapted and modified from Kosson, D. S., Cyterski, T. D., Steuerwald, B. L., Neumann, C. S., & Walker-Matthews, S. (2002). The reliability and validity of the Psychopathy Checklist Youth Version (PCL:YV) in nonincarcerated adolescent males. *Psychological Assessment*, *14*, 97–109.

[9] This example was adapted and modified from Hodgins, D. C., & Makarchuk, K. (2003). Trusting problem gamblers: Reliability and validity of self-reported gambling behavior. *Psychology of Addictive Behaviors*, *17*, 244–248.

[10] This example was adapted and modified from Powers, D. E. (2004). Validity of Graduate Record Examinations (GRE) general test scores for admissions to colleges of veterinary medicine. *Journal of Applied Psychology*, *89*, 208–219.

sion with job performance ratings, information on the validity of the new measure can be obtained. A negative correlation (i.e., those who score higher on depression generally score lower in their job performance ratings) would be expected. If no correlation is found or if a positive correlation is found (i.e., those who score higher on depression also score higher in their job performance ratings), the results would cast doubt on the validity of the new measure of depression.

Because construct validity can be difficult to understand at first, consider another example. The researchers who were validating the insomnia scale mentioned in Example 14.1 indicated that it was logical to expect that those who have higher insomnia scores should have lower general health scores. Hence, they correlated participants' insomnia scores with scores on a general health inventory and found a negative correlation, as expected. The correlation, however, was not strong ($r = -.26$), but this was also expected because in addition to insomnia, a very large number of variables impact general health. Therefore, insomnia should not be strongly correlated with general health. (pp. 140–141)[11]

In Example 14.9, the researcher validated a new measure of the construct called anxiety. Given that it is generally believed that anxiety is debilitating in many ways, the researcher correlated the anxiety scores with scores on a measure of happiness, expecting that more anxious individuals would report being less happy.

Example 14.9
A description of the construct validity of a new measure of anxiety
A negative correlation between anxiety and happiness was expected. The Kuwait University Anxiety Scale was administered. To assess self-rated happiness, subjects responded to the statement "I feel happy in general" by marking a number on an 11-point scale, anchored by 0: No and 10: Always. Correlations between happiness and anxiety were −.43 and −.44 for boys and girls, respectively. (pp. 572–574)[12]

Example 14.10 shows some other relationships that could be examined in order to estimate the construct validity of measures of various constructs.

Example 14.10
Examples of relationships and differences that could be examined in construct validity studies
For a new measure of the construct called "social anxiety," positive relationships would be expected between the social anxiety scores and amount of time spent in solitary activities such as recreational reading and playing solitaire.

For a new measure of the construct called "organizational efficiency," organizations that are more profitable should score higher on the average than less profitable organizations.

---

[11] Levine, D. W., Kripke, D. F., Kaplan, R. M., Lewis, M. A., Naughton, M. J., Bowen, D. J., & Shumaker, S. A. (2003). Reliability and validity of the Women's Health Initiative Insomnia Rating Scale. *Psychological Assessment, 15*, 137–148.
[12] This example was adapted and modified from Abdel-Khalek, A. M. (2004). Divergent, criterion-related, and discriminant validities for the Kuwait University Anxiety Scale. *Psychological Reports, 94*, 572–576.

For a new measure of the construct called "shyness," students who have high shyness scores should report participating in fewer extracurricular activities.

Distinguishing Between Construct Validity and Criterion-Related Validity

Construct validity provides indirect evidence. For instance, there are many reasons why students might participate in few extracurricular activities, with shyness being only one of them (see the last part of the previous example). Contrast this with a criterion-related validity study in which the criterion would be another measure of shyness such as teachers' ratings of students' shyness. Correlating students' self-reports of shyness on the new shyness scale with teachers' ratings of shyness provides much more direct evidence of validity than correlating self-reports of shyness with self-reports of participation in extracurricular activities.

Put another way, in criterion-related validity, two measures of the same construct are used (e.g., self-reports of shyness and teachers' ratings of shyness). In construct validity, the construct (e.g., shyness) is related to a characteristic that should be related to the construct (e.g., participation in extracurricular activities).

While criterion-related validity studies provide information that more directly bears on validity, construct validity studies are also highly desirable because they provide a more complex picture of how valid a new measure is. Ideally, both types should be reported for most new measures.

Exercise for Chapter 14

Factual Questions

1. The term *social desirability* refers to the tendency of participants to do what?

2. The term *consistency* is synonymous with what more technical term?

3. Three factors that reduce test-retest reliability are listed in this chapter. What is the first one?

4. What value of a split-half reliability coefficient is generally regarded as the lowest acceptable level?

5. To determine alpha, a test must be administered how many times to a group of examinees?
    A. Once.   B. Twice.

6. What are the two reasons why interobserver reliability might be low?

7. What type of validity is based on experts' judgments?

8. What are the names of the two types of criterion-related validity discussed in this chapter?

9. A "construct" is a label for what?

10. Which of the following provides more direct evidence of the validity of a measure?
   A. Criterion-related validity.   B. Construct validity.

Questions for Discussion

11. Consider the measure(s) you named in your preliminary research proposal (prepared after reading Chapter 11). What types of reliability information on them are already available? Will you be conducting a reliability study before using the measure(s) in your research? Explain.

12. Consider the measure(s) you named in your preliminary research proposal (prepared after reading Chapter 11). What types of validity information on them are already available? Will you be conducting a validity study before using the measure(s) in your research? Explain.

Notes:

Chapter 15
Writing Objective Measures

As noted in the previous chapter, quantitative researchers value objectivity in measurement. A tremendous number of objective measures, whose reliability and validity have already been established, are available for use by beginning researchers. These can be found by identifying those used in published research and by searching databases of measures such as the ETS Test Collection Database described in Chapter 8.

Despite the very large number of existing measures, certain research projects may require that new measures be developed. For instance, a new test may be needed to assess seniors' knowledge of a new Medicaid prescription benefit or a new attitude scale may be needed for assessing attitudes toward a new mathematics program in a school.

Going though all the steps taken by test-construction professionals when they build objective measures is a daunting task that can be learned only through several advanced courses in test construction. Nevertheless, beginning reseachers can usually build acceptable measures for research purposes by following these steps: (1) develop a plan, (2) have the plan reviewed, (3) revise the plan in light of the review, (4) write items based on the plan, (5) have the items reviewed, (6) revise the items in light of the review, (7) pilot test the measure, and (8) revise the measure in light of the pilot test. These steps will be discussed in more detail later in this chapter.

Only the three types of measures most commonly built by beginning researchers will be covered in this chapter. They are attitude scales, observation checklists, and achievement tests.

Attitude Scales

An attitude is a general orientation toward a person, group, type of person, organization, and so on. It consists of *feelings* that have the potential to lead to *actions*. Thus, to measure attitudes, questions about both feelings (e.g., feelings about attending school) and actions or potential actions (e.g., faking illness in order to be excused from school) are usually asked.

Planning an Attitude Scale

To plan an attitude scale, first identify the *components* of the object of the attitudes. For instance, for a new instructional program in math, the components might be (a) a new textbook, (b) computer software, (c) the instructors, (d) the facility, such as the classroom where the instruction takes place, and so on. The plan should specify how many attitude scale items will be written for each component, such as "five items for the new textbook," "three items for the software," and so on.

Have the plan reviewed for feedback, asking the reviewers to identify any components that might have been inadvertently omitted and asking for feedback on the proposed number of items for each component.

In addition to items on specific components, it is often a good idea to plan to have an item or two that ask for overall attitudes. Such an item might simply state, "Overall, I enjoy the program." When appropriate, an item asking for recommendations to others might also be asked to tap overall attitudes (e.g., "I would recommend this program to my friends").

Writing an Attitude Scale

While numerous approaches to the measurement of attitudes have been proposed and studied, the approach suggested by Rensis Likert in the 1930s has been found to be about as good as or better than the others for most research purposes. The basic concept of a Likert scale is simple: write straightforward statements about the object of the attitude and provide choices that vary from "Strongly Agree" to "Strongly Disagree."

Each statement in a Likert scale should deal with only one point. Otherwise, participants will find themselves in the untenable position of answering what are, in effect, two or more questions with only one set of choices. For instance, the first item in Example 15.1 asks about liking the examples and liking the illustrations. Each should be asked about separately as illustrated in the improved version in the next example.

Example 15.1
A Likert statement asking about two points (not recommended)
The examples and the illustrations in the new math textbook help me learn.
☐ Strongly Agree   ☐ Agree   ☐ Neutral   ☐ Disagree   ☐ Strongly Disagree

Improved version, with one item on each point (recommended)
The examples in the new math textbook help me learn.
☐ Strongly Agree   ☐ Agree   ☐ Neutral   ☐ Disagree   ☐ Strongly Disagree

The illustrations in the new math textbook help me learn.
☐ Strongly Agree   ☐ Agree   ☐ Neutral   ☐ Disagree   ☐ Strongly Disagree

If all of the statements in a Likert-type measure reflect favorable attitudes, some respondents may move quickly through them, answering them based on their overall attitude and not consider the content of each item carefully. To overcome this problem, about half should be favorable and half should be unfavorable. Note that an unfavorable statement can be made by using the word "not" as in this statement: "The examples in the new math textbook do not help me learn." However, research on the use of negatives such as "not" indicate that they can be confusing to some respondents, so it is best to avoid using them when writing unfavorable statements. Example 15.2 shows a statement that expresses an unfavorable sentiment without the use of the word "not."

Example 15.2
A Likert statement expressing an unfavorable sentiment without the use of "not" (recommended)
The examples in the new math textbook confuse me.
☐ Strongly Agree   ☐ Agree   ☐ Neutral   ☐ Disagree   ☐ Strongly Disagree

Reverse scoring should be used for the items expressing unfavorable sentiments. Thus, if "Strongly Agree" is given 5 points, "Agree" is given 4 points, and so on for a favorable statement, the reverse should be done for unfavorable ones (i.e., "Strongly Disagree" is given 5 points, "Disagree" is given 4 points, and so on). Having done this, the total number of points for each respondent can be counted up, resulting in an overall attitude score.

For questions asking about actions, it is often necessary to pose hypothetical situations. Example 15.3 shows a statement that asks about how respondents would act in a hypothetical situation.

Example 15.3
A Likert statement asking about an action in a hypothetical situation
If I were old enough, I would drop out of school.
☐ Strongly Agree   ☐ Agree   ☐ Neutral   ☐ Disagree   ☐ Strongly Disagree

The attitude items should be reviewed by others and revised if necessary.

Pilot Testing an Attitude Scale

After the attitude scale items have been written, they should be reviewed by others, modified, and then pilot tested. The pilot test should be conducted with respondents who will not be included in the main study. To get information on the quality of the items, two techniques can be used. First, the "think aloud" technique can be employed by asking each respondent in the pilot study to read each statement aloud and state what they are thinking as they answer each one. When doing this, it is not uncommon to find that some respondents attach different interpretations to certain items than the author did when writing them. This often leads to rewriting some items to make them clearer. The second technique is to ask respondents in the pilot study to write notes in the margins on anything that bothers them, is unclear, and so on.

Observation Checklists

An observation checklist consists of a list of behaviors (e.g., thanking a customer) and characteristics (e.g., hair is combed) for which observations should be made. A check is made for each item on the list that is exhibited by a participant.

Planning an Observation Checklist

To evaluate a construct such as "sociability," specific behaviors should be identified that are indicators of the trait (e.g., "smiles when meeting a stranger" and "tells stranger his or her name"). The context within which the observations will be made should also be put in writing in the plan. Often, an artificial or laboratory setting is used for convenience and in order to control extraneous variables. For instance, to observe how sociable participants are when they first meet someone of a different race, arrangements might be made for each participant to meet the same individuals (one of their own race and one of a different race) in a room with no other individuals present.

The plan should be reviewed, and the reviewers should be asked to note any behaviors or characteristics specified in the plan that might be difficult to observe objectively or that are not clear in meaning.

Writing Observation Checklists

Each item in an observation checklist should refer to only a single, discrete behavior. Thus, a checklist item such as "Greets the patient by name and smiles" should be rewritten to make two items, one on greeting by name and one on smiling.

Very frequently, observation checklists are used to evaluate the performance of a task. Example 15.4 shows some items that might be included in an observation checklist for evaluating the performance of student nurses when they are administering an injection of medication.

Example 15.4
Some items for an observation checklist (check mark is placed on the line to the left if the behavior is present)

_____   Checks the patient's name on the wristband.

_____   Greets the patient by name.

_____   Puts on latex gloves.

_____   Measures out the correct amount of medication.

And so on.

In addition to items that ask if a behavior is present, also consider including items that touch on *speed of behavior* (e.g., "Completes task in less than a minute"), *duration of behavior* (e.g., "Engages in conversation for more than five minutes"), and *success of the behavior* (e.g., "Reaches goal on first attempt"), when appropriate.

The items for the checklist should be reviewed by others and revised if necessary.

Pilot Testing an Observation Checklist

The pilot test should be conducted with participants who will not be participating in the main study. The key to a useful pilot test of a checklist is to have two or more observers (preferably observers who will make the observations in the main study) observe the same participants at the same time without conferring with each other. Then, the extent to which the observers agree on each checklist item should be determined. For items on which there is disagreement, consider whether the items are stated ambiguously and whether they can be made more concrete by referring to more specific behaviors.

When there are disagreements among independent observers, it sometimes helps if the researcher provides definitions. Example 15.5 shows a checklist item that had low agreement in a pilot test. The definition provided to the observers greatly increased their level of agreement.

Example 15.5
Checklist item with definition to improve agreement between independent observers

_____   Smiles broadly.

   Definition: Edges of lips noticeably curved upward *and* teeth are showing.

Achievement Tests

Most quantitative researchers rely heavily on test items that can be objectively scored.[1] By far the most popular is the multiple-choice item.

Planning an Achievement Test

Modern instruction is typically based on specific instructional objectives contained in curriculum guides. The key to successful planning of an achievement test is to base the test on the objectives. In the planning stage, decisions should be made regarding whether the test will cover all the objectives or just a sample of them. If only a sample will be covered, those that are selected should be specified in the written plan.

The plan should be reviewed, and the reviewers should be asked to comment on the adequacy of the coverage of the objectives in the curriculum guide.

Writing Achievement Test Items

A *multiple-choice* item should have one choice that is correct and two or more *distracters* (i.e., plausible incorrect choices). Plausible incorrect choices are ones that might appeal to unskilled or unknowledgeable examinees. While the distracters should be plausible regardless of the material being tested, it is easiest to understand the concept by considering a math item. Example 15.6 shows a multiple-choice item with its correct choice as well as two distracters, with the rationale as to why the distracters might be plausible stated in small print.

Example 15.6

Multiple choice items with plausible distracters

Fifty-seven people will be attending a charity event. Each person will bring three toys to be donated to the charity. What is the total number of toys that will be brought?

A. 171 (Correct choice: $57 \times 3 = 171$).

B. 151 (Distracter: Incorrect answer obtained by failing to carry the "2" in multiplication).

C. 60 (Distracter: Incorrect choice obtained by summing 57 and 3).

An ambiguity in a multiple-choice item can cause skilled examinees to make errors. These are often difficult for item writers to spot because an item writer may have one mental set, while some examinees might have another. Consider the multiple-choice items in Example 15.7. What is the ambiguity?[2]

---

[1] For the purposes of assigning grades, teachers usually supplement test scores with other measures such as short-answer tests, essay tests, term projects, performances, and so on. However, in quantitative research in which a quick snapshot of achievement is needed, especially when there will be a large group of participants and when only an assessment of factual knowledge is necessary, multiple-choice items usually provide satisfactory data.

[2] The ambiguity stems from the fact that "largest" might refer to population (in which case, the answer is New York) or to geographical size (in which case, the answer is Georgia). Note that the distracters are plausible because they all name states that are relatively large (in both senses) and they all are located east of the Mississippi River.

Example 15.7
An ambiguous multiple-choice item
What is the largest state east of the Mississippi River?
A. New York
B. Pennsylvania
C. Georgia
D. Virginia

The items should be reviewed by others and revised, if necessary.

Pilot Testing an Achievement Test

The pilot test should be conducted with participants who will not be participating in the main study. If possible, include some examinees who are typically high and some who are typically low in achievement.

Calculate the percentage who marked each multiple-choice item correctly in the pilot test and examine the results for unexpected results. For instance, did some items that seemed simple when they were written turn out to be difficult? If so, it could be that these items have ambiguities or have poorly written correct choices. Also, did some items that seemed difficult when they were written turn out to be easy? If so, something about the item might have given away the answer, such as implausible distracters or other determining factors such as the correct choice being stated more precisely and at greater length than the distracters.

Useful information can also be obtained by comparing the performance of examinees who typically are high in achievement with that of examinees who are typically low in achievement. Other things being equal, each item should be marked correctly by a larger percentage of high achievers than low achievers. Items for which the reverse is true (i.e., low achievers outperforming high achievers on an item) should be scrutinized for possible flaws. For instance, sometimes high achievers are more sensitive to ambiguities than low achievers, which can cause more high achievers to be tricked by an ambiguous item.

Concluding Comments

Students who have taken courses in test construction will recognize that this chapter only touches on the essentials of preparing good measures. Tests prepared by test construction professionals usually will have undergone much more expert and comprehensive reviews and pilot tests than those suggested here. As a consequence, beginning researchers are advised to use measures previously developed by professionals when possible.

Exercise for Chapter 15

Factual Questions

1. "This chapter strongly encourages beginning researchers to build new measures." Is the preceding statement true *or* false?
    A. True.   B. False.

2. In addition to questions about feelings, questions on attitude scales usually also ask about what?

3. In addition to planning to have attitude items about specific components, it is often a good idea to plan to have an item or two that ask for what?

4. "Reverse scoring" should be used for what?

5. When pilot testing an attitude scale, two techniques are recommended. What is the name of the first one mentioned in this chapter?

6. What is the flaw in the following observation checklist item?
    "_____ Sits quietly in class, but answers questions when requested."

7. The "key to a useful pilot test of a checklist" is to do what?

8. What is the key to successful planning of an achievement test?

9. Plausible incorrect choices in a multiple-choice item are ones that have what characteristic?

10. For a pilot test of an achievement test, what two types of examinees should be included, if possible?

Questions for Discussion

11. Will you be writing a measure for your research? If yes, why will you be writing one instead of using a previously published one?

12. If you answered "Yes" to Question 11, what type of measure will you write?

13. If you answered "Yes" to Question 11, what types of individuals will you use to review the plan for your measure and the items you write?

14. If you answered "Yes" to Question 11, do you plan to pilot test the measure? Explain.

Notes:

Chapter 16
Measurement in
Qualitative Research

As you know from Chapter 8, qualitative researchers strive for *credibility* in their measures. Some of the techniques for establishing credibility mentioned in that chapter are *member checks* (i.e., getting feedback from participants on the correctness of the re-sults), employing *prolonged engagement in the field*, and *triangulation of data sources* (i.e., using multiple sources for information on the topic).

They also strive for *dependability*. To do this, they use more than one individual to code and interpret the data as well as using *triangulation of measures* (using more than one measure to collect the same type of data from the same participants).

By far, the most common measure for collecting qualitative data in published re-search is an interview, which is described in this chapter. Focus group methodology, which is a related type of qualitative research, is described in Appendix B.

Issues in Interviewer Selection and Behavior

The background and characteristics of interviewers may influence how participants respond as well as how the interviewers conduct the interviews. Hence, care should be taken in considering who will be conducting the interviews.

Matching Interviewers and Participants

To collect credible data, interviewers need to be able to establish rapport with the participants so that they will feel comfortable in being forthcoming with information. An important consideration in establishing rapport is the match of the background character-istics of the interviewer(s) and the participants. For instance, young adult participants might be more comfortable if interviewed by a young adult interviewer. Another instance of the need to consider this issue is discussed in Example 16.1.

Example 16.1
Matching interviewers and participants

In Aboriginal communities, it is particularly important to engage a relatively unbi-ased and credible local person to gain entry to the community. Without such a local connection, Aboriginal social research is both undesirable and impossible (AIATSIS, 2000). In the current study, the local researcher had a strong knowledge of local culture that was vital to the research. It was important that he did not have any affiliations with recognized factions within the community and was well respected by most community members, as his family had lived in the district for many generations. (p. 7)[1]

Interviewer Self-Disclosure

Because the interview process and the analysis of the resulting data involve subjective decisions in qualitative research, those who will be conducting the interviews should engage in *self-disclosure* (i.e., a technical term that refers to consciously thinking about their traits and beliefs that might affect their decisions, both while conducting the interviews and analyzing the data). This self-acknowledgement should take place before any interviews are conducted, and the results of the self-acknowledgment should be noted in the report of the research. Example 16.2 shows an example of self-disclosure. It was written by a research team that was studying men's ability to attend and persist in college.

Example 16.2
A description of interviewer self-disclosure

Our research team was diverse in gender and ethnic identification. In order of authorship, the first author is a Puerto Rican and Guatemalan American woman, the second author is an African American and White man, the third author is a Mexican American and White man, the fourth author is a Mexican American woman, and the fifth author is an African American man. We unanimously agreed that, when possible, ethnic and gender match between interviewer and participant would be ideal so that language preferences and specific cultural references would be more freely shared by participants. The third author was the lead interviewer and conducted all 12 interviews. All members served as analysts in the coding of interview data and were involved in the writing of this article. Before data collection was initiated, we hypothesized that participants would discuss the importance of family and a general recognition of the low number of Latino men in university. Aside from these assumptions, we did not have any other specific expectations about the data. (pp. 5–6)[2]

Example 16.3 shows another statement of self-disclosure This qualitative study examined the experiences of therapists with Asian women.

Example 16.3
A description of interviewer self-disclosure

We (the two primary researchers) are women psychologists (European American and Taiwanese American) with backgrounds in multicultural research and experience treating diverse clients with EDs. Three Masters-level counseling students (all women; Vietnamese American and 2 European American) contributed to the data analysis. Two other women psychologists (1 Mexican American and 1 Japanese

---

[1] Kendall, E., & Marshall, C. A. (2004). Factors that prevent equitable access to rehabilitation for Aboriginal Australians with disabilities: The need for culturally safe rehabilitation. *Rehabilitation Psychology, 49,* 5–13.

[2] Cerezo, A., Lyda, J., Beristianos, M., Enriquez, A., & Connor, M. (2012). Latino men in college: Giving voice to their struggles and triumphs. *Psychology of Men & Masculinity.* Advance online publication. doi: 10.1037/a0029646

American) served as outside auditors. All four psychologists have degrees in counseling psychology and have been trained in qualitative methods.[3]

Devising Interview Protocols

An *interview protocol* describes how an interview will be conducted. The set of questions that will be asked is often called an *interview schedule*.

Semi-Structured, Open-Ended Interviews

Qualitative researchers use semi-structured interviews.[4] The protocol for this type of interview can take two forms. First, a semi-structured interview can have a core set of questions to be asked of all participants, while allowing the interviewer to add additional questions as needed to explore unexpected findings. The authors of Example 16.4 briefly describe this approach.

Example 16.4
A description of a semi-structured interview protocol
The interviews lasted between 1.5–2 hours. Students were asked to talk about their experiences with gang members and to share the types of bullying and victimization experiences they had or had witnessed. Sample questions included: 1. How would you define bullying? Can you give a few examples? 2. Can you talk a little about what types of bullying you see at this school? 3. Talk about what happens when someone or a group of kids bully other kids at school. As opposed to limiting students to a predefined set of categories requesting that they fit their views into that model, students were free to choose their own specific aspects of bullying and victimization to comment on by answering open-ended questions such as the ones above. (p. 5)[5]

Often, the additional questions that are asked in a semi-structured interview are *probes*, which request additional information relating to the questions asked. Probes are especially helpful when participants provide answers that are vague or too general in content to provide adequate insights into the topic being investigated.

Second, the protocol for a semi-structured interview can be less formal, consisting only of a list of topics about which questions will be asked instead of a standard set of questions. The list serves as a starting point for interviewers and helps them remember to cover all essential topics. This less formal type of protocol is more appropriate for use by seasoned qualitative researchers than by beginning researchers.

---

[3] Smart, R., Tsong, Y., Mejía, O. L., Hayashino, D., & Braaten, M. E. T. (2011). Therapists' experiences treating Asian American women with eating disorders. *Professional Psychology: Research and Practice, 42*(4), 308–315. doi: 10.1037/a0024179

[4] In a fully structured interview, all questions are determined in advance, and these questions are asked of all participants. When quantitative researchers conduct interview research, they usually use this type of interview.

[5] Forber-Pratt, A. J., Aragon, S. R., & Espelage, D. L. (2013). The influence of gang presence on victimization in one middle school environment. *Psychology of Violence*. Advance online publication. doi: 10.1037/a0031835

Qualitative researchers typically use *open-ended questions*. This simply means that the participants are free to answer the questions as they wish because no choices are given as possible answers.

Initial Questions to Establish Rapport

The initial questions that are asked set the tone for the rest of an interview. Thus, care should be taken to use initial questions that make participants feel comfortable. Notice how this issue is addressed in Example 16.5.

Example 16.5
A description of initial questions designed to establish rapport
The interview began with some questions about what subjects respondents were studying, their thoughts about the course, and university life in general. When some rapport had been established through the introductory questions, the interviewer then began exploring some of the issues relevant to the study. (p. 619)[6]

Using Previously Developed Interview Protocols

The use of previously developed measures is much more characteristic of quantitative research than qualitative research. Nevertheless, there are times when it may be appropriate in qualitative research. For instance, if other researchers had success in uncovering interesting findings using a particular interview protocol with one group, a subsequent researcher might find it informative to use the same protocol with some other type of group. The authors of Example 16.6 used a protocol based on interview protocols used in previous studies.

Example 16.6
Use of a previously published interview protocol (acceptable)
The primary measure was an in-depth, semi-structured interview protocol based on those used in previous studies (Gomez et al., 2001; Richie et al., 1997). (p. 70)[7]

Having Interview Protocols Reviewed

Whether a new interview protocol has been developed or an existing one identified for use in a study, it is a good idea to have it reviewed by experts whenever possible. This is especially true for beginning researchers. Example 16.7 very briefly describes such a review by experts.

Example 16.7
Description of a pilot test of an interview protocol (acceptable)
The protocols were reviewed and edited by three psychologists experienced in both general research and as interviewing techniques. (p. 341)[8]

---

[6] Martin, A. J., Marsh, H. W., Williamson, A., & Debus, R. L. (2003). Self-handicapping, defensive pessimism, and goal orientation: A qualitative study of university students. *Journal of Educational Psychology, 95,* 617–628.

[7] Noonan, B. M., Gallor, S. M., Hensler-McGinnis, N. F., Fassinger, R. E., Wang, S., & Goodman, J. (2004). Challenge and success: A qualitative study of the career development of highly achieving women with physical and sensory disabilities. *Journal of Counseling Psychology, 51,* 68–80.

Pilot Testing Interview Protocols

A pilot test of a measure in qualitative research is less crucial than in quantitative research because it is acceptable for qualitative researchers to modify their measures (e.g., interview schedules) as they collect data. Nevertheless, a pilot test of an interview protocol might help beginning researchers by giving them an opportunity to practice their interviewing skills before collecting data that will be analyzed in the main study. When a pilot test is conducted, it should be done with individuals who will not be included in the main study, which was done in Example 16.8.

Example 16.8
Description of a pilot test of an interview protocol (acceptable)
The interview protocol included questions specific to disability and was tested and refined through a pilot study. The pilot participants were five prominent women with physical and sensory disabilities located in the Washington, D.C., metropolitan area who were acquainted with the researchers (and thus excluded from the final sample). (p. 70)[9]

Formulating Questions about Demographics

In almost all cases, questions asking for demographic information (i.e., background information) should be standardized for all participants. In other words, the questions should be formulated prior to beginning the study and asked in the same way of all participants.

Many demographic questions are innocuous, such as questions about grade level, city of residence, and so on. These can be asked near the beginning of an interview, or even before, such as in Example 16.9.

Example 16.9
Sample description of demographic questions
All participants completed a brief demographic form and submitted it to the first author electronically or through regular mail prior to the interview. This form elicited information regarding the participants' age, country of origin, method of immigration (e.g., tourist visa, border crossing), length of time in the United States, and family constitution both in the United States as well as in the participants' country of origin.[10]

However, any questions that are potentially sensitive should usually be asked near the end of an interview, after the interviewer has had ample opportunity to establish rapport. Two questions that participants often are uncomfortable answering are about age of

[8] Timlin-Scalera, R. M., Ponterotto, J. G., Blumberg, F. C., & Jackson, M. A. (2003). A grounded theory study of help-seeking behaviors among white male high school students. *Journal of Counseling Psychology, 50,* 339–350.

[9] Noonan, B. M., Gallor, S. M., Hensler-McGinnis, N. F., Fassinger, R. E., Wang, S., & Goodman, J. (2004). Challenge and success: A qualitative study of the career development of highly achieving women with physical and sensory disabilities. *Journal of Counseling Psychology, 51,* 68–80.

[10] Ellis, L. M., & Chen, E. C. (2013). Negotiating identity development among undocumented immigrant college students: A grounded theory study. *Journal of Counseling Psychology.* Advance online publication. doi: 10.1037/a0031350

adults and income. To overcome resistance to answering questions about these characteristics, the interviewer should preface them with a brief explanation of the reason for asking them. Example 16.10 shows such an explanation.

Example 16.10
Sample introduction to sensitive demographic questions

The following two questions are being asked for research purposes only, and your answers will not be shared with others. While you are not required to answer them, your answers will help me in conducting the data analysis for this study.

To soften the impact of sensitive questions, an interviewer can offer choices that cover ranges of age and income, which allows respondents to respond honestly without being specific. Example 16.11 shows such a question on age that might be used with a sample of older adults.

Example 16.11
Sample question about age for a sample of older adults

Which of the following best describes your age?

Under 50 years of age; 51 to 60 years; 61 to 70 years; 71 years or older

Recording Responses and Note Taking

Recording responses—either on tape or electronically—has the advantage of producing a complete record of participants' responses. The primary disadvantage is that the presence of a recorder might inhibit some participants.

An alternative to recording is to take notes on participants' responses. While this may seem more natural to participants, it has two major disadvantages: (1) The notes will not constitute a complete record of responses, and (2) it greatly complicates the work of interviewers.

As a general rule, beginning researchers should record responses instead of making notes. The primary exception is if the heart of the interview schedule deals with highly sensitive matters, in which case participants might be less than fully forthright when responding with a tape recorder present.

Even if the interviews are tape recorded, the interviewer should make notes of important aspects of the interview as soon as possible after the conclusion of each interview. These notes might include a brief summary of the interview as well as notes on participants' body language and emotional mood. Example 16.12 shows how a researcher described her note-taking after each recorded interview.

Example 16.12
Note-taking after recorded interviews

After each interview, a written record of it was constructed, including a summary of the interview, verbatim transcription of particularly important or powerful comments, and notes on theoretical implications. (p. 944)[11]

---

[11] Willetts, M. C. (2003). An exploratory investigation of heterosexual licensed domestic partners. *Journal of Marriage and Family, 65*, 939–952.

Exercise for Chapter 16

Factual Questions

1. According to this chapter, an important consideration in establishing rapport is the match of what?

2. What is the name of the technical term that refers to consciously thinking about traits and beliefs that might affect interviewers' decisions, both while conducting the interviews and analyzing the data?

3. What do *probes* request?

4. Are there times when it might be appropriate to use a previously developed interview protocol?

5. "In a pilot study, individuals who will participate in the main study should be used." Is the preceding statement true *or* false?
   A. True.   B. False.

6. In addition to providing a brief explanation of the reasons for asking sensitive demographic questions, what else can a researcher do to soften the impact of such questions?

7. What is the primary disadvantage of tape recording responses?

Question for Discussion

8. If you will be conducting qualitative research, consider your description of the proposed measures in your preliminary research proposal (prepared after reading Chapter 10). Will you be making any changes in it? Explain.

Notes:

Part D

Techniques for Data Analysis

The first chapter in this part (Chapter 17) covers basic descriptive statistics that are widely used by quantitative researchers. Because descriptive statistics are also used by qualitative researchers to describe the demographics of their participants, this chapter will be useful to both quantitative and qualitative researchers.

Chapters 18 and 19 cover statistical methods widely used by quantitative researchers, while Chapter 20 describes two general approaches to analyzing qualitative data in more detail than they were described initially in Chapter 10.

Because entire books could be written about each major topic in this part of the book, the contents of the chapters presented here are necessarily highly selective, with an emphasis on analytic techniques most likely to be used by beginning researchers.

Notes:

Chapter 17
Descriptive Statistics for Quantitative and Qualitative Research

The function of descriptive statistics is to summarize data. Statistics that summarize, such as averages and percentages, help researchers understand and communicate data.

While statistical analysis is much more closely associated with quantitative research than with qualitative research, both qualitative and quantitative researchers often use descriptive statistics to describe demographic data (i.e., background data) such as data on age, income, and educational status of participants in their research. For instance, both quantitative and qualitative researchers might report the average age of the participants and the percentage who graduated from high school.

For the analysis of the main data generated by their studies, however, qualitative researchers use judgmental methods described in Chapters 10 and 20, while quantitative researchers use statistical methods described in this chapter as well as Chapters 18 and 19.

The coverage of statistical methods in this chapter and the following ones is highly selective. In this chapter, only descriptive statistics that are widely used by beginning researchers are presented. It is assumed that students reading this book have taken or will take a statistics course in which the computation of statistics is covered. Hence, computational procedures are described in this chapter only when a discussion of computations will help in understanding the meaning of the statistics being discussed.

Describing Nominal Data

Nominal data refers to data that consist of names or labels that contain words, not numbers. For instance, when researchers ask participants to name their country of birth, they will reply with names such as the United States, Mexico, and Canada. The most straightforward way to analyze nominal data is to calculate percentages.

A *percentage* indicates the number of participants per 100 that have some trait or characteristic. Thus, if there are 1,000 participants and 800 said that they were born in the United States, a researcher could report that "80% were born in the United States."

Example 17.1 illustrates the use of percentages in describing demographics in a *qualitative* study. Note that not only are percentages reported, but the underlying numbers of cases (i.e., *n*) are also provided in the example. Reporting the *n* associated with each percentage, often in parentheses as shown in the example, is widely recommended by statisticians.

Example 17.1

Percentages used to describe demographics in a qualitative study

With regard to religion, 38% identified as "Catholic," 33% identified as "Protestant Christian" (e.g., Evangelical, Pentecostal, etc.), and 24% identified as "other." Thirty-eight percent reported not finishing high school, 38% reported finishing high school or GED, and 19% reported having and college degree. In terms of annual income, 57% of both men and women reported earning $25,000 a year and 76.2% reported having insurance coverage in Massachusetts (e.g., Mass Health Coverage).[1]

To examine the relationship between two nominal variables, quantitative researchers build a two-way table called a *contingency table*, in which the rows are for one variable and the columns are for the other. Example 17.2 shows a contingency table in which the rows are for the nominal variable called "gender," and the columns are for the nominal variable called "level of agreement" with some proposition. The percentages in the example show a relationship between the two variables, such that women are much more likely to strongly agree than men, while men are much more likely to strongly disagree than women.

Example 17.2

A contingency table for the relationship between gender and level of agreement (two nominal variables)

	Strongly Agree	Agree	Disagree	Strongly Disagree
Men ($n = 50$)	10.0% ($n = 5$)	20.0% ($n = 10$)	30.0% ($n = 15$)	40.0% ($n = 20$)
Women ($n = 200$)	60.0% ($n = 120$)	25.0% ($n = 50$)	12.5% ($n = 25$)	2.5% ($n = 5$)

Describing Ordinal Data

Ordinal data put participants in *rank order* from high to low. For instance, a researcher could ask a teacher to rank order his or her students based on their reading comprehension skills by giving a rank of "1" to the most skilled student, a rank of "2" to the next most skilled, and so on. While it is simple to have participants ranked, rank orders convey little information. For instance, suppose Jennifer is ranked "1" in reading comprehension while Jake is ranked "2." These ranks indicate only that Jennifer is somewhat higher than Jake, but they do not indicate how much higher she is. For instance, the ranks of "1" and "2" could be obtained if Jennifer is only very slightly higher than Jake, but they could also be obtained if Jennifer is much higher than Jake.[2]

---

[1] Moreno, O., & Cardemil, E. (2013). Religiosity and mental health services: An exploratory study of help seeking among Latinos. *Journal of Latina/o Psychology*, 1, 53–67. doi: 10.1037/a0031376

[2] The obvious alternative to ranking students on the basis of their reading comprehension skills is to administer an objective test of reading comprehension that yields scores. The scores would tell "how much" skill each student has and thereby indicate how much superior Jennifer is to Jake (e.g., 1 point superior would indicate little superiority). Objective achievement tests yield *interval data*, which is the next topic in this chapter.

Because ordinal data provide such limited information, researchers tend to avoid collecting such data. If collection of ordinal data is unavoidable for some reason, the data can be summarized with the *median* and *interquartile range*, which are descriptive statistics covered later in this chapter.

Describing Ratio and Interval Data

Ratio data have three characteristics. First, they tell "how much" of a characteristic each participant has. For instance, if a researcher measures a participant's height and finds that it is 72 inches, the researcher knows that the participant has 72 units of a characteristic called height. Second, in ratio data, all units represent the same amount of the characteristic. For instance, each of the 72 inches that the participant has is the same amount of height as each other inch. Put another way, the difference between 60 and 61 inches represents the same difference in height as any other two adjoining values such as between 70 and 71 inches.[3] Third, ratio data have a true, absolute zero point. For instance, on a tape measure, researchers know where the zero point is, and it is meaningful because it truly represents "nothing," or in this example, it truly represents "no height."

Interval data have the first two characteristics of ratio data. For instance, scores on objective tests indicate how much skill examinees have (not just their rank orders), and it is reasonable to assume that the differences represented by adjoining test scores are all equal. For instance, getting 10 right instead of 9 right on a multiple-choice test is about the same amount of difference as getting 20 right instead of 19 right.

Unlike ratio data, interval data do not have a true zero. For instance, if a participant gets zero correct on a multiple-choice vocabulary test, this result indicates that he or she has no knowledge of the vocabulary on that test. It does not indicate that the participant has absolutely zero knowledge of any vocabulary. Hence, a zero on an objective test such as a multiple-choice vocabulary test is arbitrary (not absolute) because the zero point depends on what particular items were written and their difficulty.

While the distinction between ratio and interval data is useful for some mathematical purposes, both types of data are analyzed in the same way using the statistics described in the rest of this chapter in the social and behavioral sciences.

The Mean and Median

By far, the most commonly used descriptive statistic for summarizing ratio and interval data is the *mean*, which is a particular type of average. Computationally, it is the average obtained by summing all the scores and dividing by the number of scores. Examples 17.3 and 17.4 show the use of the mean to describe some demographic data that might be reported in a report on either quantitative or qualitative research. One of the symbols for the mean (i.e., *M*) is shown in Example 17.4. The upper-case *M* should be

---

[3] Note that ordinal data discussed earlier do not have this characteristic. For instance, the amount of difference represented by ranks of 1 and 2 might be small while the difference represented by ranks of 2 and 3 might be large.

used if the data are for an entire population, while the lower-case *m* should be used if the data are for only a sample drawn from a population.[4]

Example 17.3
Means used to describe demographics

The mean age of the participants was 17.4, and the mean number of years of schooling completed was 11.8.

Example 17.4
Means used to describe demographics (with the symbol M)

The average female participant was younger ($M = 34.5$ years) than the average male ($M = 38.2$ years).

The mean has a major drawback for certain data sets. Specifically, if there are some extreme scores on one side of a distribution without extreme scores on the other side to balance them out, the mean may be pulled too far toward the side with the extreme scores to be representative of the typical participant. When the distribution of a set of scores is unbalanced in this way, the distribution is said to be *skewed*. Consider the scores in Example 17.5, in which the distribution is skewed to the right because there are two very high scores (350 and 400), which are very different from the others. The mean equals 60.4, which is higher than the scores for all but two of the 25 participants. Clearly, the mean has been pulled up by the two extreme cases, which resulted in an average that is unrepresentative of the typical case.

Example 17.5
A skewed distribution of scores (mean pulled toward the high scores)

The mean number of times marijuana was reportedly smoked in the month before the 25 adolescents began treatment at a drug rehabilitation facility was 60.4.

Note: The raw scores used to compute the mean, which would not be reported in a research report are: 20, 20, 25, 26, 27, 28, 30, 31, 31, 32, 32, 32, 32, 34, 35, 35, 37, 37, 40, 40, 45, 46, 46, 350, 400.

When the mean is highly influenced by a small number of participants who are very different from most participants, there are two ways to handle the problem. First, the mean could be calculated both with and without the extreme cases with an explanation that the distribution is skewed, as illustrated in Example 17.6.

Example 17.6
Sample statement illustrating the use of the mean with a skewed distribution

The mean number of times marijuana was reportedly smoked in the month before adolescents began treatment at a drug rehabilitation facility was 60.4. Two of the 25 cases had extreme scores: 350 and 400, creating a skewed distribution. With these two cases removed in order to summarize the behavior of the vast majority of the cases, the mean is only 33.1.

---

[4] Note that all statistical symbols should be italicized to distinguish them from letters of the alphabet. For instance, "M" is a letter of the alphabet while "*M*" is the symbol for the mean.

An alternative to reporting the mean when a distribution is highly skewed is to report a different average: the *median*. The median is always the score that has 50% of the cases above it and 50% below it.[5] To obtain an approximate median, simply count up from the lowest score until half the cases are reached. The score at that point is the median. For the raw data in Example 17.5, approximately 50% of the cases are above and 50% are below a score of 32. Thus, the median is 32, which seems reasonably representative of the typical case since 23 of the 25 participants had scores ranging from 20 to 46. Note that the median is an alternative to the mean for describing skewed distributions because it is insensitive (i.e., not pulled in one direction or the other) to small numbers of extreme scores.

The Standard Deviation and Interquartile Range

The mean and median are averages that indicate the typical score for interval and ratio data. While an average is a key feature of any set of scores, it does not provide a thorough description because it does not indicate the amount by which the scores vary. To understand this, consider the following two sets of scores, which differ greatly in their variation.

Scores for Group A: 100, 100, 100
** *M* for Group A = 100.0**
Scores for Group B: 0, 100, 200
** *M* for Group B = 100.0**

Both sets of scores have an average of 100.0. However, the two sets of scores are quite different. Specifically, Group A's scores have no variation because they are all the same. The scores for Group B, in contrast, are much more varied, ranging from 0 to 200. Because variation is an important characteristic of a set of scores, statisticians have developed descriptive statistics called *measures of variation*,[6] which describe how variable a set of scores is. The two that are most frequently used are described next.

The *standard deviation* is the statistic that is almost always used to describe variation when the mean has been used as the average. To get a general understanding of the standard deviation, consider the three sets of scores in Example 17.7 on the next page. All three sets have a mean of 10.00. However, for Set X, the standard deviation equals 0.00 because all the scores are the same (i.e., they have no variation). Set Y has greater differences among the scores than Set X, which is reflected by a standard deviation of 1.49. In contrast, Set Z has the most variation (i.e., larger differences among the scores), which is reflected by a standard deviation of 7.45. Thus, the general rule is the more variation, the larger the standard deviation will be. According to most statistics textbooks, the symbols for the standard deviation are *S* when describing a whole population or *s* when describing a sample from a population. In reports published in journals, researchers often use *SD* or *sd* for populations and samples, respectively.

---

[5] Note that the mean of 60.4 in Example 17.5 has 23 cases below it and 2 cases above it. This illustrates that the mean does not always have half above and half below.
[6] *Averages* are sometimes called *measures of central tendency.*

Example 17.7
Standard deviations for three sets of scores that have the same mean but differ in their variation

Set X: 10, 10, 10, 10, 10, 10, 10, 10, 10 (no variation among scores)
   SD **for Set X = 0.00**

Set Y: 8, 8, 9, 9, 10, 11, 11, 12, 12 (modest variation)
   SD **for Set Y = 1.49**

Set Z: 0, 0, 5, 5, 10, 15, 15, 20, 20 (more variation)
   SD **for Set Z = 7.45**

The standard deviation was designed specifically to describe what is known as the *normal distribution* (also known as the *bell-shaped curve*), which is shown in Figure 17.1. This type of distribution is widely found in nature. Specifically, most of the cases are near the middle, and it is symmetrical, with fewer cases to the left (where there are lower scores) and to the right (where there are higher scores). Because it is symmetrical (not skewed), the mean is an appropriate average for such a distribution.

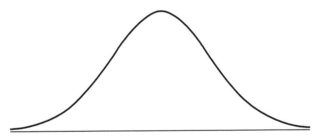

Figure 17.1. Normal curve (i.e., bell-shaped, symmetrical curve).

Suppose a researcher calculated a mean and standard deviation for a normal distribution and obtained *M* = 40.00 and *SD* = 10.00. These results would indicate that a score of 40 is in the middle of the distribution and that by going out 10 points on each side of the mean (to scores of 30 and 50), about 68% of the cases would be included. This is illustrated in Figure 17.2.

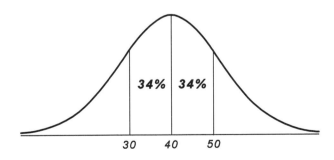

Figure 17.2. Normal curve with a mean of 40.0 and a standard deviation of 10.0 points.

The inclusion of 68% within a standard deviation unit of the mean is always true as long as distribution is normal. Put another way, when a researcher calculates the mean and standard deviation of a normal distribution, he or she is calculating the number of points that one must go out on both sides of the mean to gather up about 68% of the cases. Consider Example 17.8 in which two normal distributions with different amounts of variation are described.

Example 17.8
Statistics and interpretations for two normal distributions of scores
Statement in a research report for Study A: "The mean equals 70.0, and the standard deviation equals 5.0."

Statement in a research report for Study B: "The mean equals 70.0, and the standard deviation equals 20.0."

Interpretation by an individual who read both reports: "The middle of both distributions is the same at a score of 70, while the distribution in Study B is much more variable than the distribution in Study A. In Study B, a researcher needs to go out 20 points from the mean (to 50 and 90) to gather up the middle 68% of the cases. In Study A, the researcher needs to go out only 5 points from the mean (to 65 and 75) to gather up 68% of the cases."

Just as the mean is unduly influenced by highly skewed distributions (with some extreme scores on one side but not the other), the standard deviation is, also. Thus, for a highly skewed distribution another measure of variability known as the *interquartile range* should be used instead of the standard deviation. The definition of the interquartile range is the range of the middle 50% of the scores. To understand this, consider these scores:

5, 10, 11, 12, 15, 16, 17, 20

Ignoring the bottom 25% of the scores (the bottom two scores) and the top 25%, the middle 50% is left, as shown here:

~~5, 10,~~ 11, 12, 15, 16, ~~17, 20~~

The range of the middle 50% is 5 points (16 − 11 = 5). Thus, the interquartile range is 5 points.[7]

To see that the interquartile range is a measure of variation (differences among scores), consider this set of scores, which has much more variability than the previous set.

0, 10, 14, 20, 35, 44, 55, 60

---

[7] A more precise method of calculation, typically covered in statistics courses, is needed to calculate the precise interquartile range when there are tie scores at the points that identify the middle 50%. For instance, if there were three individuals with a score of 11 and four individuals with a score of 16, the method shown here would yield only an approximate answer.

Ignoring the bottom 25% of the scores and the top 25%, the middle 50% is left, as shown here:

~~0, 10,~~ 14, 20, 35, 44, ~~55, 60~~

The difference between 44 and 14 is 30 points, so the interquartile range is 30, which is much higher than the simple range of 5 for the entire set of scores.

Now consider a highly skewed set of scores, with a score of 476, which is much higher than the rest of the scores.

0, 10, 14, 35, 40, 44, 55, 476

If the mean and standard deviation were calculated for this set of scores, they would be greatly pulled up by the extreme score of 476, which skews the distribution. However, because the top (and bottom) 25% of the scores are ignored in the calculation of the interquartile range, it is a good measure of variability for such a highly skewed distribution. Ignoring the bottom 25% of the scores and the top 25%, the middle 50% is left, as shown here:

~~0, 10,~~ 14, 35, 40, 44, ~~55, 476~~

Because the difference between 44 and 14 is 30, the interquartile range is 30 points, which was calculated without using the very high score of 476 that skewed the distribution.

Consider Example 17.9 in which two normal distributions with different amounts of variation are described.

Example 17.9
Statistics and interpretations for median and interquartile range
Statement in a research report for Study X: "The median equals 25.0, and the interquartile range equals 2.0."

Statement in a research report for Study Y: "The median equals 25.0, and the interquartile range equals 10.0."

Interpretation by individual who read both reports: "In both studies the typical score is 25 with 50% of the cases above a score of 25 and 50% of the cases below a score of 25. However, the scores in Study Y are much more variable than the scores in Study X. In Study Y, one needs to go out 10 points on each side of the median to gather up the middle 50% of the scores, while in Study X, one needs to go out only 2 points on each side of the median to gather up the middle 50% of the scores."

A reminder: When analyzing interval and ratio data, if the distribution is not highly skewed, the mean and standard deviation should be used. When there is an obvious skew, the descriptive statistics that should be used are the median and the interquartile range.

Exercise for Chapter 17

Factual Questions

1. The term *nominal data* refers to data that consist of what?

2. To examine the relationship between two nominal variables, quantitative researchers build a two-way table called what?

3. "According to this chapter, researchers prefer to collect ordinal data when possible." Is the preceding statement true *or* false?
    A. True.   B. False.

4. Which average is obtained by summing all the scores and dividing by the number of scores?

5. Which statistic is an alternative to the mean when a distribution is highly skewed?

6. Which of the following always has 50% of the cases above it and 50% below it?
    A. The mean.   B. The median.

7. What is the name of the statistic that is almost always used to describe variation when the mean has been used as the average to describe a distribution that is not skewed?

8. A researcher obtained a mean of 100.0 and a standard deviation of 20.0 for a normal distribution. What percentage of the cases lies between scores of 80 and 120?

9. What is the definition of the *interquartile range*?

10. When there is not an obvious skew, what two descriptive statistics should be used to describe interval and ratio data?

Question for Discussion

11. Consider your description of the proposed data analysis in your preliminary research proposal (prepared after reading Chapter 11). Will you be making any changes in it? Explain.

Notes:

Chapter 18
Correlational Statistics for Quantitative Research

Basic correlational methods allow researchers to examine and describe relationships between pairs of scores for a group of participants. For instance, consider the two sets of scores in Table 18.1. They are correlated because individuals who are high in geography are also high in history. For instance, Allison has the highest geography score, and she also has the highest history score. At the same time, Wilber has the lowest geography score, and he also has the lowest history score. This type of relationship (with highs associated with highs *and* lows associated with lows) is known as a *direct relationship* (also known as a *positive relationship*).

Table 18.1
Scores on Geography Knowledge and History Knowledge Tests

Participant	Geography Score	History Score
Allison	10	12
Fernando	9	10
Betty	4	9
Brian	5	8
Wilber	3	6

While there is a direct relationship between geography and history in Table 18.1, it is not perfect because there are exceptions to the direct trend. For instance, Brian has a higher score than Betty in geography, but he has a lower score than Betty in history. In other words, the two sets of scores do not put the individuals in the exact same rank order.

A statistic known as a *correlation coefficient* provides a precise number to express the strength of a relationship. A correlation coefficient can range from 1.00 for a direct relationship with no exceptions (i.e., a perfect, direct relationship) to 0.00 for the complete absence of a relationship (i.e., no pattern). For the scores in Table 18.1, the value of the correlation coefficient is 0.90, which is close to a perfect 1.00 and thus, is very strong.

A correlation coefficient has a negative value when the relationship between two sets of scores is inverse. In an *inverse relationship* (also known as a *negative relationship*), those who score high on one variable tend to score low on another variable. For instance, consider the scores in Table 18.2 for the variables called "self-concept" and "depression." Those who are near the top of the group in self-concept (such as Joey with a score of 10) are near the bottom of the group on depression (such as Joey with a score of 2). At the same time, those who are near the bottom of the group on self-concept (such as Mike) tend to be near the top of the group on depression.

Table 18.2
Scores on Self-Concept and Depression

Participant	Self-Concept Score	Depression Score
Joey	10	2
Francine	8	1
Juanita	9	0
Brian	7	5
Wilber	7	6
June	6	8
Hector	4	8
Mildred	1	9
Mike	0	9

For inverse relationships, correlation coefficients can be as low as –1.00, which indicates a perfect, inverse relationship (with no exceptions to the trend). The relationship in Table 18.2 is not perfect because there are exceptions such as Mildred being higher than Mike on self-concept, while she is tied with Mike on depression. Still, the relationship is strong. Computing the correlation coefficient for these data yields a coefficient of –0.86.

While there are a number of different types of correlation coefficients, by far the most widely used is the *Pearson product-moment correlation coefficient*, developed by a statistician named Karl Pearson. The symbol for his statistic is a lower-case, italicized *r*. Often, it is simply called the Pearson *r*.[1]

In review, a correlation coefficient (such as the Pearson *r*) describes two characteristics of a relationship. First, it indicates whether a relationship is direct (indicated by a positive value of *r*) or inverse (indicated by a negative value of *r*). Second, a correlation coefficient indicates the strength of the trend. The relationships between the scores in Tables 18.1 and 18.2 are strong because are there only a few minor exceptions to the trends. Hence, the values of the Pearson *r* for them are near 1.00 (i.e., 0.90 and –0.86).

It is easier to spot a relationship when relationships are strong with only a few minor exceptions, such as in Tables 18.1 and 18.2. For instructional purposes, these relationships intentionally were made to be very strong. In practice, researchers often find weaker relationships. Example 18.1 shows some values of the Pearson *r* for direct (i.e., positive relationships) recently reported in published reports of research.

Example 18.1
Values of r for direct relationships recently reported in published research
For the relationship between satisfaction with life and social support, researchers reported a Pearson *r* of 0.39, indicating a weak tendency for those individuals who have *more* alcohol use disorders to experience *more* psychological distress.[2]

---

[1] For all practical purposes, consumers of research can interpret all types of correlation coefficients in the same way that a Pearson *r* is interpreted.
[2] Glaesmer, H., Grande, G., Braehler, E., & Roth, M. (2011). The German version of the Satisfaction With Life Scale (SWLS): Psychometric properties, validity, and population-based norms. *European Journal of Psychological Assessment*, *27*(2), 127–132.

For the relationship between compulsive buying behavior and perceived social status associated with buying, researchers reported a Pearson *r* of 0.60, indicating a strong tendency for individuals who have *more* compulsive buying behavior to be *more* likely to perceive buying as an indicator of social status. (p. 307)[3]

For the relationship between self-esteem and ethnic identity among Hispanics, researchers reported a Pearson *r* of 0.30, indicating a weak tendency for those who have *more* self-esteem to also have *more* ethnic identity. For whites, however, the researchers reported a very weak relationship, with *r* equal to only 0.11. (p. 341)[4]

Example 18.2 shows some values of the Pearson *r* for inverse (i.e., negative relationships) recently reported in published reports of research.

Example 18.2
Values of r for inverse relationships recently reported in published research
For the relationship between marital satisfaction and depressive symptoms among women, researchers reported a Pearson *r* of –0.36, indicating a weak tendency for those who are *more* satisfied with their marriages to have *less* depression. (p. 310)[5]

For the relationship between satisfaction with life and depression, researchers reported a Pearson *r* of –0.44, indicating a moderately strong tendency for those who have *more* satisfaction with life to have *less* depression. (p. 130)[6]

For the relationship between GPA and frequency of bullying other students, researchers reported a Pearson *r* of –0.11, indicating a very weak tendency for those who have *higher* GPAs to engage in *less* bullying behavior. (p. 60)[7]

Describing the Strength of a Relationship

A value of a Pearson *r* that is very close to 1.00 (e.g., 0.95) would be described as a "very strong" direct or positive relationship. Likewise, a value of a Pearson *r* that is very close to –1.00 (e.g., –0.95) would be described as a "very strong" inverse or negative relationship.

In contrast, a positive value of a Pearson *r* that is very close to 0.00 (e.g., 0.15) would be described as a "very weak" direct or positive relationship. Likewise, a negative value of a Pearson *r* that is very close to 0.00 (e.g., –0.15) would be described as a "very weak" inverse or negative relationship.

---

[3] Yurchisin, J., & Johnson, K. K. P. (2004). Compulsive buying behavior and its relationship to perceived social status associated with buying, materialism, self-esteem, and apparel–product involvement. *Family and Consumer Sciences Research Journal, 32,* 291–314.
[4] Negy, C., Shreve, T. L., Jensen, B. J., & Uddin, N. (2003). Ethnic identity, self-esteem, and ethnocentrism: A study of social identity versus multicultural theory of development. *Cultural Diversity and Ethnic Minority Psychology, 9,* 333–344.
[5] Cano, A., & Vivian, D. (2003). Are life stressors associated with marital violence? *Journal of Family Psychology, 17,* 302–314.
[6] Glaesmer, H., Grande, G., Braehler, E., & Roth, M. (2011) The German version of the Satisfaction with Life Scale (SWLS): Psychometric properties, validity, and population-based norms. *European Journal of Psychological Assessment, 27,* 127–132.
[7] Chapell, M., Casey, D., De la Cruz, C., Ferrell, J., Forman, J., Lipkin, R., Newsham, M., Sterling, M., & Whittaker, S. (2004). Bullying in college by students and teachers. *Adolescence, 39,* 53–64.

Table 18.3 provides some descriptive labels for beginning researchers to use when interpreting correlation coefficients. Because there is no universally accepted set of descriptors, the descriptors in Table 18.3 are merely suggestive. They represent what this author has found to be typical descriptors for varying values of r based on extensive reading of published research reports.

Table 18.3
Suggested Descriptors for Various Values of the Pearson r

Value of r	Suggested Descriptor	Value of r	Suggested Descriptor
0.85 to 1.00	Very strong	−0.85 to −1.00	Very strong
0.60 to 0.84	Strong	−0.60 to −0.84	Strong
0.40 to 0.59	Moderately strong	−0.40 to −0.59	Moderately strong
0.20 to 0.39	Weak	−0.20 to −0.39	Weak
0.00 to 0.19	Very weak	−0.00 to −0.19	Very weak

Appendix A provides additional information that can assist in interpreting the strength of a relationship.

Exercise for Chapter 18

Factual Questions

1. What is the value of a correlation coefficient when there is a perfect, inverse relationship?

2. If there is a complete absence of a relationship, what value will the Pearson r have?

3. Which of the following values of the Pearson r indicates a stronger relationship?
    A. 0.65   B. −0.75

4. What is the suggested descriptor for an r of 0.22?

5. What is the suggested descriptor for an r of 0.88?

6. What is the suggested descriptor for an r of −0.45?

7. What is the suggested descriptor for an r of −0.66?

8. In an inverse relationship, which of the following is true?
    A. Those individuals with high scores on one variable tend to have high scores on the other variable.
    B. Those individuals with high scores on one variable tend to have low scores on the other variable.

Question for Discussion

9. Consider your description of your proposed data analysis in your preliminary research proposal (prepared after reading Chapter 11). Will you be making any changes in it based on the information in this chapter? Explain.

Notes:

Chapter 19
Inferential Statistics for Quantitative Research

Inferential statistics are used by researchers who have sampled from a population. To understand the need for inferential statistics, first consider Example 19.1, in which researchers did not sample and thus, their results could not be in error due to sampling.

Example 19.1

A study with no sampling error

A team of researchers asked all 725 clients currently receiving services at a counseling center whether they would recommend the center to others. Forty-four percent of the clients answered "Yes." Because the researchers did not sample, their results were not subject to sampling errors. Thus, the researchers could state with confidence that at the time the survey was taken, only a minority (44%) would recommend the center.

Next, consider Example 19.2, in which the researchers sampled in order to have a more manageable number of participants in their study.

Example 19.2

A study with sampling error

A team of researchers drew a random sample of 225 of the 725 clients currently receiving services at a counseling center and asked the sample whether they would recommend the center to others. Forty-four percent of the clients answered "Yes." Because the researchers sampled, they realized that their results were subject to sampling errors and might not be accurate. More specifically, the researchers could not be sure whether only 44% of all 725 clients would recommend the center. This uncertainty existed because the researchers posed the question to only 225 of the 725 clients.

Margins of Error

The inferential statistic that is needed to aid in the interpretation of the results in Example 19.2 is a *margin of error*, which is based primarily on the number of participants. Specifically, the larger the sample of participants, the lower the margin of error will be. For the information in Example 19.2, the margin of error that will give the researcher 95% confidence is 6.5 percentage points.[1] In other words, the researchers can have 95% confidence that the true percentage in the population is within 6.5 percentage points of 44%. This means that they can be 95% confident that the percentage in the population who would recommend the center is somewhere between 37.5% (i.e., 44% minus

---

[1] Margins of error are standard statistics that can be computed with any of the widely used statistical programs. The same is true of the other inferential statistics in this chapter.

6.5%) and 50.5% (i.e., 44% plus 6.5%). In other words, an allowance of 6.5 percentage points should be made because of random sampling, which does not always produce precisely correct results.

A margin of error must have some degree of confidence associated with it. The 95% confidence level mentioned in the previous paragraph is probably the most commonly used. Standard statistical computer programs will also produce the 99% margin of error. As it turns out, for the data in Example 19.2, the 99% margin of error is 8.5 percentage points, meaning that the researchers can be 99% confident that the true percentage in the population who would recommend the center is somewhere between 35.5% and 52.5%. Notice that for a larger degree of confidence, a larger margin of error must be used. In this example, the margin is 6.5 percentage points for 95% while it is 8.5 percentage points for 99% confidence.

Standard statistical software will also produce margins of error for means. For instance, for a given sample, a mean might equal 44.0 and the 95% margin of error might equal 3.0 points. A researcher with such a result could be 95% certain that the true mean in the entire population is somewhere between 41.0 (i.e., 44.0 minus 3.0) and 47.0 (i.e., 44.0 plus 3.0).

The Null Hypothesis

The *null hypothesis* needs to be considered any time a researcher has sampled at random and finds a difference. Specifically, the null hypothesis states that a difference may have been created by errors caused by random sampling, These errors are simply called *sampling errors*.[2] Consider Example 19.3 in which there is a difference between percentages that might have been caused by sampling error.

Example 19.3
A study with a difference that may have been caused by sampling error
A team of researchers drew a random sample of 200 male students and a random sample of 200 female students and asked how they planned to vote on an issue that will be presented in an upcoming student body election. They obtained this result: 60% of the men and 40% of the women planned to vote "Yes." The researchers cannot be certain of the apparent "gender gap" because they sampled instead of polling the entire population. In this case, the null hypothesis says that the 20 percentage point difference between 60% and 40% was created by sampling error, which is the same as saying that there is no true difference between the populations of men and women; a difference exists in the study only because of random samples that are not representative. The null hypothesis for differences between percentages can be tested with the chi-square test, which is discussed below.

It is important to distinguish between "research hypotheses," which state what researchers predict they will find, and the "null hypothesis," which always asserts that the difference may have been created by sampling error. Thus, a research hypothesis is a

---

[2] Another way to state the proposition is that "there is no true difference." Statisticians define a "true difference" as the difference that would be obtained if an entire population and not a sample had been studied.

judgmental hypothesis made by a researcher, while the null hypothesis is a statistical hypothesis that comes into play whenever random sampling has been used.

The Chi-Square Test

The *chi-square test* is a test of the null hypothesis involving differences among percentages. To understand it, consider again the results in Example 19.3. What could have created the 20-point difference in that example? From a statistical point of view, the answer is that there are two possible explanations:[3]

1. There is no difference in the population, but a difference was found in the sample due to random sampling, which created sampling error. This explanation is called the *null hypothesis*.

2. There is a difference between men and women in the population, and this difference has been reflected in the results obtained with the sample. This explanation is called the *alternative hypothesis* because it is an alternative to the null hypothesis.

The chi-square test establishes a probability that the null hypothesis is a correct hypothesis. For the example being considered, it establishes the probability that random error alone would produce a 60%–40% split, given a total sample size of 400. If the probability is sufficiently low, the null hypothesis can be rejected, leaving only the alternative hypothesis as a viable alternative. As it turns out, a standard statistical software program will indicate that for the data in the example being considered, the probability is less than 1 in 1,000. By almost all standards, this would be considered a very low probability. Because this is so low, the null hypothesis should be rejected because it is a very unlikely explanation for the 20-point difference.

In the social and behavioral sciences, any probability of 5 or less in 100 is usually regarded as sufficiently low to reject the null hypothesis. Thus, for instance, if the probability that the null hypothesis is true is .05 in a given study, the null hypothesis would be rejected as probably being an incorrect hypothesis. In other terms, the decision is being made that the difference under consideration is probably not a chance (i.e., random) difference.

The .05, .01, and .001 levels are the most commonly reported in published research. However, any probability of .05 or less (such as .04, .03, .02, and so on) would lead to rejection of the null hypothesis by conventional standards.

When the null hypothesis for a specific difference (such as 40% versus 60%) has been rejected based on an inferential statistical test such as the chi-square test, researchers declare the difference to be *statistically significant*. In other words, saying that a difference is "statistically significant" is equivalent to saying that "the null hypothesis has been rejected as an explanation for the difference."

---

[3] From a nonstatistical point of view, it is also possible that the researcher deliberately or inadvertently created some type of bias such as by asking the question using different words with women than were used with men. Care in conducting a study can rule out such an explanation.

The symbol for chi-square is χ^2, and the symbol for probability is p. Example 19.4 shows a statement from a published research report using these symbols. Note that chi-square is not a descriptive statistic. Instead, it is an inferential statistic that was used to get the probability, which is the end result of a significance test. In other words, showing the value of chi-square is like showing the answer to a substep in a math problem. It is not presented for interpretation by consumers of research.

Example 19.4
Expression of statistical significance based on a chi-square test
Compared with males, light and nondrinkers, female heavy drinkers [HD] endorsed the highest percentage of lifetime depression rates [female HD = 33.3% male HD = 9.1%; χ^2 (5, 581) = 12.28, p = .031].[4] (p. 163)

For all inferential tests, including the chi-square test, degrees of freedom (*df*) must be calculated and used to obtain the probability. In Example 19.4, the numbers 5 and 581 are the degrees of freedom for this example. They are indicated by being in parentheses. Often, values of the degrees of freedom are indicated by using the symbol *df*, as in *df* = 5, 581. Regardless of the way the degrees of freedom are shown, showing them is similar to showing the answer to a substep in an arithmetic problem. It is not a value to be interpreted. Only the value of p leads to an interpretation.[5] In short, the only value of interest to the typical consumer of research for the results such as those in Example 19.4 is the probability level of p = .031, which is less than p = .05. When the value of p is low, p indicates that it is unlikely that the null hypothesis is true. If something is unlikely to be true, then we reject it.

The *t* Test

The *t* test is widely used to test the null hypotheses relating to means and correlation coefficients.

The *t* Test for Means

A major use of the *t* test is to obtain the probability that sampling error created the difference between two means (i.e., the probability that the null hypothesis is true for the difference between two means).[6]

Example 19.5 shows how the results of two *t* tests might be reported. Note that $p > .05$ means that "p is greater than .05" (odds are more than 5 in 100). By conventional standards, p must equal or be less than .05 for the null hypothesis to be rejected. Also note the use of *ns*, which is a standard abbreviation for "not significant."

---

[4] Based on results reported in Cheng, A. W., Lee, C. S., & Iwamoto, D. K. (2012). Heavy drinking, poor mental health, and substance use among Asian Americans in the NLAAS: A gender-based comparison. *Asian-American Journal of Psychology, 3,* 160–167. doi: 10.1037/a0028306

[5] Before computers, researchers had to calculate the values of chi-square and the degrees of freedom and use these two values when reading a probability table to get the probability for a particular difference.

[6] If there are two medians instead of two means to be compared, a *median test* can be used to determine statistical significance. This test is interpreted in the same way as a *t* test.

Example 19.5

Statement regarding statistical significance based on a t test for the difference between pairs of means

A national sample of 620 married and 531 single adults was surveyed. The difference in average number of minutes per day spent exercising ($m = 7.1$ for married and $m = 8.1$ for singles) was not statistically significant ($t = .59$, $p > .05$, ns), and, therefore, the null hypothesis was not rejected. In contrast, the difference between the averages in time spent in social activities ($m = 46.7$ for married and $m = 69.0$ for singles) was highly significant ($t = 3.26$, $p < .001$). Thus, the null hypothesis was rejected for this difference. (p. 267)[7]

The *t* test can be used for testing the difference between only one pair of means at a time. The use of ANOVA for testing one or more pairs in a single analysis is discussed later in this chapter.

The *t* Test for Correlation Coefficients

When a correlation coefficient is based on a sample from a population, the null hypothesis says that there is no true correlation (i.e., whatever degree of correlation that exists in the sample is not present in the population as a whole). For instance, the correlation coefficient in Example 19.6 was obtained with a national sample of 3,551 adults. The null hypothesis says that the *r* for this sample was created by the random sampling process and that in the population as a whole there is no relationship. Because the probability that this is true is less than 5 in 100, the null hypothesis was rejected by the researcher. Note that standard statistical software programs automatically report the associated value of *p* whenever a correlation coefficient is computed.

Example 19.6

Statement regarding statistical significance of a correlation coefficient based on a t test

The correlation between perceiving their work to be meaningful and reporting that they have learning opportunities was direct, moderately strong, and statistically significant ($r = .53$, $p < .05$). Thus, the null hypothesis that there is no true relationship between these variables was rejected. (p. 407)[8]

Note that while the value of *t* is almost always reported when reporting on the significance of the difference between two means, it is customary to omit the value of *t* when reporting the significance of a correlation coefficient.

---

[7] Loosely based on results reported in Lee, Y. G., & Bhargava, V. (2004). Leisure time: Do married and single individuals spend it differently? *Family and Consumer Sciences Research Journal, 32,* 254–274. Note that it is customary to report the standard deviations immediately after reporting the means.

[8] Loosely based on results reported in Voydanoff, V. (2004). The effects of work demands and resources on work-to-family conflict and facilitation. *Journal of Marriage and Family, 66,* 398–412. Note that it is customary to report the means and standard deviations for the two variables that were correlated before presenting the results of the significance test.

The *F* Test (ANOVA)

Frequently, researchers have more than two values of the mean whose significance needs to be determined in a single comparison. An extension of the *t* test known as an *F* test might be used in this case. The *F* test is conducted using a set of procedures known as Analysis of Variance (ANOVA). Like the *t* test, the *F* test is a test of the null hypothesis. It can be used to determine the significance of the set of differences among any number of means.

For instance, consider a research team that conducted an experiment in which three methods of reinforcing behavior were administered to first-grade students. Group A received verbal praise for raising their hands during lessons, Group B received token rewards for the same behavior, while Group C was designated as the control group, which received no special reinforcement. Suppose that the means in Table 19.1 were obtained. (p. 121)[9]

Table 19.1
Mean Number of Times Students Raised Their Hands During a Lesson

Group A (Verbal Praise)	Group B (Token Rewards)	Group C (Control)
$M = 6.00$	$M = 5.50$	$M = 2.33$

There are three differences associated with the means in Table 19.1. They are

1. Group A (6.00) has a higher mean than Group B (5.50),
2. Group A (6.00) has a higher mean than Group C (2.33), and
3. Group B (5.50) has a higher mean than Group C (2.33).

The null hypothesis says that the set of differences immediately above is the result of sampling error (i.e., there is no true difference). In effect, it says that the random sampling that was used to draw students for each of the three groups produced three groups of students that differed in their classroom behavior only by the luck of the draw (e.g., by chance, Group A consisted of students who tend to raise their hands more often).

The *F* test can be used to test the null hypothesis. As it turns out, the *F* test for the data in Table 19.1 yields a probability of less than .05 ($p < .05$). This means that it is unlikely that the set of three differences, as a whole, was created at random. Thus, the null hypothesis is rejected and the set of differences is declared to be statistically significant.

Note that the significant value of *F* only indicates that the set of differences as a whole probably has some nonrandom differences. To determine which specific pairs of means are significantly different from each other, another test known as a *multiple comparisons test* (based on the *t* test) should be used. A multiple comparisons test indicates the following:[10]

---

[9] This example is based on one in Patten, M. L. (2012). *Understanding research methods: An overview of the essentials* (4th ed.). Glendale, CA: Pyrczak Publishing.

[10] There are a number of multiple comparisons tests that usually yield similar results. The one used for these comparisons is known as *Scheffé's test*. Multiple comparisons tests are also known as *post hoc tests*.

1. Group A is *not* significantly superior to Group B because p is greater than .05 ($p > .05$),

2. Group A is significantly superior to Group C because p is less than .05 ($p < .05$), and

3. Group B is significantly superior to Group C because p is less than .05 ($p < .05$).

The type of F test just considered is conducted using a set of procedures known as a *one-way ANOVA*, which can be found on any standard statistical software. Also, such software will automatically conduct multiple comparisons tests.[11]

Statistical Versus Practical Significance

Statistical significance indicates only that whatever difference(s) is/are being considered is/are unlikely to have been created at random (by chance). Thus, a statistically significant difference is not necessarily of any practical significance.

A major consideration in determining practical significance is *cost in relation to benefit*. Suppose an experimental group achieves, on the average, a statistically significant five points more than a control group on a multiple-choice achievement test but that the treatment given to the experimental group costs substantially more than the conventional treatment in terms of time, money, and effort. These costs would call into question whether the benefit (five points) is great enough to justify the cost.

Another important consideration is whether statistically significant results suggest actions that are questionable from an ethical or legal standpoint. If so, this would limit practical significance.

The third and final major consideration is *acceptability*. Actions suggested by a statistically significant result might be perfectly ethical and legal but be unacceptable to clients, students, teachers, social workers, and others who have a stake in whatever process is being examined. Objections by major stakeholders limit practical significance.

Exercise for Chapter 19

Factual Questions

1. Inferential statistics should be used by which of the following?
      A. A researcher who has studied an entire population.
      B. A researcher who has sampled from a population.

2. Which hypothesis attributes differences to random error?
      A. The null hypothesis.   B. The alternative hypothesis.

3. Would a probability of p less than 1 in 100 usually be regarded as statistically significant?

---

[11] Such software will also perform more advanced analysis of variance procedures, which are beyond the scope of this book.

4. When a difference is declared to be statistically significant, what decision has been made about the null hypothesis?

   A. Reject the null hypothesis.   B. Do not reject the null hypothesis.

5. What is the name of the significance test discussed in this chapter that tests the null hypothesis involving percentages?

6. Can the *t* test be used to test for the overall significance of a set of three means?

7. What does the null hypothesis say about a correlation coefficient based on a sample from a population?

8. The acronym "ANOVA" stands for what words?

9. What is the name of the test used to compare pairs of means after a statistically significant *F* test?

10. Three considerations for determining practical significance are discussed in this chapter. What is the first one that is discussed?

Question for Discussion

11. Consider your description of the proposed data analysis in your preliminary research proposal (prepared after reading Chapter 11). Will you be making any changes in it based on the information in this chapter? Explain.

Chapter 20
A Closer Look at Data Analysis
in Qualitative Research

Nine specific techniques for analyzing qualitative data are covered in Chapter 10. Not all of the techniques need to be used in a given qualitative study, but the use of at least any three or four of the nine by beginning researchers is highly recommended.[1]

In Chapter 13, the use of descriptive statistics to present an analysis of the demographics of participants in qualitative research was discussed.

The purpose of this chapter is to present a closer look at the analysis of qualitative data by examining how researchers who have published qualitative research describe their data analysis procedures, with an emphasis on the two general approaches for analyzing qualitative data that were introduced in Chapter 10 (i.e., the grounded theory approach and the consensual qualitative approach).

Self-Disclosure and Bracketing in Data Analysis

As you may recall from Chapter 16, individuals who will be collecting data, such as conducting interviews, should engage in *self-disclosure* (i.e., consciously thinking about their traits and beliefs that might affect their decisions, both while conducting the interviews and analyzing the data). Self-disclosure should be followed by *bracketing*, which refers to setting aside any individual's beliefs and concerns in order to be able to view the phenomena under investigation from the point of view of the participants. In Example 20.1, a research team describes this step, which is an important first step in analyzing qualitative data.

Example 20.1
A description of bracketing
The first step is for the researchers to set aside their own preconceived ideas about the phenomenon under investigation [and] to understand it through the voices of the study participants. This process is called *epoche* or *bracketing* (Husserl, 1970; Moustakas, 1994). Epoche requires that looking precede judgment and that judgment of what is "real" or "most real" be suspended until all the evidence (or at least sufficient evidence) is in (Ihde, 1977, p. 36). As such, epoche is an ongoing analytical process rather than a single fixed event (Patton, 1990, p. 408). (pp. 62–63)[2]

---

[1] The techniques, which are covered near the end of Chapter 10, are enumeration, selecting quotations, intercoder agreement, diagramming, peer debriefing, auditing, member checks, identifying the range of responses, and discrepant case analysis.
[2] Iwasaki, Y., MacKay, K. J., & Ristock, J. (2004). Gender-based analyses of stress among professional managers: An exploratory qualitative study. *International Journal of Stress Management, 11*, 56–79.

A Closer Look at the Grounded Theory Approach

Example 20.2 serves as a reminder of the three basic types of coding in the grounded theory approach that are discussed in Chapter 10.

Example 20.2

Microanalysis in the grounded theory approach

Grounded theory is a methodology for developing theory that is grounded in data gathered in diverse ways, but systematically collected and analyzed. Theory is mostly generated through coding techniques (i.e., *open coding*, *axial coding*, and *selective coding*) that encourage the constant comparison of the data with an emerging conceptual framework of plausible relationships between theoretical concepts. The data collection and analytic procedures occur in stages that are not discrete and may not follow each other in a strict linear sequence. (p. 200)[3]

In Example 20.3, the researcher cites the need for a microanalysis of data in order to develop theories when using the grounded theory approach.

Example 20.3

Microanalysis in the grounded theory approach

According to Strauss and Corbin, it is through microanalysis of the data that theory can be developed: "It is through careful scrutiny of data, line by line, that researchers are able to uncover new concepts and novel relationships and to systematically develop categories in terms of their properties and dimensions" (Strauss & Corbin, 1998, p. 71). (p. 379)[4]

The first step in the grounded theory approach to analysis is *open coding*, in which distinct, separate segments of the responses of participants are identified and given names (i.e., codes). Example 20.4 describes how researchers conducted open coding in their research. Notice that the initial coding was done *independently* (i.e., without consulting with each other), which is recommended so that the individuals who are analyzing the data are not unduly influenced by each other at this stage of the analysis.

Example 20.4

A description of the first step (open coding) in the grounded theory approach

Following Strauss and Corbin's (1998) framework, open coding was performed to identify the central concepts and their dimensions within the data. The first two authors reviewed the entire data set three times, with an eye toward identifying recurrent themes discussed by contributors. On the fourth review, they employed the constant comparative method to make sense of the data by identifying themes that permeated the discourse (Glaser & Strauss, 1967). In particular, the identification of the themes was based on the frequency, extensiveness, and intensity of related discourse (Krueger, 1998), without emphasizing any one of these features over an-

---

[3] Borrayo, E. A., & Jenkins, S. R. (2003). Feeling frugal: Socioeconomic status, acculturation, and cultural health beliefs among women of Mexican descent. *Cultural Diversity and Ethnic Minority Psychology, 9,* 197–206.

[4] Roldán, I. (2003). The experience of the Puerto Rican family when a member has HIV/AIDS. *Families in Society: The Journal of Contemporary Human Services, 84,* 377–384.

other. Another pass was completed wherein the first two authors independently re-read the transcripts to identify points of departure from the developed framework. This reading allowed for refinement of the themes to capture the issues in the discourse more completely. Through discussion among the authors, we collapsed common themes and identified those that were unique. Next, the first author reread the discourse.[5]

Example 20.5 also describes the open coding stage of a grounded theory analysis. Notice that a very large number of codes were initially developed. They were then reduced to just 17 key categories in the second stage called *axial coding*, which was introduced in Chapter 10 and is described in Example 20.6 below.

Example 20.5

Another description of the first step (open coding) in the grounded theory approach
The first phase of data analysis involved *open coding*, in which transcripts were broken down into small, discrete parts (e.g., a word, phrase, or group of sentences) labeled as *concepts* (all terminology is from Strauss & Corbin, 1998). Each transcript was coded by one team member and then recoded by a second team member; disagreements were resolved by consensus, and final coding was reviewed by the faculty advisor. This process resulted in approximately 1,400 distinguishable concepts. (p. 70)[6]

Example 20.6

A description of the second step (axial coding) in the grounded theory approach
The next phase of coding involved the creation of *categories*, higher order labels that encompass several concepts. The research team developed sets of categories from the generated concepts of all transcripts (guided, in part, by categories obtained in the previous Gomez et al., 2001, and Richie et al., 1997, studies), which were further synthesized into one master category list. This step of the analysis resulted in 59 categories, which were then organized into 17 *key categories* (*axial coding*) in order to group together similar categories (e.g., the categories "Mother Influences" and "Father Influences" were grouped with several other categories into a key category labeled "*Family/Community Background, Influences*").[7]

The last steps in the grounded theory approach are to develop a *core category* and describe the *process* by which variables interact and are related to each other. Developing a core category is called *selective coding*, and describing the process is sometimes called *developing a story line*, which will become the heart of the narrative in a report on qualitative research. Example 20.7 describes how selective coding was used by a team of researchers, and Example 20.8 shows a description of the development of a story line.

---

[5] Jennings, Kelsall, V., Aloia, L. S., & Solomon, D. H. (2012). Stressors experiences by women within Marine Corps families: A qualitative study of discourse within an online forum. *Military Psychology*, *24*, 363–381. doi: 10.1080/08995605.2012.695255
[6] Noonan, B. M., Gallor, S. M., Hensler-McGinnis, N. F., Fassinger, R. E., Wang, S., & Goodman, J. (2004). Challenge and success: A qualitative study of the career development of highly achieving women with physical and sensory disabilities. *Journal of Counseling Psychology*, *51*, 68–80.
[7] Ibid.(2004).

Example 20.7

A description of the third step (selective coding) in the grounded theory approach

The data were again examined to determine how the multiple categories were related. *Selective coding* was used to determine core categories, relate them to other categories, validate the relationships, and fill in categories that needed refinement and development. This required reexamining the data to see how the categories were connected. From this, a theoretical framework was developed (Strauss & Corbin, 1990). (p. 407)[8]

Example 20.8

A description of developing a story line in the grounded theory approach

In the final process of grounding the theory, a *story line* began to emerge from the data during selective coding, and the researchers task was to explicate the story line by connecting the categories in terms of their relationships to one another. While explaining the story line, the researchers linked actions and phenomena into interactional sequences to bring "process" into the analysis (Strauss & Corbin, 1990). The authors described process as a way of giving "life to the data" and connecting the data further with consequences and interactions among the phenomena. (p. 342)[9]

A key element throughout the analysis of data using the grounded theory approach is *constant comparison* (mentioned previously in Example 20.2), which is a technical term that refers to constantly comparing each new element of the data with all previous elements that have been coded in order to establish and refine categories. While this is being done, the analysis focuses on similarities and differences in the data that might be accounted for by a core idea.

A Closer Look at the Consensual Qualitative Approach

The methods used in consensual qualitative research (CQR) to analyze data were described in Chapter 10. A brief overview of the steps in this approach is presented in Example 20.9.

Example 20.9

Overview of the CQR method

The components of CQR consist of using open-ended questions, reliance on words to describe phenomena, studying a few cases intensively, paying attention to context, and applying inductive reasoning. The three general steps of the CQR process involve partialling the interview responses into domains (i.e., topic areas), constructing core ideas (i.e., brief summaries) for all the material within each domain for every interviewee, and developing categories that describe themes in the core ideas within domains across cases (Hill & Thompson, 1997). In CQR, a primary

---

[8] Chapin, M. H., & Kewman, D. G. (2001). Factors affecting employment following spinal cord injury: A qualitative study. *Rehabilitation Psychology, 46*, 400–416.

[9] Timlin-Scalera, R. M., Ponterotto, J. G., Blumberg, F. C., & Jackson, M. A. (2003). A grounded theory study of help-seeking behaviors among white male high school students. *Journal of Counseling Psychology, 50*, 339–350.

team of judges engages in a consensus method of agreement; then one or two audi-tors review the consensus judgments made by the primary team, and their com-ments are considered by the team in the process of revisiting the interview data.... (p. 132)[10]

Because CQR emphasizes reaching consensus (i.e., unanimous agreement), re-searchers must establish how and when the consensus-building process will be con-ducted. Example 20.10 describes how one team of researchers did this.

Example 20.10
Consensus building in the CQR method

The analysis team met weekly to discuss individual interpretations of the data, mov-ing toward consensus about the meaning of the data. Although it was impossible to quantify the consensus process in a meaningful way, we took care to seek input from every group member as equitably as possible. On a few occasions, we audio-taped our group analysis meetings, and a review of those tapes indicated that we all shared opinions and that we had many involved and extensive discussions before we reached consensus, particularly early in the analysis process. (p. 277)[11]

The first step in the CQR method is to *code into domains*. This refers to segmenting the data into groups according to the topics they cover. After each member of the re-search team has done this, they meet and discuss and refine the domains until they reach unanimous agreement on them.

The next step is to *develop core ideas within domains*. This is done by writing short summaries (i.e., abstracts) that reduce the original ideas of participants into fewer words. Example 20.11 describes how one team conducted this step. Notice that initially, the re-searchers worked independently in developing core ideas. Working independently at this point is highly recommended.

Example 20.11
Abstracting core ideas in the CQR method

Domains represent clusters of common notions (i.e., categories) derived from the independently created themes. Core ideas (i.e., notions derived from the categories and domains) serve to detail and holistically integrate the data, while remaining close to the original data source (Hill et al., 2005, 1997). In extracting categories and domains from the data, the research team members presented, discussed, and negotiated their own analytical impressions of the data until a consensus was reached. These preliminary results (i.e., categories, domains, themes) were then sent to the external auditors for their feedback in an effort to curtail groupthink tenden-cies among research team members and to encourage diverse viewpoints. After re-

---

[10] Wiseman, H., & Shefler, G. (2001). Experienced psychoanalytically oriented therapists' narrative ac-counts of their personal therapy impacts on professional and personal development. *Psychotherapy: The-ory, Research, Practice, Training, 38*, 129–141.

[11] Juntunen, C. L., Barraclough, D. J., Broneck, C. L., Seibel, G. A., Winrow, S. A., & Morin, P. M. (2001). American Indian perspectives on the career journey. *Journal of Counseling Psychology, 48*, 274–285.

ceiving this feedback, the research team met to incorporate the perspectives of the external auditors in order to compile the final categorization of domains and categories through consensus. [12]

The third step in CQR is to have the domains and core ideas developed in the first two steps audited by an outside expert. How this was done in one qualitative study is described in Example 20.12.

Example 20.12
Auditing domains and core ideas in the CQR method
At this point, the auditor reviewed the work that was completed thus far. The auditor worked to ensure that the data were appropriately listed within each domain, every important point in the domain had been abstracted, and the wording of the core ideas was clear. Then, the auditor met with the primary research team to discuss her suggestions. As with other aspects of the analysis, a consensus version was then developed. (p. 161)[13]

The next step in CQR is called *cross-analysis*. In this step, the core ideas are grouped into categories based on similarities. This results in a higher level of generalization (i.e., the results are becoming less specific and more general). The results of the cross-analysis are also reviewed by one or more independent auditors. Example 20.13 describes this step.

Example 20.13
Cross-analysis in the CQR method
Next, a cross-analysis was completed with all 11 of the initial cases. In this stage of data analysis, we coded the core ideas within each domain into categories. (Categories represent the similarities between cases culled from the core ideas.) This process began with each team member independently assigning categories to several domains. We then met as a team to argue to consensus. This resulted in the revision of several categories. After reaching agreement on all categories within each domain, the team reviewed the results to ensure consensus on the final version. After consensus was reached on the categories, the auditor then reviewed this portion of the data analysis. The team met to review and discuss the auditor's suggestions. Changes were made to the wording of the categories to represent the overarching themes present in the data. (p. 305)[14]

---

[12] Steinfeldt, J. A., Foltz, B. D., Kaladow, J. K., Carlson, T. N., Pagano, Jr., L. A., Benton, E., & Steinfelt, M. C. (2010). Racism in the electronic age: Role of online forums in expressing racial attitudes about American Indians. *Cultural Diversity and Ethnical Minority Psychology*, *16*(3), 362–371. doi: 10.1037/a0018692

[13] Kim, B. S. K., Brenner, B. R., Liang, C. T. H., & Asay, P. A. (2003). A qualitative study of adaptation experiences of 1.5-generation Asian Americans. *Cultural Diversity and Ethnic Minority Psychology*, *2*, 156–170.

[14] Schultheiss, D. E. P., Palma, T. V., Predragovich, K. S., & Glasscock, J. M. J. (2002). Relational influences on career paths: Siblings in context. *Journal of Counseling Psychology*, *49*, 302–310.

Finally, there is a *stability check*, which can be done by examining additional data, if available. Internal stability can also be examined by determining the extent to which each category was general, typical, or variant, as described in Example 20.14.

Example 20.14
Stability check in the CQR method
After the initial cross-analysis was complete, the remaining two cases (omitted in the initial analysis…) were added back in to determine whether the designations of "general," "typical," and "variant" changed…, and also to assess whether the team felt that new categories were warranted to accommodate the final two cases. The remaining cases did not alter categories that were labeled *general* if they applied to all cases, *typical* if they applied to at least half (but not all) of the cases, and *variant* if they applied to fewer than half but at least two cases.… [Hence], the findings were deemed stable. (p. 469–470)[15]

Exercise for Chapter 20

Factual Questions

1. Self-disclosure should be followed by *bracketing*, which refers to what?

2. In the grounded theory approach, what is the name of the first type of coding?

3. In the grounded theory approach, what is the name of the type of coding in which a core category is developed?

4. In the grounded theory approach, what is the technical name that refers to constantly comparing each new element of the data with all previous elements that have been coded in order to establish and refine categories?

5. In the consensual qualitative approach, which of the following involves writing summaries (i.e., abstracts)?
      A. Coding into domains.   B. Developing core ideas within domains.

6. "Because the purpose of consensual qualitative research is to reach unanimous agreement (i.e., consensus), it is never appropriate for researchers to work independently at any point when using this approach." Is the preceding statement true *or* false?
      A. True.   B. False.

---

[15] Knox, S., Burkard, A. W., Johnson, A. J., Suzuki, L. A., & Ponterotto, J. G. (2003). African American and European American therapists' experiences of addressing race in cross-racial psychotherapy dyads. *Journal of Counseling Psychology, 50,* 466–481.

7. In the consensual qualitative approach, what is the title given to the outside expert who reviews the work of the researchers?

8. In the consensual qualitative approach, the "general" category refers to what percentage of the cases?

Question for Discussion

9. Consider your description of the proposed data analysis in your preliminary research proposal (prepared after reading Chapter 11). Will you be making any changes in it based on the information in this chapter? Explain.

Part E

Issues in Conducting Surveys

Basic issues in participant selection were covered in Chapter 7 in Part A of this book. The first chapter in this part (Chapter 21) explores this issue in more detail, especially as it relates to survey research.

Because survey researchers frequently describe participants' demographics in detail, Chapter 22 provides more information on this topic, especially for the collection of potentially sensitive information.

Chapter 23 provides information on how to assemble a questionnaire and administer survey research.

Students who wrote preliminary research proposals for survey research based on the material in Part A of this book should reconsider their proposals in light of the material in the next three chapters. Students who do not plan to conduct a survey should find the material in this part of the book helpful when reading reports of experimental research.

Notes:

Chapter 21
Issues in Participant Selection
for Surveys

Surveys are a type of nonexperimental, quantitative research.[1] Their purpose is to describe the characteristics of one or more populations as they exist without experimental treatments. Although surveys may be used to gather qualitative data, the term *survey* is usually reserved for studies in which quantitative data are collected.

Selecting unbiased samples is emphasized in survey research. As you know from Chapter 7, a random sample, by definition, is an unbiased sample. In random sampling, each member of the population being studied is given an equal chance of being selected. Chapter 12 illustrates how to draw a random sample using a table of random numbers. That chapter also describes stratified random sampling, systematic sampling, cluster sampling, and consideration of how to determine an appropriate sample size.

This chapter deals with two major sources of bias in surveys: (1) using the postal system to conduct what are called *direct mail surveys*, in which questionnaires are mailed out through the US postal system and returned in the same way and (2) using the Internet to conduct email and online surveys. Because the response rate to both of these types of surveys is almost always less than 100%, and very often substantially less, such surveys are presumed to be biased in favor of individuals who are better educated, have high literacy skills, or have frequent access to the Internet. Techniques for increasing the response rates to direct mail surveys and online surveys are discussed below. Then, techniques for improving biased, convenience samples are described.

Participant Issues in Conducting Direct Mail Surveys

Often, the most efficient way to reach respondents who reside in geographically diverse locations is via the postal service. Response rates to direct mail surveys vary widely and, sometimes, they are exceptionally low. Example 21.1 shows the response rates reported in three published research reports.

Example 21.1
Examples of response rates to mailed questionnaires
1. To assess whether current public attitudes and behaviors support traffic safety advancement in the United States, a survey containing items that had been endorsed by traffic safety experts was mailed to a nationally representative sample of U.S. households. Completed surveys were returned by 46% of recipients.[2]

---

[1]Large portions of this chapter were drawn directly from *Conducting a Survey* (2007) by Lawrence T. Orcher, Pyrczak Publishing. Reprinted with permission. No further reproduction permitted without written permission from the publisher.
[2]Girasek, D. C. (2013). Gauging popular support for traffic safety in the United States. *Accident Analysis and Prevention, 50,* 1112–1117. doi: 10.1016/j.aap.2012.09.001

2. A questionnaire on training in clinical psychology was mailed to 2,100 members of the American Psychological Association. Of these, 11 were returned as undeliverable. Of the remaining 2,089, 571 were completed and returned, yielding a 27.3% response rate. (p. 150)[3]

3. A self-administered anonymous questionnaire on perceptions of generic drugs for the treatment of epilepsy was completed by 47 patients with epilepsy. These 47 patients represent a response rate by postal mail of only 6.7% of potential participants who were contacted by mail.[4]

Researchers use a number of techniques to increase response rates to direct mail surveys. One technique is to offer an incentive such as a physical reward. A reward does not have to be large or expensive, nor does it have to be awarded directly to the participants, as illustrated in Example 21.2.

Example 21.2

An incentive offered to increase response rate to a mailed questionnaire

A questionnaire on mandatory continuing education of clinicians was mailed to 300 medical psychologists. As an incentive to participate, the researchers indicated that they would make a small contribution to the American Cancer Society for every completed questionnaire that was returned. A total of 168 usable questionnaires were returned, yielding a response rate of 56%. (p. 319)[5]

Another step that can be taken to increase the response rate is to personalize the survey by having the questionnaires mailed by a person or an agency that the potential respondents will recognize. An example of this technique is described in Example 21.3.

Example 21.3

Personalization of a mailed questionnaire to increase response rate

Researchers prepared a questionnaire on the intention of individuals with HIV/AIDS to return to work. The researchers negotiated with AIDS service agencies to mail the surveys to clients from the agencies. The questionnaire was headed with each respective agency's name, and cover letters were printed on each respective agency's letterhead and signed by that agency's executive director. The response rate was 37%. (p. 183)[6]

The researchers who conducted the study in Example 21.3 also offered a $1 bill as an incentive to complete and return the questionnaires. In addition, they mailed a reminder letter one week after the questionnaires were mailed. Finally, a second copy of the

---

[3] Dohm, F.-A., & Cummings, W. (2003). Research mentoring and men in clinical psychology. *Psychology of Men & Masculinity, 4*, 149–153.

[4] Ngo, S. N. T., Stupans, I., & McKinnon, R. A. (2013). Generic substitution in the treatment of epilepsy: Patient attitudes and perceptions. *Epilepsy & Behavior, 26*(1), 64–66. doi: 10.1016/j.yebeh.2012.10.032

[5] Sharkin, B. S., & Plageman, P. M. (2003). What do psychologists think about mandatory continuing education? A survey of Pennsylvania practitioners. *Professional Psychology: Research and Practice, 34*, 318–323.

[6] Martin, D. J., Brooks, R. A., Ortiz, D. J., & Veniegas, R. C. (2003). Perceived employment barriers and their relation to workforce-entry intent among people with HIV/AIDS. *Journal of Occupational Health Psychology, 8*, 181–194.

questionnaire might be sent for those who misplaced the original one. All of these techniques will typically increase response rates from what they otherwise would be.

Example 21.4 also illustrates the use of follow-ups.

Example 21.4

Mailing a reminder postcard and second copy of the questionnaire to increase response rate to a mailed questionnaire

Surveys were mailed to all active U.S. district court judges in November 1998 ($N = 619$). Judges who had not responded within a few weeks received a postcard prompting them to complete the survey; judges who did not respond to the prompt were sent a second survey several weeks later. (p. 312)[7]

Successive mailings of a questionnaire to nonrespondents will usually increase the total response rate. However, response rates to the third and successive mailings are usually too low to justify the cost.

Additional steps that can be taken to improve response rates are:

1. Enclose a self-addressed, stamped envelope.

2. Keep the vocabulary and grammar as simple as possible, especially when writing a questionnaire for the general public, many of whom may have poor language skills.

3. Avoid using technical jargon in questions designed for the general public. For instance, the term "curriculum" is jargon that might be unfamiliar to some parents of schoolchildren. Instead, ask about "subjects taught," "skills to be learned," and so on.

4. Keep the questionnaire as short as possible to achieve the research purposes. Long questionnaires tend to reduce response rates.

5. If possible, point out how the results of the survey will directly benefit the participants. For example, for a survey to be used in planning an elementary school library, a researcher might say, "The results of this survey will help us in planning library activities for your children."

Participant Issues in Conducting Internet Surveys

The Internet offers an opportunity to reach geographically diverse samples at little cost, assuming that the researcher has the technical expertise to upload the questionnaire and download the data without incurring the cost of a consultant to assist with these activities.

Email Surveys

A survey in which a researcher asks questions in an email or an attachment to an email and asks the respondents to click "Reply" and answer the questions is called an *email survey*. This type of survey works best when the researcher has only a few simple

---

[7] Krafka, C., Dunn, M. A., Johnson, M. T., Cecil, J. S., & Miletich, D. (2002). Judge and attorney experiences, practices, and concerns regarding expert testimony in federal civil trials. *Psychology, Public Policy, and Law, 8*, 309–332.

questions to ask. In published research, email surveys are relatively rare. Instead, researchers conduct what are called *online surveys*, which are described next.

Online Surveys

In an online survey, a researcher emails potential respondents and asks them to click on a link that takes them to an Internet site that is professionally designed for posting and analyzing the data from quantitative questionnaires. The Guide to Online Research that is included in the Learning Resources for this text describes some free and inexpensive sites for conducting online surveys.

Like direct mail surveys, response rates to online surveys can vary dramatically from survey to survey, as illustrated in Example 21.5.

Example 21.5
Examples of response rates to online surveys

1. Participants who were randomly selected to take part in the survey received a notification email from Knowledge Networks informing them that the survey was available for them to take. In the email, participants were provided with a hyperlink that directed them to the questionnaire. As shown, Figure 1 illustrates how the study sample (*n* = 1,006) was derived from the initial eligible population. Cooperation rate of this study was 46.1%.[8]

2. An online survey was developed and administered to estimate how often psychiatry residents train at correctional facilities and to explore the residency directors' attitudes toward this training. The survey contained two factual and eight opinion questions assessing their experiences with and attitudes toward resident training in correctional facilities, and allowed for free responses. Ninety-five people participated out of 492 for a response rate of 20%.[9]

3. We randomly selected two institutions from each of the 11 Football Bowl Subdivision conferences and one from the independent schools. Using publicly available online and paper campus directories, we drew a purposive sample of 13,604 faculty from the 23 universities to maximize the representation of faculty with campus governance involvement and with experience teaching student-athletes. A total of 3,005 individuals completed the survey, for a response rate of 23 percent.[10]

Obviously, online research is biased against individuals and households that do not have access to the Internet. As indicated in the Guide to Online Research included in the Learning Resources, older individual members of minority groups and those with modest incomes or education are less likely to use the Internet than their opposite counterparts.

---

[8]Girasek, D. C. (2013). Gauging popular support for traffic safety in the United States. *Accident Analysis and Prevention, 50*, 1112–1117. doi: 10.1016/j.aap.2012.09.001

[9]Fuehrlein, B. S., Jha, M. K., Brenner, A. M., & North, C. S. (2013). Availability and attitudes toward correctional psychiatry training: Results of a national survey of training directors. *The Journal of Behavioral Health Services & Research*, no pagination specified. doi: 10.1007/s11414-013-9336-0

[10] Lawrence, J., Ott, M. (2013). Faculty perceptions of organizational politics. *Review of Higher Education: Journal of the Association for the Study of Higher Education, 36*(2), 145–178. doi: 10.1353/rhe.2013.0011

Techniques for Improving Convenience Samples

The following techniques may improve sampling when an "ideal" sample cannot be drawn for a survey.

Consider Adjusting the Research Problem

Some researchers might want to adjust the research purpose in light of the accessibility of potential participants. For instance, if a researcher has access to a good sample of psychology majors (with assistance of the psychology department), a research purpose involving all undergraduates on a campus might be changed to involve only psychology majors.

Use Diverse Locations and Times

Suppose that a sample will be obtained by approaching students on campus and asking them to agree to be interviewed for a survey. For such a project, using only one location such as at the campus cafeteria entrance might unnecessarily bias the sample because students who tend to use the cafeteria might be systematically different from those who do not. Thus, soliciting participation at the entrances to a variety of buildings on campus probably will provide a superior sample to one conducted at only the entrance to the cafeteria.

In addition to striving for diversity in location, a researcher might strive for diversity in times. For instance, seeking participation of only students arriving for morning classes might unnecessarily bias the sample because those who attend morning classes might be systematically different in a variety of ways from students who attend afternoon and evening classes.

Use Population Demographics When Planning the Sample

The office of institutional research on most campuses routinely compiles demographic information (i.e., background information) on the student body, and this information is generally available to the public. Demographics can be used by researchers who are trying to draw a representative sample of a student body. For instance, consider a researcher learns that the office of institutional research indicates that 15% of the students in the population are graduate students. This researcher can plan to survey graduate-level classes until about 15% of the projected sample size consists of graduate students.

Example 21.6 illustrates another way this technique can be implemented.

Example 21.6
Using population demographics when planning a survey

A student knows that 60% of the undergraduates on a campus are women, based on population demographics supplied by the office of institutional research. The student plans to interview 30 undergraduates by approaching them at various locations on campus. To have the sample be representative in terms of gender, the student wants 18 (60% of the 30) of the participants to be women and 12 to be men. Thus, the student plans to stop approaching women for interviews once 18 have been obtained; likewise, the student plans to stop approaching men once 12 have been obtained.

Use Population Demographics When Analyzing the Data

Consider a student who used the campus mail (with permission) to solicit students to participate in a survey. After calculating the average age of the respondents, the student compares the average to the average age of the population, as determined by the office of institutional research. Finding that the average age of the respondents is much higher than the average age in the population, the student deletes some of the questionnaires submitted by older respondents, thus making the sample more representative of the population in terms of age.[11]

Track Information on Nonvolunteers

Nonvolunteers are potential participants who were contacted but refused to participate. Consider that a student solicits students at various locations on campus to be interviewed for a survey. Keeping track of the rates of participation at the various locations might reveal, for instance, a higher rate of participation from students entering the cafeteria than from students entering classroom buildings. Even if the influence of this on the results is not clear, this differential in rates of participation should be noted in the research report in order to advise readers of a potential bias in sampling.

For mailed surveys, keeping track of zip codes can shed light on how representative a sample is. For instance, if 30% of the questionnaires were mailed to one of the zip codes but only 20% of the responses were posted in that zip code, the student could report this discrepancy, noting that caution should be used in interpreting the results.[12]

Consider Seeking a Community-Based Sample

In some academic fields, much research is conducted using campus-based samples. When replicating or extending previous research based on campus samples, using a community-based sample could be an important strength. For instance, if a series of studies have been conducted using biased campus samples (e.g., introductory psychology students who volunteer for course credit), a term-project survey using a community-based sample would extend knowledge of the research problem, even if the community-based sample is also biased.

Obviously, community-based samples can be obtained by soliciting participation in public places. In addition, community groups and organizations such as social clubs, religious institutions, and neighborhood councils might provide access to their members, especially if the results have the potential to help the groups and organizations.

---

[11] When deleting in this example, it is best to identify all respondents over a certain cut-off age and then select at random the ones to be deleted. The obvious disadvantage of deleting responses is that the sample size will be reduced. Students who have more advanced training in statistics may prefer to "weight" the results, giving less weight to the responses of the older participants without deleting any of them.

[12] Note that individuals living in one zip code often differ in important ways (such as income) from those in other zip codes. Techniques for mailed surveys are discussed in Chapter 10.

Concluding Comments

As a general rule, obtaining a representative sample is more important than using a large sample. Thus, if forced to choose, it is usually better to work with a smaller representative sample than a larger biased sample.

Exercise for Chapter 21

Factual Questions

1. Are surveys a form of experimental research? Explain.

2. "Because the response rate to online surveys is almost always less than 100%, such surveys are presumed to have biased samples." Is the preceding statement true *or* false?
   A. True.   B. False.

3. "Direct mail surveys are presumed to be unbiased." Is the preceding statement true *or* false?
   A. True.   B. False.

4. "Resending a questionnaire to nonrespondents usually increases response rates." Is the preceding statement true *or* false?
   A. True.   B. False.

5. "In the three examples of response rates to Internet surveys, all examples have response rates of 90% or more." Is the preceding statement true *or* false?
   A. True.   B. False.

6. "The terms in an email survey and an Internet survey are synonymous." Is the preceding statement true *or* false?
   A. True.   B. False.

7. "Because the purpose of consensual qualitative research is to reach unanimous agreement (i.e., consensus), it is never appropriate for researchers to work independently at any point when using this approach." Is the preceding statement true *or* false?
   A. True.   B. False.

8. Do online surveys have an obvious bias? Explain.

Question for Discussion

9. Consider your description of the proposed participant selection procedures in your preliminary research proposal (prepared after reading Chapter 11). Will you be making any changes in it based on the information in this chapter? Explain.

Chapter 22
Issues in Measuring Demographics
in Surveys

Demographics are background characteristics of the participants such as age, highest level of education, and gender.[1]

There are two reasons for collecting demographics. First, some research problems require it. For instance, if a research purpose is to compare men and women on some variable, gender will need to be determined. The second reason for collecting demographics is to enable a researcher to describe a sample in enough detail that readers of the research report can get a good idea of what types of individuals participated in the survey.

Determining Which Demographics to Collect

There are an almost limitless number of types of demographic information that might be collected. Table 1.1 in Chapter 1 provides a list of some that are commonly examined in surveys.

As a general rule, only demographics deemed to be relevant to the research problem should be collected. For instance, for a survey on voting behavior of students in college elections, the demographics of age, major in college, and political affiliation might be relevant, while health status and hobbies would be peripheral, at best.

Writing Demographic Questions

Use straightforward language and simple statements and questions to pose demographic questions. The following guidelines address some issues in posing such questions.

Questions on Sensitive Variables

The impact of requesting information on potentially sensitive matters can be somewhat mitigated by providing a range of values from which participants may choose. For instance, many individuals regard their income as a private matter. Asking participants to indicate the range within which their income falls may make revealing this information more acceptable. Example 22.1 illustrates how this might be done. Notice that the important term "household" is underlined to draw attention to it since individual income is often much lower than household income.

---

[1] Most of this chapter was drawn directly from *Conducting a Survey* by Lawrence T. Orcher, Pyrczak Publishing. Reprinted with permission. No further reproduction permitted without written permission from the publisher.

Example 22.1
A demographic item presenting a range of values (recommended)
What is your approximate <u>household</u> income before taxes?
☐   Under $10,000
☐ $10,000 to less than $20,000
☐ $20,000 to less than $35,000
☐ $35,000 to less than $50,000
☐ $50,000 to less than $75,000
☐ $75,000 to less than $100,000
☐ $100,000 or more

When presenting a range of values, be sure to include exhaustive choices (i.e., a set of choices that will include all participants). For instance, in Example 22.2, the choices are not exhaustive because there is no choice for anyone under 18 years of age. The improved version in Example 22.3 starts with the choice "17 years or under."

Example 22.2
A demographic question without exhaustive choices (not recommended)
What is your age?
☐ 18–24 years
☐ 25–44 years
☐ 45–64 years
☐ 65 years or over

Example 22.3
An improved version of Example 22.2
What is your age?
☐ 17 years or under
☐ 18–24 years
☐ 25–44 years
☐ 45–64 years
☐ 65 years or over

When presenting a range of values, consider how many individuals are likely to fall into each range. For instance, for a survey of undergraduates, the improved version in Example 22.3 would likely have the vast majority of respondents in the second range of values (18 to 24), with only a scattering above and below this range. For such a population, more differentiation among the participants in terms of age could be obtained with the choices in Example 22.4.[2]

---

[2] Note that for undergraduates, age is less sensitive an issue than for older adults, so age might be asked with an open-ended question.

Example 22.4

An improved version of Example 22.3 for undergraduates

What is your age?

☐ 17 years or under

☐ 18–19 years

☐ 20–21 years

☐ 22–23 years

☐ 24 years or over

A potentially sensitive issue is racial and ethnic background. The difficulty in writing items on this variable arises because preferred terms change over time and because various members of the same group may prefer different terms. In Example 22.5, which was used in a questionnaire prepared by an insurance company, alternative terms are provided within three of the choices (e.g., Black/African American) to accommodate changing preferences for terms. Notice that the choice for "Other" would allow participants to indicate mixed ancestry.

Example 22.5

Demographic items on race/ethnicity with alternative terms for race/ethnicity in three choices

Which of the following best describes your racial or ethnic background?

Please check one.

☐ Asian

☐ Black/African American

☐ White/Caucasian

☐ Hispanic (may be any race)

☐ Native American/American Indian

☐ Other. Please specify: _____

Because it is difficult to write satisfactory items on race/ethnicity, it is helpful to examine how professional survey researchers have written such items. Example 22.6 shows an item used by the United States Census Bureau in the last census. Notice that even with such a detailed item, the bureau has allowed for individuals to print the name of some "Other" group.

Example 22.6

Demographic item used by the Census Bureau

Is Person 1 Spanish/Hispanic/Latino?

Mark ☒ in the **"No"** box if **not** Spanish/Hispanic/Latino.

☐ **No,** not Spanish/Hispanic/Latino	☐ Yes, Puerto Rican
☐ Yes, Mexican, Mexican Am., Chicano	☐ Yes, Cuban
☐ Yes, other Spanish/Hispanic/Latino – *Print group*:	

Providing Definitions

Carefully consider all terms in demographic questions to determine if definitions or explanations should be provided. It is especially important to provide these when using technical terms with which participants may not be fully familiar. For instance, in a study of breast cancer survivors, researchers requested demographics on a number of variables such as current age, prior health status, and age at diagnosis. In addition, they asked about the type of cancer using three technical terms (i.e., localized, regional, and invasive). They provided explanations of the terms, as indicated in Example 22.7.

Example 22.7
Explanations offered for technical terms[3]
Type of cancer was assessed by asking women whether they had localized, regional, or invasive disease, with the following explanations: local = no lymph nodes are involved; regional = cancer has spread past the breast to the underarm lymph nodes; and invasive = cancer has spread beyond the underarm lymph nodes.

Providing Exhaustive Choices

As mentioned earlier, the choices in an item should be exhaustive (i.e., provide a choice for each possibility). Sometimes, it is difficult to spot deficiencies in the exhaustiveness of the choices. Consider Example 22.8, which at first glance may seem adequate. Notice, however, that there is no choice for a participant who did not finish elementary school. In addition, the choice "college graduate" is ambiguous because it is not clear if it includes graduates of two-year colleges. In contrast, consider Example 22.9, which shows how the United States Census Bureau asked about highest level of education completed. Example 22.9 is clearly superior to Example 22.8 because Example 22.9 has exhaustive choices, and each choice is defined by indicating the number of years associated with it.

Example 22.8
Demographic item that fails to provide exhaustive choices and is ambiguous
Highest level of education completed:
- ☐ Elementary
- ☐ Secondary
- ☐ Some college
- ☐ College graduate

Example 22.9
Improved version (Census Bureau version) of Example 22.8
Highest level of education completed:
- ☐ Elementary (0 to 8 years)
- ☐ Some high school (1 to 3 years)
- ☐ High school graduate (4 years)
- ☐ Some college (1 to 3 years)
- ☐ College graduate (4 or more years)

---

[3] Bellizzi, K. M., & Blank, T. O. (2006). Predicting posttraumatic growth in breast cancer survivors. *Health Psychology, 25*, 47–56.

Providing Spaces for Responses to Open-Ended Questions

As a general rule, choices that participants can quickly check off should be provided. However, for some items of information, there may be so many possible choices that providing choices would be unwieldy. For instance, asking participants for zip codes is best done with an open-ended question because there are so many possible zip codes. Consider Example 22.10. Note that five boxes are provided, one for each number in a basic zip code (i.e., the zip code without a four-number extension).

Example 22.10
An open-ended question with boxes for the answer
What is the zip code for your residence? Write one number in each box.

□ □ □ □ □

For non-numerical entries, such as words that may vary greatly in the number of letters (or even the number of words) in response to an open-ended item, be careful to provide an appropriate amount of space. Too much or two little space might confuse participants. For instance, for the question, "What is the name of your neighborhood?" posed to residents of Los Angeles, more than one or two lines of space might suggest that the researcher is seeking more than a simple answer such as "Wilshire District."

Pilot Testing Demographic Questions

A pilot test of the demographic questions should be conducted with individuals who will not be participating in the main survey. An effective way to pilot test is to ask each individual to "think aloud" as they consider and respond to the questions. Often, this can reveal flaws in demographic questions. For instance, in response to the question, "Are you in a relationship?" a pilot study participant might state this thought, "I've been dating someone for two weeks. I wonder if that counts as a relationship." Such a statement would suggest that the term "relationship" needs to be defined within the item.

Organizing and Introducing Demographic Questions

Whether presented in a questionnaire or in an interview schedule, all demographic items should be grouped together and placed at the end of the questionnaire or schedule. This is recommended because when demographic questions are asked first, they blur the purpose of the instrument (making the questionnaire or schedule seem insignificant) and may be viewed as intrusive, especially if sensitive demographics are sought.

Just before asking the demographic questions, a brief explanation should be given for asking them. For instance, in an interview, the interviewer might state, "Now, I have a few questions about your background. This information is needed for the statistical analysis and categorization of your answers." Giving participants an explanation helps blunt resistance to answering questions that some participants might view as invasive of their privacy.[4]

Exercise for Chapter 22

Directions: Share your answers to this exercise with other students who may still be considering which demographic questions to ask and how to phrase them.

1. List demographic variables that might help readers of your research report visualize relevant characteristics of your sample.

2. Are any of the variables you listed in response to Question 1 potentially sensitive? Might participants view questions about them as an invasion of privacy? Explain.

3. Write two demographic questions you intend to ask in your survey. Have them reviewed by other students and rewrite the questions based on suggestions the students make for improving them.

---

[4] Note that assurances of confidentiality and anonymity should be given at the beginning of the questionnaire or interview, which are discussed in the next chapter. If some demographic questions are especially sensitive, these assurances might be repeated just before the demographic questions are asked.

Chapter 23
Issues in the Use of Questionnaires in Surveys

This chapter provides guidelines on the organization and administration of instruments. It covers both questionnaires and interviews.

Preparing Instruments for Administration

Before administering an instrument, the following steps should be taken in order to make it an efficient and effective measurement tool.

Give a Questionnaire a Title

A questionnaire should be given a title that clearly indicates the types of variables covered.

Consider a questionnaire for a survey in which the researcher wants to compare the political activism (e.g., voting, signing petitions, attending demonstrations) of undergraduates majoring in political science with that of undergraduates with other majors. The title of the questionnaire in Example 23.1 is inadequate because it could apply to any number of issues. The title in Example 23.2 is superior.

> **Example 23.1**
> *A vague questionnaire title (not recommended)*
> Undergraduate Opinion Survey

> **Example 23.2**
> *A questionnaire title that names a specific variable (recommended)*
> Undergraduates' Political Activism Survey

Prepare an Introduction

Participants should be given a brief introduction, which should indicate (a) the purpose of the survey, (b) the sponsor (i.e., the individual or group paying for and conducting the survey), (c) the approximate amount of time it will take to complete the questionnaire or interview, and (d) whether responses will remain confidential. This is illustrated in Example 23.3.

> **Example 23.3**
> *A brief introduction for a questionnaire or interview*
> The purpose of this survey is to explore undergraduates' current and future levels of participation in political processes. I am conducting this survey as part of a term project for my course in political science methodology. The survey will take less than five minutes of your time, and your cooperation will be greatly appreciated.

Your responses will remain confidential, and the research report will present only group averages and percentages.

When stating the purpose of the survey, point out any potential benefits that might accrue either to the individual responding or to a group of individuals. For instance, in the introduction to a questionnaire on reference-room services at a college library, a researcher might point out that the information collected through the survey might help in restructuring the services to the benefit of all students who use the library.

Group the Items by Topic

If there is more than one question on each of several subtopics, group the items by topic. In a questionnaire, provide subheadings for each group of questions, such as those in Example 23.4. In an interview schedule, introduce each group with a statement such as, "First, I have a few questions about your selection of a health plan."

> **Example 23.4**
> *Subheadings for groups of questions*
> About Your Selection of a Health Plan (3 questions)
> About Your Primary Care Physician (5 questions)
> About Specialists (3 questions)
> About Prescription Drugs (4 questions)
> Demographics (6 questions)

Conclude with a "Thank You" and Provide Contact Information

The instrument should end with a thank-you statement. In addition, because participants should be treated as "participants" and not "objects" or "subjects," they should be informed of how to contact the researcher in the future if they have any concerns or desire feedback on the results.

Group Administration of Questionnaires

Sometimes questionnaires are administered to groups of individuals, such as all members of a class. Because potential participants should be given the right to decline to participate, determine in advance what individuals who decline should be instructed to do while waiting for other students who are participating. Should they be asked to wait quietly at their desks during the administration? Should they be told they are free to leave the classroom for a specified number of minutes?

Advantage of Group Administration

Administering a questionnaire to one or more groups (such as class sections) is an efficient way to obtain a large sample.

Disadvantage of Group Administration

Naturally existing groups, such as class sections of a sociology course, are called "clusters" (see the information on cluster sampling in Chapter 12). Each cluster tends to be homogeneous in important respects. For instance, an evening section of the course might have older students who are employed full time during the day. Thus, the responses from such a group might not represent the full diversity of students taking sociology courses.

Individual Administration of Questionnaires

Questionnaires can be handed out to individuals instead of groups. For instance, a researcher could set up a small table outside buildings on campus and solicit individual respondents to have a seat at the table and respond to the questionnaire.

Advantage of Individual Administration

Administering a questionnaire to individuals usually will provide a more diverse sample than administration to naturally existing groups (see the "Disadvantage of Group Administration").

Disadvantage of Individual Administration

Administration to one individual at a time will take more effort and time than administration to groups.

Advantages of Face-to-Face Interviews

Participation rates when potential participants are approached on a face-to-face basis can be higher than when they receive an impersonal mailed questionnaire. In addition, an interviewer might get insights into participants' understanding of the interview questions through comments and facial expressions. For instance, some respondents may express difficulty in understanding what a question is driving at, which might be noted in the research report with a suggestion that the question be reworded in future studies.

Exercise for Chapter 23

1. If you will be using a questionnaire, write a title for it, and ask other students to provide feedback on it. Report the result of these activities here.

2. If you will be using a questionnaire, prepare a brief introduction for your questionnaire, and ask other students to provide feedback on it. Report the result of these activities here.

3. If you will be using a questionnaire, which of the following methods do you plan for administration? Explain the reason for your choice.

    A. Group administration
    B. Individual administration

Part F

Issues in Conducting Experiments

The first chapter in this part (Chapter 24) contains a general introduction to experimentation. It also explores the issue of the external validity of experiments, which refers to the extent to which it is reasonable to generalize the results to a population.

Chapter 25 deals with the issue of the internal validity of experiments, which refers to the extent to which the causes of changes in participants' behavior can be identified with confidence. Also, three true experimental designs, all of which have high internal validity, are discussed.

Chapter 26 presents experimental designs that might be used when it is not possible to use a true experimental design.

Students who wrote preliminary research proposals for experiments based on the material in Part A of this book should reconsider their proposals in light of the material in the next three chapters. Students who do not plan to conduct an experiment should find the material in this part of the book helpful when reading reports of experimental research.

Notes:

Chapter 24
Introduction to Experimentation and Threats to External Validity

In experiments, researchers administer treatments to participants in order to determine the effects on one or more outcome variables. Thus, the general purpose of experiments is to explore cause-and-effect relationships. Example 24.1 briefly summarizes an experiment.

Example 24.1
A description of an experiment
College students who had public speaking anxiety were identified. Each student was assigned at random to either the experimental group or control group. The experimental group received small group counseling designed to treat their anxiety. The other group was designated as a control group and received no special treatment. A self-report measure of public speaking anxiety was administered to all participants at the beginning (i.e., a pretest) and at the end (i.e., a posttest) of the experiment. The hypothesis was that those who received the small group counseling would report a significantly greater reduction in public speaking anxiety from pretest to posttest than the control group.

In Example 24.1, there were two treatments. The first treatment was small group counseling. The second treatment was "no special treatment," which was the control condition. Note that in experimentation, a control condition is counted as one of the treatments. A set of treatments in an experiment is called the *independent variable*.

The outcome variable in Example 24.1 is the amount of self-reported public speaking anxiety. In an experiment, the outcome variable is called the *dependent variable*.

Controlling the Hawthorne Effect in Experimentation

The *Hawthorne Effect* refers to the tendency of participants to improve simply because they are being studied. This effect was first documented in experiments at the Hawthorne Western Electric Plant in Illinois, in which industrial psychologists noticed improvement in workers' productivity even when treatments that should decrease productivity were given.

The Hawthorne effect could influence the results of the experiment described in Example 24.1. For instance, the group counseling in and of itself might not be effective in reducing public speaking anxiety. However, the participants in the experimental group might have a reduction in public speaking anxiety simply as a result of receiving special attention. To control for this, an *attention control group* might be used. For instance, in the experiment in Example 24.1, instead of having a control group that receives no special treatment, the control group might be given special attention by being given a treatment that should not affect public speaking anxiety (perhaps small group counseling on making career choices without any reference to public speaking anxiety). Then, if the experimental group has a greater reduction in anxiety than the attention control group, it cannot be simply because of the attention provided by group counseling because both groups received attention through counseling.

Example 24.2 describes a study in which there was an attention control group and another control group that received no special attention.

Example 24.2
An experiment with an "attention control group" to control for the Hawthorne effect

Researchers identified a pool of individuals who were mildly depressed. At random, the researchers formed three groups: (1) an experimental group that received telephone counseling for their depression, (2) an attention control group that also received telephone counseling but the counseling was on stress management (not depression), and (3) a control group that received no special treatment other than that ordinarily provided by their primary care physicians. The outcome variable was depression as measured by the Hamilton Rating Scale for Depression. (pp. 785–789)[1]

Using Multiple Independent and Dependent Variables

A given experiment can have more than one independent variable (i.e., more than one set of treatments). In Example 24.3, there are two independent variables: (1) the level of personalization and (2) the level of immersion.

Example 24.3
An experiment with two independent variables

In an experiment in which college students were taught a science lesson via a computer game, there were two independent variables. The first independent variable was the level of personalization with two treatment categories: (1) high personalization in which the first individual such as *I* and *you* was used in the lesson and (2) low personalization in which the third individual was used. The second independent variable was the level of immersion, which also had two treatment categories: (1) high immersion in which the game was presented with head-mounted displays that convey the sense of physical presence and (2) low immersion in which the game was presented with standard desktop computers. The two independent variables with two levels each created four experimental conditions, resulting in four groups of participants, as illustrated below. Individual students were assigned at random to the four conditions. Retention of the science material was the dependent variable. (p. 165)[2]

---

[1] Abstracted from Lynch, D., Tamburrino, M., Nagel, R., & Smith, M. K. (2004). Telephone-based treatment for family practice patients with mild depression. *Psychological Reports*, *94*, 785–792.
[2] Abstracted from Moreno, R., & Mayer, R. E. (2004). Personalized messages that promote science learning in virtual environments. *Journal of Educational Psychology*, *96*, 165–173.

	High immersion (HI)	Low immersion (LI)
High personalization (HP)	*Group 1* received HP and HI	*Group 2* received HP and LI
Low personalization (LP)	*Group 3* received LP and HI	*Group 4* received LP and LI

By examining two independent variables at the same time in the same experiment, researchers can examine how the variables work together to produce differences on the dependent variable. In statistics, this is called an *interaction* of the independent variables. While it is possible to include more than two independent variables in an experiment, the statistical analysis and interpretation for more than two can be difficult for beginning researchers.

In addition, researchers frequently examine more than one dependent variable (i.e., outcome variable) in an experiment. In Example 24.4, there are six dependent variables.

Example 24.4
An experiment with six dependent variables
College women were randomly assigned to examine one of three types of magazines: (1) fashion magazines, (2) fitness-and-health magazines, and (3) news magazines. Each participant examined magazines for 15 minutes. The purpose of the experiment was to determine the effects of the types of magazines on these six dependent variables: (1) depression, (2) trait anxiety, (3) eating disorders, (4) fear of fat, (5) self-esteem, and (6) body satisfaction. (p. 1093)[3]

The number of dependent variables to be examined in an experiment is limited only by the number of outcomes that might reasonably be expected to be influenced by the independent variable and the willingness of participants to complete multiple measures such as six questionnaires.

External Validity of Experiments[4]

External validity refers to the ability to generalize the results of an experiment to individuals in a population outside of the experimental setting. A *threat to external validity* is a circumstance that limits the ability to generalize. Five threats are described next.

Selection Bias

The first threat to external validity is called *selection bias*. This refers to any bias that might have occurred in the selection of individuals to be participants in an experiment. As you know from Chapter 12, *random selection* (such as drawing names out of a

---

[3] Abstracted from Cameron, E. M., & Ferraro, F. R. (2004). Body satisfaction in college women after brief exposure to magazine images. *Perceptual and Motor Skills, 98*, 1093–1099.
[4] Except where noted, the technical terms used in the remainder of this chapter were originally suggested by Campbell, D. T., & Stanley, J. C. (1966). *Experimental and quasi-experimental designs for research*. Chicago: Rand McNally.

hat or using a table of random numbers) is the key to preventing bias in sampling. If there are to be two groups in an experiment, for instance, the ideal is to select a sample of individuals at random from a population to be in the experimental group and to select a second sample of individuals at random from the same population to be in the control group.

Unfortunately, researchers usually cannot obtain random samples from well-defined populations, often because they must rely on volunteers to be participants in experiments. For instance, in Example 24.5, the 22 participants in the experiment were not drawn using random selection and, therefore, constitute a biased sample of the 158 first-year law students in the population. This reduces the external validity of the experiment.

Example 24.5
An experiment with selection bias

A team of researchers sent a letter to all 158 first-year law students, inviting them to participate in an experiment in which a treatment for reducing stress would be tested. Included with the letter was an informed consent form. Twenty-nine of the 158 returned completed consent forms, and 22 of these completed the study. Using volunteers instead of using random selection limited the external validity of the study because of *selection bias*. (p. 45)[5]

Reactive Effects of Experimental Arrangements

Much experimental research is conducted in laboratory settings (or college classrooms that are used as laboratories). The setting can have an effect on how the participants respond to the treatments. Consider Example 24.6, in which the effects of drinking alcohol on participants' reactions while driving were studied in a laboratory setting. The results found in such a setting might not apply to natural settings in which individuals drink alcohol.

Example 24.6
A laboratory experiment with limited external validity due to reactive effects of experimental arrangements

College students in an experimental group were asked to each drink three beers over a three-hour period in a psychology lab. A control group was asked to do the same thing but was given a nonalcoholic beer to drink. Reaction times of students in both groups were measured at the end of each hour using a computer simulation of driving. The researcher's interest was in documenting the impairment to reaction times caused by alcoholic beer when driving automobiles. However, the applicability of the results to actual driving situations was limited by conducting the study in a laboratory.

An obvious reason for conducting the study in Example 24.6 in a laboratory setting with computer simulation is to limit potential harm that might result if reaction times were measured in real driving situations. Another reason is that in laboratory settings, researchers have more control, such as control over how much alcohol is consumed as

---

[5] Based on Sheehy, R., & Horan, J. J. (2004). Effects of stress inoculation training for 1st-year law students. *International Journal of Stress Management, 11*, 41–55.

well as control over how quickly it is consumed. In a study conducted in a natural setting such as in a bar, a researcher would find it difficult to control these factors, which could have a major impact on the results. Thus, experiments are often brought into a laboratory setting to increase experimenters' control. Doing this, however, usually limits the external validity of the experiments.

Any artifact of an experiment, such as conducting an experiment in a laboratory setting, can cause participants to display different *reactions* than would normally occur in response to the treatments. Hence, this threat to validity is called the *reactive effects of experimental arrangements*.

Reactive effects can occur whenever anything about the experimental setting is unlike the natural setting in which the behavior ordinarily occurs. For instance, the presence of recording equipment, research assistants, and safety devices in an experiment can lead to results that would not occur in a natural setting.

Reactive Effects of Testing

This threat to external validity is sometimes also called *pretest sensitization*. It refers to the possibility that the pretest in an experiment might sensitize participants to a treatment. Perhaps, for instance, a movie will be shown that will illustrate the importance of mathematics in everyday life in order to see if it will improve students' attitudes toward mathematics. However, if a pretest consisting of an attitude toward a math scale is administered, participants may react differently to the movie than they would if no pretest had been given. Thus, the experimental results might not apply to members of the population if the population (in natural settings) does not receive a pretest before being shown the movie. In other words, the experiment will only show how well the film worked when a pretest is given first. It will not show how well it works in a natural setting in which no pretest is given.

To avoid pretest sensitization, one might conduct an experiment without a pretest, a possibility that is discussed in Chapter 26. Another way to avoid it is to use *unobtrusive measures*, which is discussed next.

Obtrusiveness of Measurement[6]

Measurement at any point in an experiment (not just on a pretest as discussed above) might obtrude on participants and cause them to react differently than they would if there were no measurement. In other words, what is learned about the effectiveness of a treatment in an experiment in which participants are aware that their behavior is being measured might not indicate how effective the treatment will be when the treatment is used in a natural setting with no measurement. This threat to external validity is called *obtrusiveness of measurement*.

To avoid this threat, experimenters sometimes use *unobtrusive measures*. For instance, one-way mirrors are frequently used when they are judged not to infringe on participants' rights. Another common method is to ask for reports from others who are normally present. For instance, the drinking behavior of husbands after treatment for alco-

---

[6] This threat to external validity was not included in Campbell and Stanley's (1966) work.

holism in an experiment might be measured by asking their wives to report on it rather than by asking the participants themselves.

Unobtrusive measures also can often be used in experiments conducted in natural settings (often called *field experiments*) through observation from a distance or through indirect observation, which was used in Example 24.7. In the example, the observation was indirect because the restaurant tabs (rather than the customers themselves) were examined without the participants' knowledge. In fact, participants were totally unaware that they were in an experiment, and, therefore, unaware that measurement was occurring.[7]

Example 24.7
A field experiment with an unobtrusive measure
To determine the effects of soft and loud background music (the independent variable) on how much customers spent while dining (the dependent variable), a researcher varied the volume at random. The average purchase amount, or "restaurant tab," was higher for customers who heard soft background music. (p. 1025)[8]

Multiple-Treatment Interference
This threat to external validity of experiments occurs whenever the same participants are given more than one treatment. For instance, a group of participants might be given token rewards that can be exchanged for privileges for a week and then be given verbal praise as a reward for the second week. What is learned in such an experiment about the effects of verbal praise during the second week would have limited external validity (i.e., limited generalizability) to a population that is first given tokens. This is because at the point the participants received praise in the experiment, they had already been subjected to a different treatment (i.e., token rewards). For instance, during the second week, some of the participants might be annoyed because tokens were no longer being given, which might cause them to be less responsive to the verbal praise than they otherwise would be.

Concluding Comments
To the extent to which it is reasonable to believe that the results of an experiment apply to a population in a natural setting, an experiment is said to have good external validity. While it is often not possible to avoid all the threats to external validity discussed in this chapter, steps should be taken to eliminate as many as possible.

---

[7] Ethical problems might arise in such an experiment if the researcher directly observed the customers to identify them or became aware of their identity by examining credit card slips.

[8] Lammers, H. B. (2003). An oceanside field experiment on background music effects on the restaurant tab. *Perceptual and Motor Skills, 96*, 1025–1026.

Exercise for Chapter 24

Factual Questions

1. A control group received ordinary teacher-led instruction with a textbook in solving math word problems. At the same time, an experimental group received the same instruction as the control group except that they also practiced numerous word problems presented in a new workbook. The hypothesis was that using the new workbook would increase the number of correct answers on a test of the ability to solve math word problems. In this example, what is the dependent variable?

2. A set of treatments in an experiment is called what?
     A. The independent variable.   B. The dependent variable.

3. To control for the Hawthorne Effect, what type of control group should be used?

4. "A given experiment can have more than one dependent variable." Is the preceding statement true *or* false?
     A. True.   B. False.

5. What is the name of the threat to external validity that results from nonrandom selection of individuals to participate in an experiment?

6. Suppose an experiment was conducted in a psychology lab and the participants reacted differently to the treatments than they otherwise would have reacted in a natural setting. This illustrates what threat to external validity?

7. What are the two names given in this chapter for the possibility that the pretest in an experiment might sensitize participants to a treatment?

8. Suppose a group of participants was first given Treatment X in an experiment and then was given Treatment Y. What is the name of the threat to external validity that warns that what was learned about the effectiveness of Treatment Y might not apply in a population without first administering Treatment X?

Question for Discussion

9. If you are preparing a proposal for an experiment, will you be making any changes in it based on the information in this chapter? Explain.

Notes:

Chapter 25
Threats to Internal Validity and True Experiments

The previous chapter covered the *external validity* of experiments, which refers to the ability to generalize the results of an experiment to individuals in a population outside of the experimental setting (i.e., in a natural setting). In this chapter, the *internal validity* of experiments will be considered.

To understand internal validity, first recall that the basic purpose of an experiment is to explore cause-and-effect relationships. An experiment is said to have good internal validity if it is conducted in such a way that the independent variable is the only viable explanation for changes observed in participants. It is easiest to understand this by considering an experiment that has very weak internal validity, which is the case in Example 25.1, which has only one group of participants.

Example 25.1
An experiment with poor internal validity and an inappropriate conclusion
At the beginning of first grade, a team of teachers measured students' knowledge of the letters of the alphabet. Then the team taught letter recognition using a new instructional computer program, which constituted the independent variable. After two months of instruction, the team again measured students' knowledge of the letters. They found a statistically significant increase in the average score from pretest to posttest. Because the difference was larger than what chance alone would create, they concluded that the independent variable must be the cause of the increased knowledge.

The conclusion in Example 25.1 is inappropriate because the experiment is subject to several *threats to internal validity*, which are alternative explanations regarding the cause of the difference (i.e., the increased knowledge). These are discussed next.

History

An important threat to internal validity is called *history*,[1] which refers to any event external to the experiment that might have caused the observed change in participants' behavior. For instance, the parents of the students in Example 25.1 might have felt that it was time for their children to learn the letters of the alphabet and taught them to their children at home. Perhaps a popular children's television program covered the letters of the alphabet, and the students learned the letters from the television program and not from the computer program. These and a host of other external events, most of which would be unknown to the researchers, might have caused the students' average score to increase. Thus, an appropriate conclusion would be that the increase might have been

---

[1] The technical terms used in this chapter were originally suggested by Campbell and Stanley (1966).

caused by the computer program, but it also might have been caused by other external events. Because it is not clear whether the independent variable was the cause of the change observed in this experiment, it has poor internal validity.

Controlling History with a True Experiment

To fully control the threat called history, *true experiments* should be conducted. All true experiments have more than one group of participants, and the participants are assigned to the groups at random. A basic true experiment has two groups with pretests and posttests for each group. This experimental design can be diagrammed as follows, with the two rows of symbols representing two groups, the letter "R" indicating that individual participants were assigned to the groups at random. The letter "O" stands for "observation," which is defined as any type of measurement, with the first "O" in each line standing for a pretest and the second standing for a posttest. Finally, the "X" stands for an experimental treatment that was administered to the top group, and the absence of the "X" for the bottom group indicates that they are a control group.

$$R \quad O \quad X \quad O$$
$$R \quad O \qquad O$$

How does this true experimental design control for the effects of history? Quite simply, it does so by having a control group that will be influenced by the same external events. Thus, if participants are learning the names of the letters of the alphabet by watching a television program instead of via the computer program in Example 25.1, both groups will increase by about the same amount due to watching the television program. Thus, only if the experimental group's mean increases more than the control group's mean will the conclusion that the computer program probably caused the increase be justified.

Maturation

The experiment in Example 25.1 is also subject to the threat called *maturation*, which refers to natural developmental changes, which are most noticeable in young children. Perhaps, for instance, the participants' maturational increase in visual acuity might be responsible for an increase in recognizing the letters of the alphabet.

Like the threat called history, the threat called maturation can be controlled by conducting a true experiment, which has an experimental group and a control group formed at random. Because of the random assignment to groups, both groups will be equally likely to experience the same maturational influences. In other words, the control group will probably mature at about the same rate as the experimental group. Thus, if the experimental group gains more than the control group, maturation is not a good explanation for the difference between groups.

Instrumentation

Instrumentation is the threat that refers to possible changes in a measure or measurement process. For instance, perhaps the researchers who administered the posttest in

Example 25.1 were more alert and noted more correct answers than when they administered the pretest, accounting for the difference from pretest to posttest.

In addition to changes in human observers' abilities, other examples of instrumentation are (1) tests reproduced on paper fading over time, making them more difficult to read, (2) noisy testing conditions during the pretest but not during the posttest, (3) accidental changes in testing time limits, with more generous time limits given on the posttest than on the pretest, and (4) failure of the test administrator to read all the directions to participants on the pretest but reading all the directions on the posttest.

Within a true experiment with randomly assigned experimental and control groups, both the experimental and the control group would tend to change from pretest to posttest at the same rate because of instrumentation (i.e., both groups should be affected about equally by changes in the measures). If the experimental group gains more than the control group, "because of instrumentation" would not be a good explanation for the difference in the rate of change.

Testing

Testing is the threat to internal validity that results from learning how to take a particular test with the result that performance is increased on the posttest. In some research literature, this threat is called the *practice effect*, which helps to explain its meaning. In effect, the pretest in Example 25.1 might have provided the students the opportunity to practice their test-taking skills, resulting in an improved performance on the posttest. This threat is most likely to occur when participants are children who have had little experience taking tests, as well as with participants of any age when an unusual or novel method of testing is used.

Like the other threats to internal validity, this threat is controlled by using a true experimental design with a randomly assigned control group, which will also have the benefits of practicing on the pretest. Thus, if the experimental group gains more than the control group, the threat called testing is not a good explanation for the difference between the gains of the two groups.

Statistical Regression

Statistical regression (also called *regression toward the mean*) refers to the tendency of participants who are extremely high or extremely low to score closer to the mean on retesting. It is a phenomenon that was originally noted in the biological sciences. For instance, if only individuals who are extremely tall are considered, their offspring will have an average height closer to the average of the population than the average of the parents. In other words, the offspring are regressing toward the mean of the population. What is happening is that "errors," such as being extremely tall, tend to correct themselves on retesting (or in this instance, in subsequent generations).

The same phenomenon has been observed on psychological and educational tests (i.e., those who are extremely low on one testing will, on average, be higher on retesting as well as those who are extremely high on one testing will, on average, be lower on retesting). Thus, if the students in Example 25.1 had been selected because they had extremely low scores, they would tend to score higher on retesting (on the posttest) because of statistical regression.[2]

Like the other threats to internal validity, this threat is controlled by using a true experimental design with participants who have extreme scores randomly assigned to experimental and control groups both drawn from the same extreme pool of potential participants. Both groups will, therefore, be likely to regress toward the mean at the same rate, eliminating statistical regression as a good explanation for the difference in the amount of gain for the two groups.

Selection

Selection is a threat to the validity of an experiment when two (or more) nonequivalent groups are compared. Note that whenever nonrandom assignment is used to form the experimental and control groups, the groups are presumed to be nonequivalent.[3] Example 25.2 describes such an experiment.

Example 25.2
An experiment with nonequivalent groups
A sociology professor conducted an experiment in which her morning Introduction to Sociology class served as the experimental group that received immediate feedback on the results of weekly quizzes via computer. Her evening Introduction to Sociology class served as the control group that received feedback at the next class meeting. A pretest that measured knowledge of basic concepts in sociology was administered at the beginning of the course to both classes. On the pretest, both groups were similar on the average with both groups having low scores. On the posttest at the end of the course, the morning class scored significantly higher than the evening class.

Although the two groups in Example 25.2 were similar to each other on the pretest, they could have been quite different on other important variables that might affect achievement. For instance, more of those who signed up for the morning class might have been full-time students, while more of those who signed up for the evening class might have been part-time students with full-time jobs during the day, giving them less time to study. On the other hand, students who signed up for the evening class might have liked to party late at night and, thus, did not register for the morning class so they could sleep

---

[2] The explanation for this is that some of those who have very extreme scores on psychological and educational tests have large errors in their scores. For instance, some students might make a clerical error and put all their answers on an answer sheet in the wrong spaces. On retesting, these types of errors will tend to wash out, raising the scores of some individuals in the low group, which, in turn, will raise the average for the low group.

[3] Note the difference between the threat to internal validity in this chapter called *selection* and the threat to external validity called *selection bias* in the previous chapter. *Selection bias* refers to how the participants for an experiment were drawn from a population, while *selection* refers to how individuals who have already been selected are assigned to groups within an experiment. For instance, an experiment that has *selection bias* because of the use of volunteers could still have random assignment to experimental and control groups. Such an experiment could be said to have low external validity because of *selection bias* but good internal validity because assignment to groups was done at random.

in. Such students may be less studious than other students. These and many other possibilities might have led to the superior performance of the experimental group. Thus, the experiment has flawed internal validity because of the way the individuals became part of the two groups (by signing up for a class section that suited them rather than by being assigned to the class sections at random).

The way to prevent selection bias is to form the two groups at random, such as pulling half the names out of a hat to form an experimental group and using the remaining half as the control group. Because random selection has no favorites, those students who are randomly assigned to the experimental group would be equally likely to be full-time students as those randomly assigned to the control group, for instance.

True Experimental Designs

As you know from the discussion so far in this chapter, the threats to internal validity can all be controlled through random assignment to groups in an experiment. Earlier in the chapter, you saw the following design, which is the "two-group randomized groups design." You should recall from the discussion earlier in this chapter that "R" stands for random assignment, "O" stands for observation or measurement, and "X" stands for an experimental treatment.

$$R \quad O \quad X \quad O$$
$$R \quad O \qquad O$$

This design can be easily extended to have more than two groups. For instance, an experiment might have three treatment groups and a control group. By using subscripts to the right of the Xs to stand for the various treatments, the design would look like this:

$$R \quad O \quad X_1 \quad O$$
$$R \quad O \quad X_2 \quad O$$
$$R \quad O \quad X_3 \quad O$$
$$R \quad O \qquad O$$

Recall that it is the random assignment that makes the experiment a "true experiment" because random assignment to groups forms two groups that are equivalent except for random errors. Random errors can be evaluated using inferential statistical tests such as the t test, which was covered in Chapter 19.[4]

Notice that it is not the pretest that makes the two groups "equivalent." Equivalency is the result of random assignment. Thus, logically, it is not necessary to have a pretest in order to have a true experiment. The following design is for a "two-group, posttest-only randomized groups design."

$$R \quad X \quad O$$
$$R \qquad O$$

---

[4] Because random assignment has no favorites (i.e., is unbiased), as the sample size becomes larger, it becomes less likely that the two groups formed at random will differ in important ways from each other. Thus, sample size is a major consideration in inferential statistical tests.

Not having a pretest gets around the threat to external validity called "reactive effects of testing," which was discussed in the previous chapter, as well as the threat to internal validity simply called "testing" in this chapter. For either of these to exist, there must be a pretest. Thus, not having a pretest excludes them from consideration.

An advantage of having a pretest is that the amount of growth or change can be determined from the beginning of an experiment on a pretest to the end on a posttest. The "Solomon four-group design," which is diagrammed next, allows researchers to find out how well a treatment works with and without a pretest. In this design, there are two experimental groups that receive the same treatment but one group is administered a pretest while the other group is not pretested. Likewise, there are two control groups: one that is given a pretest and one that is not given a pretest. Using the symbols discussed earlier, the Solomon four-group design is diagrammed as follows.

R O X O
R O   O
R   X O
R   O

Concluding Comments

External validity, which was discussed in the previous chapter, refers to the extent to which it is appropriate to generalize the results of an experiment to a population (i.e., the extent to which the results are applicable to the population from which the sample was drawn). *Internal validity* refers to the extent to which researchers can be confident that the treatments are the source of differences observed within an experiment. Because of the differences in their meaning, it is possible for an experiment to have low external validity (e.g., using a group of volunteers for an experiment) but have high internal validity (e.g., assigning the volunteers at random to the experimental and control groups). Likewise, it is possible for an experiment to have high external validity (e.g., drawing individuals at random from a population to be in an experiment) but low internal validity (e.g., allowing the participants to select the treatments they want to receive instead of assigning treatments at random).

If individuals are assigned at random to the comparison groups in an experiment, the experiment is said to be a *true experiment*. By using a true experiment, all the threats to internal validity discussed in this chapter are controlled.

Exercise for Chapter 25

Factual Questions

1. Which of the following refers to the appropriateness of generalizing the results of an experiment to a population?
    A. External validity.   B. Internal validity.

2. What is the name of the threat to internal validity that refers to any event external to the experiment that might have caused the change in participants' behavior?

3. In experimental designs, the letter "O" stands for what?

4. In experimental designs, the letter "X" stands for what?

5. What is the name of the threat to internal validity that refers to possible changes in the measure?

6. What is the name of the threat to internal validity that is also called the "practice effect"?

7. What is the threat to internal validity that is created by comparing nonequivalent groups?

8. Is it necessary to have a pretest in order to have a true experiment?

9. How can all the threats to internal validity be controlled?

10. Is it possible for an experiment to have high external validity but low internal validity?

11. Is it possible for an experiment to have low external validity but high internal validity?

Question for Discussion

12. If you are preparing a proposal for an experiment, will you be making any changes in it based on the information in this chapter? Explain.

Notes:

Chapter 26
Pre-Experiments and
Quasi-Experiments

True experimental designs, which have random assignment to comparison groups, were discussed in the previous chapter. Using random assignment to groups controls all the threats to internal validity discussed in that chapter. Unfortunately, it is often not possible to assign individual participants at random to treatment groups. In this chapter, some experimental designs that do not have random assignment will be considered.

Pre-Experiments

As its name suggests, a *pre-experiment* can be thought of as an activity that is done before formal experimentation begins. In their seminal work, Campbell and Stanley (1966) identified three pre-experimental designs and cautioned that they are so weak that they are of almost no value in exploring cause-and-effect relationships.

The first pre-experimental design was illustrated in Example 25.1 in the previous chapter in which there was only one group of participants who were given a pretest, followed by a treatment, followed by a posttest. The design of the experiment is as follows:

O X O

Because there is only one row of symbols, there is only one group in the experiment. As indicated in the previous chapter, the letter "O" stands for observation (i.e., any type of measurement), and the letter "X" stands for an experimental treatment. Example 26.1 shows another example of an experiment with this design.

Example 26.1
An experiment that illustrates the one group pretest-posttest pre-experimental design
A clinical psychologist whose specialty was obsessive-compulsive disorders assessed all clients before beginning therapy to determine the extent of their disorder. The psychologist faithfully administered cognitive therapy in all therapy sessions. After six months of therapy, each client was assessed again. The psychologist found improvement on the average from the first assessment to the second. While this was heartening, the psychologist realized that factors other than the cognitive therapy might have influenced the clients and helped improve their condition.

Because there is no randomized control group in Example 26.1, all the threats to internal validity discussed in the previous chapter are possible explanations for the psychologist's observations.[1] For instance, the threat called "history" (events external to the experiment) might have operated. Perhaps, for example, a self-help book became popular

---

[1] The threats to internal validity, which are covered in the previous chapter, are history, maturation, instrumentation, testing, statistical regression, and selection.

while the six-month experiment was being conducted, and reading it helped some of the clients, pulling up the average posttest score.[2]

The next pre-experimental design also has only one group. The group is given a treatment followed by a test. There is no pretest. This design is called a "one-shot case study," which is diagrammed here:

$$X \quad O$$

Because this design does not have a pretest, it is impossible to know if there has even been any change in the participants. For instance, suppose the posttest average is 20.0. Without a pretest, there is no way to know whether it was higher or lower or exactly 20.0 before the treatment was administered. Without knowing whether there has been a change, it is meaningless to talk about the cause of a change. Furthermore, without a control group, it is impossible to know whether the posttest scores are higher, the same, or lower than they would be without the treatment. The design is subject to all the threats to internal validity discussed in the previous chapter and, thus, is essentially of no value for exploring cause-and-effect relationships.

The final pre-experimental design is called the "static-group comparison design." It has an experimental and a control group with each receiving a posttest but no pretest. The design is as follows:

$$X \quad O$$
$$\overline{}$$
$$O$$

The dashed line separating the two groups in this design indicates that the groups are "intact groups" (i.e., groups that existed prior to the experiment that were not formed for the purpose of the experiment). For instance, students in one class section might serve as the experimental group while students in another class section might serve as the control group. Because the two classes were formed on a nonrandom basis, it is likely that the two groups were different from the start. Thus, without a pretest, it would be impossible to know whether whatever difference that is observed on the posttest existed even before the treatment.

While Campbell and Stanley (1966) urged researchers to avoid the preceding three pre-experimental designs because they provide almost no information on cause-and-effect, some beginning researchers might use them in a preliminary pilot test prior to beginning a more formal experiment. For instance, by administering the treatment even without a control group, a researcher can learn how participants react to it in general terms (e.g., do they complain about it? Do they think it is silly? Are there any unexpected side effects?). This type of information can help in refining treatments before conducting a formal experiment. Likewise, by administering the test, even if there is only a posttest with no pretest, researchers can learn how participants react to it in general terms (e.g., do they complain that the directions are confusing?, do they understand how to record their answers?, do they have questions about ambiguous questions?, and so on). This type of

---

[2] Note that if there had been a randomized control group, it would have been equally likely to be influenced by the threat called history. Then history would not be a causal explanation if the experimental group improved more than the control group.

information can help researchers improve their tests and other observational methods prior to conducting a more formal experiment.

Quasi-Experimental Designs

A number of quasi-experiments were discussed by Campbell and Stanley (1966). In their seminal book, they define these as designs that are not as good as true experimental designs with random assignment but are still of some value for exploring cause-and-effect relationships. However, the results of using them should be interpreted with a fair degree of caution. Three popular quasi-experimental designs will be discussed next.

The "nonequivalent control group design"[3] is diagrammed like this:

$$\begin{array}{ccc} O & X & O \\ \hline O & & O \end{array}$$

In this design, there are two groups: an experimental group that receives the treatment and a control group. Individuals are not assigned at random. Instead, the groups are pre-existing groups (i.e., intact groups). This design is most useful when the pretest scores are similar for the two groups. Also, to the extent that the two groups are similar on relevant demographics (e.g., age, educational level, and so on), this design yields useful data. Example 26.2 illustrates this quasi-experimental design.

Example 26.2
An example of the quasi-experimental design called the "nonequivalent control group design"
Students in one class were given a series of anti-tobacco presentations in the classroom over a 2-wk period. Another class was the control group, which was not given the presentations. On the pretest, both groups were similar, on the average, in their attitudes toward tobacco. In addition, the two groups were also almost identical, on the average, in age, socioeconomic status, and major in school. A posttest was given to both groups at the end of the experiment.

Consider how the threat to internal validity called "history" might have caused the experimental group in Example 26.2 to change from pretest to posttest. A new round of televised anti-smoking public service announcements that were broadcast at the time of the experiment, for instance, might cause those in the experimental group to become more negative in their attitudes toward tobacco from pretest to posttest. The public service announcements would constitute another explanation for change in the experimental group. However, to the extent that the two groups in this design are equal to begin with (not only in terms of attitude toward smoking on the pretest but also in terms of key demographics), the control group will be as likely to view the same public service

---

[3] Campell and Stanley (1966) use the term "nonequivalent" groups whenever the groups are not randomized. Despite the term, however, the two groups in this design might be quite similar, as discussed shortly. Campbell, D. T., & Stanley, J. C. (1966). *Experimental and quasi-experimental designs for research*. Chicago: Rand McNally.

announcements as the experimental group and to react to the announcements in the same way. Thus, history will not be a viable explanation if the experimental group's attitudes change more than the control group's attitudes.[4]

A key problem with the design being considered is that no matter how similar the two groups are known to be at the time of the pretest, they may differ in some systematic way that is unknown to the researcher. For instance, unknown to the researcher, the guidance counselor might have assigned more problem students to the control group class because this class had a teacher who was good at handling discipline problems. This difference might be the cause of changes in favor of the experimental group. Problem students might be less inclined to adopt negative attitudes toward tobacco, which might explain a difference in Example 26.2. It is important to notice that because randomization favors no particular type of student, both groups would have been about equal on all unknown variables if random assignment had been used. Hence, the true experimental design called the "two-group randomized groups design" is superior to this quasi-experimental design.

The second quasi-experimental design is called the "time-series design," which is conducted with only one group of participants. This design is especially useful when the dependent variable is a variable that naturally fluctuates from time to time without any special treatment. In Example 26.3, for instance, students' inappropriate behavior such as calling out in class when it is inappropriate might vary greatly from day to day.

Example 26.3
An example of the quasi-experimental design called the "time-series design"
A classroom was observed for one hour every day for five days. During each observational period, the researcher counted the number of times students called out in class when it was inappropriate. The researcher noted that there was variation from day to day, with students calling out more often on some days than on others. Then the researcher instructed the teacher to start giving extra verbal praise only to students who do not call out. During this phase of the experiment, the researcher continued to observe the class for one hour a day for five days. Once again, the researcher found variation in the calling-out behavior from day to day. However, overall, there was a noticeable decrease in calling-out behavior after the extra verbal praise was initiated. The results are diagrammed in Figure 26.1.

In Example 26.3, there are, in effect, five pretests (the five observations prior to treatment). *Baseline* is the technical name for a series of pretests. There are also five posttests (sometimes called "follow-up tests"). Thus, the design of the study looks like this:[5]

O O O O O X O O O O O

The pattern of results shown in Figure 26.1 suggests the experimental treatment (extra verbal praise) was effective in reducing the calling-out behavior because overall there

---

[4] The public service announcements are an example of the threat to internal validity called "history." In the discussion of the quasi-experimental designs in this chapter, only the threat to internal validity called "history" will be illustrated.
[5] Having multiple pretests and posttests is a key element of this design. However, the number of pretests and posttests may vary from experiment to experiment.

was more of the behavior during the baseline period (i.e., the five pretests) than on the posttests. Note that "history" might be a threat to the internal validity of this experiment. For instance, perhaps unknown to the researcher, the school principal gave a stern lecture to the students at the time the treatment was being given, and it was the lecture and not the extra praise that caused the change in the results from before treatment to after treatment. This possibility is much less likely in the next quasi-experimental design.

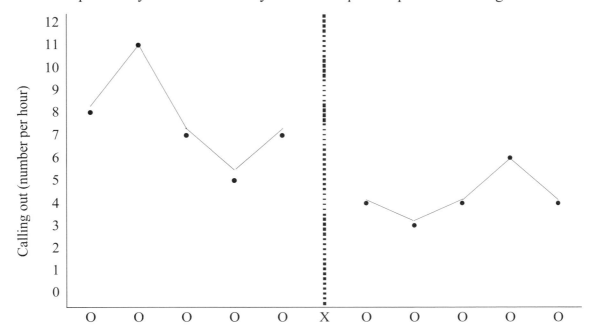

Figure 26.1. Results of the experiment described in Example 26.3.

The third quasi-experimental design is called the "equivalent time samples design," which involves only one group of participants. The design is illustrated by Example 26.4.

Example 26.4
An example of the quasi-experimental design called the "equivalent time samples design"

A researcher planned to observe students in a classroom for 1 hour on each of 10 days. Before beginning, the researcher randomly selected 5 of the 10 days. These five days became the days on which a treatment would be given (i.e., extra praise for not calling out in the classroom). The remaining five days were designated as the control condition on which extra praise would not be given. On the days when the extra praise was given, there was less calling-out behavior than the days on which no extra praise was given.

The design of the study in Example 26.4 is shown next. Note that each pair of XO symbols represents a treatment accompanied by an observation. The days with X_1 are the days when the treatment (extra praise) was given, while the days with the X_0 are the days when the treatment was not given. The days for the treatment were selected at random.

$$X_0O \quad X_1O \quad X_0O \quad X_0O \quad X_0O \quad X_1O \quad X_1O \quad X_0O \quad X_1O \quad X_1O$$

In the equivalent time samples design, it is very unlikely that the threat called "history" would be an explanation for the pattern of changes. For instance, it would be very unlikely that the school principal would give stern lectures by coincidence just on those days when the extra praise was given.

A key problem with this design is "multiple-treatment interference," which is a threat to external validity discussed in Chapter 24. Specifically, the amount of change observed, strictly speaking, only applies to a population that is given some days with extra praise and some days with none. From this design, it is not clear how well extra praise would work by itself without some intervening days on which the extra praise is not given. In other words, how students respond to the extra praise in the experiment may hinge, in part, on the fact that they also experience days with no praise.

Concluding Comments

For most experimental purposes, the true experimental designs covered in the previous chapter are the most desirable. All true designs have random assignment to treatment conditions. If it is not possible to use random assignment, the quasi-experimental designs covered in this chapter might be used to obtain useful information about cause-and-effect sequences. As a general rule, pre-experimental designs, which are also discussed in this chapter, should be avoided except when they are used only as preliminary pilot studies conducted prior to formal experimentation in order to try out and refine the treatments and measures that will be used later.

Exercise for Chapter 26

Factual Questions

1. According to Campbell and Stanley (1966), which of the following are so weak that they are of almost no value in exploring cause-and-effect relationships?
   A. Pre-experiments.   B. Quasi-experiments.

2. In experimental designs, what does the dashed line stand for?

3. Do all the pre-experimental designs have only one group of participants?

4. What do all true experiments have that none of the quasi-experiments have?

5. The social welfare clients in one city were given experimental counseling on job placement. The clients in another city served as the control group. There was a pretest and posttest for each group. What is the name of this design?

6. In some experiments, a series of pretests are given before a treatment is given. What is the technical name for these pretests?

7. Which of the following is superior in terms of controlling the threat to internal validity called "history"?
     A. Equivalent time samples design.   B. Time-series design.

8. In the equivalent time samples design, how should the days for treatment be selected?

9. What is a key problem with the time-series design?

Question for Discussion

10. If you are preparing a proposal for an experiment, will you be making any changes in it based on the information in this chapter? Explain.

Notes:

Part G

Putting It All Together

Introduction

This final part contains only Chapter 27, which describes how to write reports of empirical research. A solid research proposal written in light of the guidance in Chapter 11, and revised while reading the subsequent chapters in this book, can serve as the keystone for writing a corresponding research report because almost all of what is in a proposal will become part of the final research report. Of course, the research report will also include the quantitative or qualitative results as well as a discussion of them.

Notes:

Chapter 27
Writing Reports of
Empirical Research

A research proposal can be used as the foundation of a research report. The basic elements in a research proposal, which were presented in Chapter 11, are shown below.[1] Note that the subtitle, "A Research Proposal," has been removed, and the section called "Analysis" (used to describe the proposed method of analysis in the proposal) has been changed to "Results" because this section of a research report is used to describe the statistical qualitative outcomes.

The titles of the major sections are shown in bold. The sections on participants, measures, and procedures are subsections under the main heading of "Method."[2]

For both proposals and research reports, the title should be a brief statement that names the major variables in the research hypothesis, purpose, or question. In addition, if the research is specifically aimed at certain types of individuals (such as "Residents of King County"), the types of individuals should be mentioned.

The Influence of X on Y among Residents of King County
~~A Research Proposal~~

Introduction[3]
Literature Review
Method
Participants
Measures
Procedures (or Experimental Procedures)
~~Analysis~~ **Results**
Discussion[4]
References

---

[1] This chapter was written based on the assumption that Chapter 11 on writing proposals has already been carefully considered. Note that a number of important aspects of research writing covered in Chapter 11 are not covered again in this one.

[2] In American Psychological Association style, main headings such as "Method" are centered, while second-level headings such as "Participants" are flush left.

[3] As noted in Chapter 11, in a report of research for a thesis or dissertation, the introduction is typically presented in Chapter 1, and the literature review is presented in Chapter 2. For a report prepared for a term project, instructors may require that it begin with a literature review in which the introductory statements are integrated.

[4] Variations are permitted. For instance, "Discussion" might be called "Conclusions and Implications," or "Summary and Discussion," and so on.

The Abstract

An abstract is a brief summary that is placed below the title.[5] In most cases, an abstract of 150 words or less is appropriate, except in the case of theses and dissertations, in which longer abstracts may be expected.

At a minimum, an abstract should indicate (1) the general purpose of the research, (2) the types of individuals who served as participants, and (3) the general nature of the results. Example 27.1 shows a short abstract of a quantitative study that contains the three elements.

Example 27.1

An abstract for a quantitative study that (1) indicates the purpose, (2) identifies the type of participants, and (3) describes the overall results

To evaluate a multicultural smoking prevention curriculum, 16 schools were randomized to receive the multicultural curriculum or a standard curriculum. Program effects on one-year smoking initiation among 1,430 never-smokers were assessed. Hispanic boys who received the multicultural curriculum were less likely to initiate smoking than those who received the standard curriculum; effects were insignificant among other groups. (p. 263)[6]

Example 27.2 shows an abstract for a qualitative study. If a study is qualitative, it is customary to mention this in the abstract, as is done in the example.[7] If a particular method of qualitative research such as "consensual qualitative research" has been used, this might also be mentioned in the abstract.

Example 27.2

An abstract for a qualitative study that (1) indicates the purpose, (2) identifies the type of participants, and (3) describes the overall results

The main objective of this investigation was to explore more fully the facilitators and barriers that may contribute to or prevent the engagement and retention of Latinos/as in eating disorders (EDs) treatment. A qualitative design based on grounded theory was used to guide in-depth interviews with five Latinas (mean age 31.2 years) with history of EDs and with five Latino mental health providers (mean age 36.4 years). Six main themes were found in the discussion with patients and mental health providers: immigration stress, treatment experience in the United States, facilitators of help seeking, barriers to help seeking, treatment needs, and facilitators of treatment retention. For patients, lack of information about EDs and lack of bilingual treatment were identified as practical barriers. Other emotional factors such as stigma, fear of not being understood, family privacy and not being ready to change were identified as barriers to seeking help. Among facilitator factors that encouraged patients to seek help, the most salient were the perception of the sever-

---

[5] Abstracts are almost universally included in research reports. Often, they are also included in research proposals.
[6] Based on Unger, J. B., Chou, C.-P., Palmer, P. H., Ritt-Olson, A., Gallaher, P., Cen, S., Lichtman, K., Azen, S., & Johnson, C. A. (2004). Project FLAVOR: 1-year outcomes of a multicultural, school-based smoking prevention curriculum for adolescents. *American Journal of Public Health, 94,* 263–265.
[7] By convention, the fact that a study is quantitative is seldom mentioned in an abstract.

ity of the ED and emotional distress. For treatment retention, family support was a key element among patients. For providers, offering short-term treatment and directive treatment were seen as relevant factors for treatment retention in Latinos. A culturally sensitive intervention model for Latinas with EDs in the United States is discussed addressing four levels: patient, family, providers, and system.[8]

The Introduction and Literature Review

The purpose of a literature review is twofold: (1) to establish the context for the research study and (2) to justify the study by establishing that the problem area is important. An introduction and literature review for a research report should be written along the lines described in Chapter 11 for introductions and literature reviews in proposals.

If an introduction or literature review is more than two or three double-spaced pages, consider using subheadings to guide the reader. See Sample Literature Review 3 at the end of this book for an example of the use of subheadings in literature reviews.

The Method Section

The method section of a research report almost always has a subsection on participants as well as one on measures. In addition, a subsection on procedures is often desirable. A subsection on procedures is needed whenever there are important physical steps that were taken in order to conduct the research that were not fully described under "Participants" and "Measures." See the description of how to write the method section presented in Chapter 11. Note that in a research proposal, the future tense should be used (e.g., "The ABC Test *will be* administered to…"), while in a research report the past tense should be used (e.g., "The ABC Test *was* administered to…").

The Results Section

Many qualitative and quantitative researchers provide demographic information on participants in the subsection on participants. Other researchers prefer to summarize the demographic data at the beginning of the results section. Often, demographics can be effectively communicated with a table such as Table 27.1. Information in such a table is much easier to comprehend than information in a paragraph or two in which the statistics are embedded within sentences.

---

[8] Reyes-Rodriguez, M. L., Ramirez, J., Davis, K., Patrice, K., & Bulik, C. M. (2013). Exploring barriers and facilitators in eating disorders treatment among Latinas in the United States. *Journal of Latina/o Psychology*. No pagination specified. doi: 10.1037/a0032318

Table 27.1
Demographic Characteristics of Participants

Demographic characteristic	Percentage	Mean and standard deviation
Gender		
Men	48%	
Women	52%	
Employment status		
Full time	55%	
Part time	35%	
Unemployed	10%	
Age		$m = 21.70$ $sd = 2.30$
Annual income		$m = \$27,554$ $sd = 6,000$

When writing the results section of either a qualitative or quantitative study, keep in mind that no matter how strong the trends in the data are, they are subject to errors such as those in measurement and sampling. Thus, it is always inappropriate to use the term *prove* (such as in the statement, "The results conclusively *prove* that..."). Empirical research offers only degrees of evidence, not proof. Thus, researchers should refer to the degree of confidence they have in their results based on the evidence provided by the data. For instance, if the results are especially strong, a researcher might state that "the data strongly suggest that..." If they are moderately supportive, a researcher might state that "the data offer some evidence that..." If they are weak, a researcher might state that "the data provide very modest evidence that..."

Example 27.3 shows a statement of results for a quantitative study in which means were compared. Notice in the example that the relevance of the results to the research hypothesis is explicitly stated, which is recommended.

Example 27.3
Sample statement of results for a study in which two means were compared
On the XYZ test, the mean for the girls ($m = 59.80$, $sd = 7.00$) was higher than the mean for the boys ($m = 44.00$, $sd = 6.00$). The difference between the means was statistically significant ($t = 5.38$, $df = 121$, $p < .05$).[9] This result is consistent with the first research hypothesis, which predicted that girls would be superior.

Example 27.4 shows a statement of results for a quantitative study in which a correlation coefficient answered the research question. Notice that although only the correlation coefficient was needed to answer the question, the means and standard deviations were also reported, which is standard in statistical reporting.

---

[9] See Chapter 19 to review the *t* test. Note that the degrees of freedom (*df*) are often reported even though they are simply a mathematical substep in getting the probability value (*p*).

Example 27.4
Sample statement of results for a correlational study

The mean on the vocabulary test was 23.50 (*sd* = 4.60), and the mean on the reading comprehension test was 34.60 (*sd* = 3.90). The Pearson correlation coefficient (*r* = .53, *p* < .05) indicates a moderately strong relationship between vocabulary and reading comprehension. This answers the first research question, which asked: To what extent are the vocabulary and reading comprehension scores of children in the XYZ School District correlated?

Typically, reports of the results of qualitative studies are much longer than reports of results for quantitative studies. This is due to the structure of quantitative studies, in which the results are expressed as numbers. In qualitative studies, the results are expressed in words and must be justified, such as with quotations from participants. The quotations provide readers with glimpses of the raw data, and, hence, help readers understand the basis for the results. In addition, quotations help readers visualize the participants because they permit an assessment of their language skills. Typically, most quotations are short. Each quotation should be introduced by stating what principle, theme, or type of outcome it illustrates. This is done in Example 27.5.

Example 27.5
Short quotation used in a report of qualitative results with introductory statement

Student B, a soft-spoken male identified as being an externalizer, said,

> They call me and my friends "beaners" or like "wetbacks." Or they ask me where my green card is and stuff, and they tell us to "go back to our country." I could tell them that this is my country.

He added that other hurtful and racist statements were made that he did not want to share. Later in the interview, he returned to this subject by saying, "Some [White kids] are racists to my friends" and that "[the White kids] always want to fight."[10] (pg. 7)

In addition to quotations, it is often helpful to readers if the major findings of a qualitative study are diagrammed, which is illustrated in Chapter 10.

The Discussion Section

The discussion section often begins with a brief summary of the preceding material in the research report. At a minimum, the summary should state the general purpose of the study and indicate the major results. As a service to readers, it is also helpful to indicate in the summary whether the major results are consistent with those discussed earlier in the literature review. This is illustrated in Example 27.6.

---

[10] Balagna, R. M., Young, E. L., & Smith, T. B. (2013). School experiences of early adolescent Latinos/as at risk for emotional and behavioral disorders. *School Psychology Quarterly*. Advance online publication. doi: 10.1037/spq0000018

Example 27.6
Sample statement in the discussion that describes the consistency of results with previous research

In keeping with past work (Ano & Pargament, 2012; Wood et al., 2010), our results found positive correlations between traits such as neuroticism, trait anger, and anger at God. Similarly, Wood et al.'s (2010) finding of an inverse relationship between conscientiousness and anger at God was replicated in our findings. We also demonstrated, in both samples, that general anger at God correlated negatively with agreeableness, which was not documented in previous work but expected, because agreeableness is associated with diminished expression of anger. Collectively, these findings reinforce the assertion that intense anger at God is associated with indicators of poor mental health (Exline et al., 2011; Wood et al., 2010). (p. 5)[11]

The summary part of the discussion is typically followed by a discussion of the limitations (i.e., weaknesses) of the study. This discussion helps readers who may not be aware of the weaknesses. Also, it protects researchers from being charged with naively failing to recognize weaknesses. Example 27.7 shows portions of a long paragraph that describes the limitations of a study.

Example 27.7
Sample statement of limitations of a study in the discussion section

The current findings must be considered in the context of the limitations of this study. First, a convenience nonrandom sampling method was used to select the participants, and as a result, the sample may not be representative of the population under study. Moreover, although certain nonparental caregivers fit the profile for the study under consideration, the present study only had parental participants. A related limitation to the current study is that the representation of the sample may be skewed toward those families who were more comfortable with incorporating coping humor with....[12]

In addition to limitations, any special strengths of the study should be pointed out. Often, a strength is that the study is the first to examine certain variables or the first to examine them in a particular way, as illustrated in Example 27.8.

Example 27.8
Sample statement of the strength of a study in the discussion section

This study represents the first attempt (that we are aware of) to study the relationship between number of siblings and social skills using third-party ratings.... (p. 348)[13]

---

[11]Grubbs, J. B., Exline, J. J., & Campbell, W. K. (2013, April 1). I deserve better and God knows it! Psychological entitlement as a robust predictor of anger at God. *Psychology of Religion and Spirituality*. Advance online publication. doi: 10.1037/a0032119

[12] Rieger, A., & McGrail, J. P. (2013). Coping humor and family functioning in parents of children with disabilities. *Rehabilitation Pscyhology, 58*(1), 89–97. doi: 10.1037/a0031556

[13] Downey, D. B., & Condron, D. J. (2004). Playing well with others in kindergarten: The benefit of siblings at home. *Journal of Marriage and Family, 66,* 333–350.

Implications should also be described in the discussion section. When possible, a statement of implications should refer to specific actions that might be fruitful, as illustrated in Example 27.9 in which the authors indicate in the last sentence that campuses might collect and disseminate information.

Example 27.9
Sample statement of the specific implications

Despite its limitations, this study has important implications for alcohol education and prevention.... Findings reported here add weight to the general theoretical proposition that alcohol abuse and associated consequences are at least partially influenced by malleable cognitive processes. Campus alcohol education and prevention efforts have the potential to change students' beliefs...or expectations regarding the effects of alcohol. Collecting and disseminating campus data on the acceptance of risky drinking behaviors may be one method of changing alcohol expectancies and reducing alcohol-related harm. (p. 39)[14]

The discussion section should also include suggestions for future research. To be useful to readers, these suggestions should be as specific as possible. Example 27.10 shows such a statement.

Example 27.10
Sample statement suggesting future research

The current study leaves topics to be further explored in future studies. First, in order to identify international students who may require extra guidance and encouragement to nudge them into utilizing counseling services, future studies need to examine attitudes and characteristics of students who have not sought counseling services but are in need of them. Second, it will be beneficial to examine the factors that cause the possible discrepancy between stated purpose and actual focus of counseling.... (p. 341)[15]

If the discussion section of a research report is long, consider using subheadings for each of these elements: "Summary," "Limitations and Strengths," "Implications," and "Suggestions for Future Research."

References

The reference list should be placed immediately after the discussion. This is illustrated in Chapter 4.

Whatever style manual is being used for formatting references, it is important to pay attention to all details, including punctuation and placement of the various elements in a reference. Errors in formatting a reference list can reflect poorly on research writers.

---

[14] Fearnow-Kenny, M. D., Wyrick, D. L., Hansen, W. B., Dyreg, D., & Beau, D. B. (2001). Normative beliefs, expectancies, and alcohol-related problems among college students: Implications for theory and practice. *Journal of Alcohol and Drug Education, 47,* 31–42.
[15] Yi, J. K., Lin, J.-C. G., & Kishimoto, Y. (2003). Utilization of counseling services by international students. *Journal of Instructional Psychology, 30,* 333–342.

Exercise for Chapter 27

Factual Questions

1. The title of a research report should be a brief statement that names what?

2. According to this chapter, except for theses and dissertations, an abstract of about how many words is appropriate in most cases?

3. Is it customary in an abstract to mention that a study is "qualitative" *or* to mention that a study is "quantitative"?

4. Subheadings for participants, measures, and procedures appear under what major heading in a research report?

5. Many researchers provide demographic information in the subsection on participants. Other researchers present this information in what other section of their research reports?

6. According to this chapter, is it ever appropriate to use the word "prove" in the discussion of the results of empirical research? Explain.

7. The results section tends to be longer for which type of report?
   A. Reports of quantitative research.   B. Reports of qualitative research.

8. According to this chapter, suggestions for future research should be made in which section of a research report?

Appendix A

A Closer Look at Interpreting Correlation Coefficients

Chapter 18 presents an overview of correlation coefficients. This appendix provides additional information for students who will be conducting correlational research.

As indicated in Chapter 18, the value of a correlation coefficient (Pearson r) can vary from 0.00 to +1.00 for direct relationships. For inverse relationships, the values can vary from 0.00 to –1.00. General guidelines for interpreting the strength of relationships, first presented in Chapter 18 are repeated here:

Table A.1
Suggested Descriptors for Various Values of the Pearson r

Value of r	Suggested Descriptor	Value of r	Suggested Descriptor
0.85 to 1.00	Very strong	–0.85 to –1.00	Very strong
0.60 to 0.84	Strong	–0.60 to –0.84	Strong
0.40 to 0.59	Moderately strong	–0.40 to –0.59	Moderately strong
0.20 to 0.39	Weak	–0.20 to –0.39	Weak
0.0 to 0.19	Very weak	–0.00 to –0.19	Very weak

The descriptive labels shown above (e.g., "very weak") are based on extensive reading by this writer of correlational studies published in academic journals. In other words, these labels seem to be the ones most frequently associated with various values of r in published literature.

An additional approach to interpreting values of r is accomplished by computing a statistic called the *coefficient of determination* and converting it to a percentage. Computationally, this is quite easy to do. To compute the coefficient of determination, simply square r. For instance, for an r of 0.50, the coefficient of determination equals $0.50 \times 0.50 = 0.25$. Note that the symbol for the coefficient of determination is r^2, so this result can be expressed as $r^2 = 0.25$. To get a percentage that can be used in interpreting a correlation coefficient, simply multiply r^2 by 100. Thus, for instance, $r^2 = 0.25 \times 100 = 25\%$.

Now consider the meaning of the percentage of 25%. Suppose, for instance, that College Board scores were correlated with freshman grades earned at a college, and it was found that $r = 0.50$, which was shown in the previous paragraph as having a percentage of 25% associated with it. Obviously, there would be differences in the College Board scores; these *differences* are referred to as *variance*. Also, there would be variance in freshman grades. Then the percentage of 25% can be said to indicate the percent of the variance in freshman grades that is predicted or accounted for by College Board scores.

Not surprisingly, then, the percentage being considered here is called the *variance accounted for*.[1]

Now consider the interpretation of this variance accounted for, which equals 25%. This percentage indicates that College Board scores account for 25% of the variance (differences) in freshman grades. Conversely, then, 75% of the variance is *unaccounted for*. In more general terms, College Board scores are 25% effective in predicting freshman grades. As you can see, this is a far-from-perfect prediction. In fact, it is 75% away from a perfect prediction. The result of this example could be reported as shown in Example A.1.

Example A.1
Sample statement of results with variance accounted for

The correlation between College Board scores and freshman grades was direct and moderately strong ($r = 0.50$, $r^2 = 0.25$), indicating that 25% of the variance in freshman grades is accounted for by College Board scores, leaving 75% of the variance in freshman grades unaccounted for.

Consider another example. Suppose that scores on an employment test were correlated with subsequent job performance ratings, and r was found to equal 0.20, which should be classified as a weak relationship according to the table near the beginning of this appendix. To assist in the interpretation, the percentage of variance accounted for could be computed (i.e., $0.20 \times 0.20 = 0.04 \times 100 = 4\%$). Example A.2 shows how this result might be expressed.

Example A.2
Sample statement of results with variance accounted for

The correlation between employment test scores and subsequent job performance ratings was direct and weak ($r = 0.20$, $r^2 = 0.04$), indicating that only 4% of the variance in job performance ratings is accounted for by employment test scores, leaving fully 96% of the variance in job performance ratings unaccounted for.

Now consider an inverse relationship. Suppose that self-concept scores were correlated with anxiety scores, and r was found to equal –0.20, which should be classified as a weak relationship. To assist in the interpretation, the percentage of variance accounted for could be computed (i.e., $-0.20 \times -0.20 = 0.04 \times 100 = 4\%$). Notice that the percentage is positive even though the correlation is negative. Reporting of the negative correlation with a positive percentage to interpret it is illustrated in Example A.3.

Example A.3
Sample statement of results with variance accounted for

The correlation between self-concept scores and anxiety scores was inverse and weak ($r = 0.20$, $r^2 = 0.04$), indicating that only 4% of the variance in anxiety scores is accounted for by self-concept scores, leaving fully 96% of the variance in anxiety scores unaccounted for.

---

[1] An alternative term for *variance accounted for* is *explained variance*.

At this point, it should be clear that a Pearson r is not a proportion that can be converted to a percentage by simply multiplying it by 100. Instead, to get a percentage for the purposes of interpretation, the value of r must first be squared, which yields the coefficient of determination. The coefficient of determination can be multiplied by 100 to obtain a percentage that can be presented in the results section of a research report.

Notes:

Appendix B

Focus Group Methodology in Qualitative Research

Beginning researchers who will be conducting their first qualitative research project are encouraged to collect their data using semi-structured interviews. Data collected in this manner will be sufficiently complex and far-reaching to provide a beginning researcher with a comprehensive experience in conducting qualitative research. Three alternative approaches are briefly described in this appendix, with an emphasis on focus groups, which is for all practical purposes an extension of the interview method.

A *focus group* consists of about 8 to 12 participants who meet as a group with a moderator who leads the group discussion. The advantages of focus groups over one-on-one interviews and the limitations of focus groups are as follows:

> The group experience can help overcome a reluctance to speak to someone perceived as more powerful and to overcome the limitations imposed by low literacy skills or limited experience thinking and speaking about certain issues. Disadvantages include possible bias or "group think" responses.... The potential for socially desirable responses may be especially pronounced because the respondents may attempt to please not only the moderator but also other session participants.[1]

Typically, the moderator has a list of questions or specific topics to be presented to the group, which is called a protocol. Table B.1 shows protocol topics and questions used in a qualitative study of stress among male and female professional managers.[2]

Table B.1
Outline of Focus-Group Questioning Protocol

Comments or Questions
Opening comments
Welcome and statements regarding the purpose of the study, focus group procedures, and ethical issues.
Opening question
"Please tell us a little bit about yourself."
Introductory question
"Stress is prevalent in our everyday lives because many people feel stressed. In thinking about your daily life, what does stress mean to you?"
Transition questions
"Is stress a negative factor in your life? If so, explain how it is negative."
"Is stress a positive factor in your life? If so, in what ways is it positive?"
Subprobe: "What is it about stress that makes it good or bad?"

Table B.1 continued on next page

---

[1] Salazar, Napolitano, Scherer, & McCauley (2004, p. 149).
[2] Table B.1 was reproduced with permission from Iwasaki, MacKay, & Ristock (2004).

Table B.1 continued

Key questions

"What are the things that contribute to stress in your life?"

Subprobe: (a) "How does this work? Does one thing contribute to stress more than others or does the combination of many things contribute to stress?" (b) "Do you have any particular health concerns that contribute to your feelings of stress? Can you tell us more about this?" (c) "Besides possible health concerns, is there anything else that adds to your feelings of stress?" (d) "Does being a manager contribute to your feelings of stress? If so, describe how."

Ending questions

"All things considered, what would you say is the major cause of stress in your life?"

"Is there anything about stress that we haven't talked about that you would like to raise before we leave tonight?"

A group discussion of about 90 minutes in duration is usually appropriate to explore most issues, although strict time limits do not need to be observed, as can be seen in Example B.1 where the focus groups' meeting times varied from 1.5 to 2 hours. In the example, also note that fewer than the recommended 8 to 12 participants per group were used. Also, notice that the study had more than one group, which is typical and recommended.

Example B.1

A focus group study with varying numbers of participants and varying durations

Four focus groups of 2 to 5 children/adolescents ($n = 14$), one focus group of 3 stepparents, and two focus groups of college students ($n = 17$) were conducted by the primary investigator. Each group lasted approximately 1.5 to 2 hours.[3]

An important decision when establishing the groups is whether to form homogeneous groups. In Example B.1, the researchers restricted the homogeneity of each group by holding focus group discussions separately with (1) children/adolescents, (2) stepparents, and (3) college students. This is desirable whenever one type of participant (such as children) might feel intimidated by having a discussion with another type of participant (such as stepparents).

Oftentimes, additional information can be obtained by including both homogeneous and heterogeneous groups. For instance, in Example B.2, the researchers had two homogeneous groups (men only and women only) as well as a heterogeneous group of men and women. This permits the researchers to compare what members of each gender say when segregated with what they say when integrated, obviously providing additional richness to the study.

Example B.2

A focus group study with two varying homogeneous groups (by gender) and one mixed group

Twelve individuals who met the above criteria and agreed to participate were recruited for each of the three focus groups ($N = 36$ people): (a) women-only group

---

[3] Doyle, Wolchik, & Dawson-McClure (2002, p. 130).

(12 women), (b) men-only group (12 men), and (c) mixed-gender group (6 women and 6 men).[4]

To analyze focus group data, methods described earlier in this book (e.g., grounded theory, described in Chapters 10 and 20) can be used. However, group dynamics should be carefully considered while analyzing the data, making the process of analysis more complex than the analysis of data from one-on-one interviews. Hence, in most cases, beginning researchers are encouraged to avoid the focus group approach to qualitative research until they have first become proficient at conducting and analyzing interview data.

Two other qualitative approaches that yield data that are even more difficult to analyze than focus group data are *participant observation* and *nonparticipant observation*. In participant observation, the researcher joins a group of participants and interacts with them in their natural environment. For instance, suppose a researcher is interested in studying a school that has notoriously low achievement. As a participant observer, the researcher could join the faculty and work with them on a daily basis while gathering data. On the other hand, in nonparticipant observation for the same problem, the researcher would observe the teachers and students without becoming a member of the group. The complexity of analyzing data from both these approaches stems from the need to analyze not only what participants say (as in interviews and focus groups) but also to consider their actions in the natural context, creating a much more complex data set than most beginning researchers are prepared to tackle.

---

[4] Iwasaki, MacKay, & Ristock (2004, p. 61).

Notes:

Appendix C

An Overview of Program Evaluation

Concerted efforts to systematically evaluate programs date back to the 1960s, when the administration of President Johnson introduced a large number of educational and social programs that had the aim of reducing poverty in the United States. Since that time, legislators and other leaders have looked to the results of program evaluation in an effort to determine how to allocate limited resources to achieve the maximum effect.

Typically, the time frame for conducting a full evaluation of a program is too long for beginning researchers because most programs must be given a substantial amount of time, such as a year or more, to produce their effects. In addition, many beginning researchers may not have the contacts and cooperation from program administrators to conduct full-scale evaluations. This appendix is designed to provide starting points for researchers who are not limited by these constraints and wish to evaluate a program.

In the ideal, one or more program evaluators should be consulted while an application for program funds is being prepared because among the important parts of any program proposal is the plan that has been made to evaluate it. Consulting with program evaluators at this early stage will help assure that an adequate program evaluation plan is included.

Program evaluators can be of special assistance in the planning stages by conducting a *needs assessment*, which is the first aspect of program evaluation. The goal of a needs assessment is to determine what clients, such as parents and their students, think their needs are. Usually, this is done by preparing a questionnaire that asks for the input of clients in terms of (1) to what extent they want to have a particular type of program and (2) what they think the specific program goals and activities should be. For new program areas, program evaluators might also use qualitative methods to assess the needs of the proposed clients. The outcomes of the needs assessment can be incorporated into the program proposal as an important justification for funding a program.

Once a program is funded, the program evaluator should be involved in assessing the implementation of the program by conducting what is termed a *formative evaluation*. This aspect of evaluation examines the extent to which the actual program is consistent with the program that was proposed. This stage can be thought of as the auditing stage, in which the program activities are assessed not only in terms of whether they are consistent with those described in the program, but also whether the activities are timely based on a timeline that should have been included in the program proposal.

To understand formative evaluation, consider a program designed to increase elementary students' scientific thinking. The program might be executed by teachers in four schools with the assistance of consultants. The formative evaluation should begin at the very beginning of the program by checking to see that the materials needed in the classroom were ordered and delivered on time. Likewise, checks should be made to assure that the program implementers (in this instance, teachers) have been given the information and training necessary to execute the program properly from the beginning. After the program is underway, the program evaluators should check to see whether the prescribed activities are being conducted by the teachers in a manner consistent with those described in the program proposal. For instance, observations might be made to see if the teachers are actually using the new materials, and, if so, whether they are using them in the prescribed manner. Feedback should be given to the teachers so that they can adjust their behavior, if necessary. Finally, the program evaluator should make periodic checks (such as by testing) to see if students are moving in the desired direction (in this case, improving in their scientific thinking). Failure to move in the desired direction might require that fundamental changes be made in the program long before the end of the program year. Thus, the overarching purpose of the formative evaluation is to provide information and guidance that will help the program succeed.

The third aspect of program evaluation is *summative evaluation*, which refers to an evaluation in terms of the ultimate outcomes of the program. At a minimum, this is done by measuring at the beginning of the program (i.e., some type of pretest) as well as at the end (i.e., posttest) to determine the overall amount of change.

Because individuals change naturally over time without an intervening program, it is quite helpful to have a control or comparison group. Because random assignment to the program condition and to a control group is rarely possible, comparison groups tend to be similar groups (such as students in another similar school district) who are not receiving the program. Without random assignment, conclusions must be drawn very cautiously. Nevertheless, the data obtained by using such a nonrandomized comparison group can be quite informative.

When using a nonrandomized comparison group for a summative evaluation, the program group and the comparison group will often be found to be at least somewhat different, on average, on the pretest. A difference on the pretest, of course, may help account for any group differences on the posttest. To adjust for this, a statistical technique called *analysis of covariance* can be used.[1] Specifically, it provides an estimate of what the average posttest scores would have been for each group if the two groups had been equal on the pretest. These estimates are called *adjusted posttest means* because they have been adjusted in light of initial differences between the groups.[2] Analysis of covariance also tests for the statistical significance of the difference between the adjusted posttest means. A significant difference in favor of the program group, of course, is desirable. Caution should be used, however, because the adjustments made by analysis of covariance are only estimates based on certain assumptions that might not hold in any particular case.

If a comparison group is not available, it might be possible to use data on a larger group as a basis for making estimates about the effectiveness of a program. For instance, a nationally standardized test of scientific thinking skills could be administered as a pretest and posttest to the program group. If the average student in the program group increases in his or her percentile rank, this would indicate that the program group is pro-

---

[1] Analysis of covariance is typically taught in a second-level course on statistics.
[2] The adjustments are made based on the size of the differences between the posttest means as well as the correlations between the pretest and posttest scores. The greater the correlation, the greater the adjustment.

gressing at a greater rate than the national group, which would be encouraging. Using a larger group for comparison purposes is not limited to using standardized tests in educational settings. For instance, changes in crime rates from the beginning to the end of a crime prevention program in a community might be compared with changes in crime rates nationally or statewide.

In summary, there are three aspects to program evaluation. First, there is *needs assessment*, which helps to shape the plans for and to justify a proposed program. Second, there is *formative evaluation*, which helps to assure that the program is properly implemented and that the clients are making progress. Finally, there is *summative evaluation*, which assesses clients' overall progress in achieving the program goals, typically by examining changes in clients' behavior from the beginning to the end of the program with a comparison group when possible.

Notes:

Appendix D

Ethical Issues in Conducting Research

The purpose of this appendix is to provide an overview of some basic ethical principles that should guide researchers when conducting research. The most important principle for beginning researchers is this: *Consult with individuals who are experts in ethics as they relate to research.* The expert might be the instructor of a class or it might be a committee of individuals whose purpose is to review research proposals from an ethical perspective.[1] Most colleges and universities as well as large school districts have such committees. This advice is important because it would take an entire book to cover ethical principles in detail.[2] Thus, an appendix such as this one can provide only general guidance, which should be supplemented by expert advice.

Informed consent is a basic procedure for protecting human participants in research. To be informed, the participants (or their guardians) must be told who is conducting the research and how the researchers can be contacted before, during, and after the research. Then, they need to be informed of the purpose of the research. Next, they should be informed of the benefits of the research as well as the possible risks. In addition, the participants should also be informed of any steps that will be taken to protect them from harm and to maintain confidentiality. Also, as a condition of their consent, participants need to be informed that they may withdraw at any point during the study without penalty. To avoid misunderstandings, the informed consent information normally should be presented in writing and signed by the participants, who should be given a copy to keep.[3]

An important issue in developing the informed consent procedures arises whenever researchers believe that a certain level of *deception* is necessary in order to achieve the research purposes. Typically, this issue arises when researchers fear that fully informing participants of the purpose of the research may contaminate or confound the results of the research. For instance, if an experimental treatment designed to change attitudes is to be tried out in a study, informing participants in advance that the purpose of the study is to change their attitudes may lead some participants to be more receptive to the treatment than they otherwise would be, and it might also lead other participants to consciously resist being influenced by the treatment. One approach to this problem is to inform participants of only a very general purpose (e.g., "studying human reactions to stimuli") while providing them with a disclosure that important aspects of the purpose of the study will be shared with participants only at the end of the research. Beginning researchers should normally avoid research topics in which deception is needed in the informed consent process, at least without explicit approval from experts on ethics in research.

---

[1] Such committees are often called *institutional review boards.*
[2] See Sales and Folkman (2000) for in-depth coverage on the role of ethics in research with human participants.
[3] Informed consent procedures vary. Therefore, it is important to obtain a copy of the consent procedures at the researcher's institution.

Debriefing refers to providing a detailed explanation of the purpose of the research to participants at the conclusion of the research. A full debriefing also provides an opportunity for participants to ask questions and to express any lingering concerns about the research project and its effects on them. At a debriefing, the participants should be reminded how to contact the researchers at a later date. This is desirable because possible harm might not become evident immediately to the participants who therefore might need additional information and guidance from researchers at a later date.

As a point of courtesy as well as an important possible benefit to participants, researchers should offer to share the results of the study with the participants after the data have been analyzed. This can be done in writing or in a group meeting.

Special care should be taken to maintain *confidentiality* of the data. Questionnaires, transcripts of interviews, and other documents that might reveal the identity of participants should be carefully stored until such time as identifying information can be removed. This includes making sure that any research assistants or others who might need to handle the documents agree to hold the information confidential.

If any of the issues raised in this appendix or raised by experts who are consulted cannot be easily resolved to everyone's satisfaction, beginning researchers should seek another research topic that has fewer ethical dilemmas.

Sample Literature Review 1

Associations Between Marital Happiness, Problems, and Health

The association between health and involvement in interpersonal relationships is well established. Married individuals are consistently found to have better health and well being than their unmarried counterparts

5 (Waite & Gallagher, 2000). Stably married individuals are less likely to develop chronic health problems when compared with their divorced or widowed counterparts, with a longer marital duration further protecting health (Dupre & Meadows, 2007). Indeed, the association

10 between marital status and health has been found for both men and women (Kaplan & Kronick, 2006), across multiple countries (e.g., Gardner & Oswald, 2004), and for multiple health outcomes (e.g., Pienta, Hayward, & Jenkins, 2000). However, research sug-

15 gests that the beneficial impact of marriage on well being extends beyond the status of being married. Ample evidence exists suggesting that the quality of marital relationships also impacts health, with higher-quality marriages being associated with higher levels of

20 health and well being (e.g., Proulx, Helms, & Buehler, 2007) and long-term, poor quality marriages being associated with poor overall health (Hawkins & Booth, 2005).

In a meta-analysis on the associations between mari-

25 tal quality and spouses' well being, Proulx, Helms, and Buehler (2007) found that the marital relationship is a stronger predictor of well being than the reverse. The bulk of studies contributing to this finding were short-term longitudinal studies assessing the impact of mari-

30 tal quality at baseline on changes in spouses' health over the course of the study, and few studies examined both directions of effect (i.e., marital quality impacting change in health as well as health impacting change in marital quality). Indeed, little is known about the pos-

35 sible reciprocal associations between marital quality and health over significant periods of time. The purpose of the present study is to examine the reciprocal, or coupling, associations between two marital characteristics—one positive, one negative—and individuals'

40 self-reported health over the course of 20 years of marriage.

Several theoretical perspectives have informed the study of the unidirectional associations between changes in marriage and health, including life course

45 theory (Elder & O'Rand, 1995), stress generation models (Hammen, 1991), and socioemotional selectivity theory (Carstensen, Isaacowitz, & Charles, 1999). Each of these theories has received empirical support but they have not been applied to the dynamic assessment

50 of change in both marital quality and health. We argue here for a "doubly developmental" approach to the understanding of marital quality and spousal well being (Kurdek, 1998). Such an approach highlights the reciprocal nature of interpersonal relationships and individ-

55 ual well being, recognizing that the direction of change in both constructs is mutually influential. What is particularly important about this perspective is recognition that trajectories of change in risk factors (e.g., health or other indicators of well being) may produce different

60 effects than static levels of these factors. Thus, because of spouses', especially aging spouses' (Carstensen, 1992), identification with their marriage, the quality of that marriage may have direct impact not just on current levels of health, but on changes in health as the

65 marriage unfolds. Further, although changes in health are normative as individuals age, these changes may set the stage for considerable shifts in power, leisure time and abilities, energy, and allocation of personal and financial resources in a marriage (Booth & Johnson,

70 1994), potentially undermining its success.

Marital Quality and Changes in Health

Cross-sectional research suggests that, when compared with single individuals, being in a satisfying and well-adjusted marriage is associated with health bene-

75 fits such as better cardiovascular, mental, and physical health (Holt-Lunstad, Birmingham, & Jones, 2008). Cross-sectional research has also demonstrated that negative aspects of marriage are associated with poorer health (e.g., Bookwala, 2005). If, as some researchers

80 have suggested, marital quality declines over time (i.e., conflict increases and happiness declines; Kurdek, 1999; Umberson, Williams, Powers, Liu, & Needham, 2006), then declines in marital quality may result in subsequent changes in health for married individuals.

85 Longitudinal studies using community-based samples have found a link between changes in marital quality and perceptions of health (Umberson et al., 2006; Wickrama, Lorenz, & Conger, 1997). Using three

90 waves of data spanning 8 years of mostly midlife marriage from the American's Changing Lives study, Umberson, Williams, Powers, Liu, and Needham (2006) found that negative marital experiences increased over time and positive marital experiences declined. These changes, in turn, were linked with diminishing reports 95 of self-rated health as spouses aged. Alternatively, using latent growth curve analyses and three waves of data spanning 3 years' time in early midlife, Wickrama, Lorenz, and Conger, (1997) found that as married individuals' marital quality (a composite of items 100 assessing marital happiness, satisfaction, and stability) improved, reported symptoms of physical illness declined for both men and women. Both of these studies conceptualize marital quality as the independent variable, and thus, do not tell us whether changes in physi-105 cal health might also be influencing changes in marital quality.

The studies cited above use either positive or negative conceptualizations of marital quality and, like other studies, underscore the varying effects that posi-110 tive and negative marital quality may have on health in mid and later life. Negative aspects of marital quality in long-term marriages may be especially important to consider, as marital strain has been shown to affect health cumulatively over time and more aggressively at 115 older ages among continuously married individuals (Umberson et al., 2006). Alternatively, positive aspects of long-term marriages may be particularly important in the health–marriage link given that long-term marriages have endured and thus may be characterized by 120 sustained positive qualities. The marital relationship in middle and older age is particularly salient (e.g., Carstensen, 1992) and, when combined with the normative declines in health associated with aging, positive aspects of marriage might be especially important in pro-125 tecting spouses' health.

Changes in Health Predicting Marital Quality

In recent studies assessing changes in marital quality and health, health has been less frequently conceptualized as the independent variable than has marital qual-130 ity. Early work on this topic, often focused on specific disease entities like rheumatoid arthritis and cancer, demonstrated consistent cross-sectional relationships between illness and decreased marital satisfaction (e.g., Hawley, Wolfe, Cathey, & Roberts, 1991). In one of 135 the first studies to assess if declines in health were associated with corresponding declines in marital quality, Booth and Johnson (1994) analyzed individuals over two waves spaced 3 years apart and found that respondents who experienced a decline in self-rated health 140 also reported small but significant declines in marital happiness. There was no association found between declines in self-rated health and self-reported divorce proneness. Subsequent research has been mixed, with some studies verifying the findings in Booth and John-145 son's work (e.g., Northouse, Templin, Mood, &

Oberst, 1998), others finding the opposite direction of effects (e.g., declining health relating to increases in marital quality; Swensen & Fuller, 1992), and still others finding no association (e.g., Yorgason, Booth, & 150 Johnson, 2008). Given these mixed findings regarding how changes in health may be related to marital quality, additional research appears warranted.

References

Bookwala, J. (2005). The role of marital quality in physical health during the mature years. *Journal of Aging and Health, 17,* 85–104. doi: 10.1177/0898264304272794

Booth, A., & Johnson, D. R. (1994). Declining health and marital quality. *Journal of Marriage and the Family, 56,* 218–223. doi: 10.2307/352716

Carstensen, L. L. (1992). Social and emotional patterns in adulthood: Support for socioemotional selectivity theory. *Psychology and Aging, 7,* 331–338. doi: 10.1037/0882-7974.7.3.331

Carstensen, L. L., Isaacowitz, D. M., & Charles, S. T. (1999). Taking time seriously: A theory of socioemotional selectivity. *American Psychologist, 54,* 165–181. doi: 10.1037/0003-066X.54.3.165

Dupre, M. E., & Meadows, S. O. (2007). Disaggregating the effects of marital trajectories on health. *Journal of Family Issues, 28,* 623–652. doi: 10.1177/0192513X06296296

Elder, G. H., & O'Rand, A. (1995). Adult lives in a changing society. In K. S. Cook, G. A. Fine, & J. S. House (Eds.), *Sociological Perspectives on Social Psychology* (pp. 452–475). Needham Heights, MA: Allyn and Bacon.

Gardner, J., & Oswald, A. (2004). How is mortality affected by money, marriage, and stress? *Journal of Health Economics, 23,* 1181–1207. doi: 10.1016/j.jhealeco.2004.03.002

Hammen, C. L. (1991). The generation of stress in the course of unipolar depression. *Journal of Abnormal Psychology, 100,* 555–561. doi: 10.1037/0021-843X.100.4.555

Hawkins, D. N., & Booth, A. (2005). Unhappily ever after: Effects of long-term, low-quality marriages on well-being. *Social Forces, 84,* 451–471. doi: 10.1353/sof.2005.0103

Hawley, D., Wolfe, F., Cathey, M., & Roberts, F. (1991). Marital status in rheumatoid arthritis and other rheumatic disorders: A study of 7,293 patients. *The Journal of Rheumatology, 18,* 654–660.

Holt-Lunstad, J., Birmingham, W., & Jones, B. Q. (2008). Is there something unique about marriage? The relative impact of marital status, relationship quality, and network social support on ambulatory blood pressure and mental health. *Annals of Behavioral Medicine, 35,* 239–244. doi: 10.1007/s12160-008-9018-y

Kaplan, R. M., & Kronick, R. G. (2006). Marital status and longevity in the United States population. *Journal of Epidemiology and Community Health, 60,* 760–765. doi: 10.1136/jech.2005.037606

Kurdek, L. A. (1998). The nature and predictors of the trajectory of change in marital quality over the first 4 years of marriage for first-married husbands and wives. *Journal of Family Psychology, 12,* 494–510. doi: 10.1037/0893-3200.12.4.494

Kurdek, L. A. (1999). The nature and predictors of the trajectory of change in marital quality for husbands and wives over the first 10 years of marriage. *Developmental Psychology, 35,* 1283–1296. doi: 10.1037/0012-1649.35.5.1283

Northouse, L. L., Templin, T., Mood, D., & Oberst, M. (1998). Couples' adjustment to breast cancer and benign breast disease: A longitudinal analysis. *Psycho-Oncology, 7,* 37–48. doi: 10.1002/(SICI)1099-1611(199801/02)7:1<37::AID-PON314>3.0.CO;2-#

Pienta, A. M., Hayward, M. D., & Jenkins, K. R. (2000). Health consequences of marriage for the retirement years. *Journal of Family Issues, 21,* 559–586. doi:10.1177/019251300021005003

Proulx, C. M., Helms, H. M., & Buehler, C. (2007). Marital quality and personal well-being: A meta-analysis. *Journal of Marriage and Family, 69,* 576–593. doi: 10.111/j.1741-3737.2007.00393.x

Swensen, C., & Fuller, S. (1992). Expression of love, marriage problems, commitment, and anticipatory grief in the marriages of cancer patients. *Journal of Marriage and Family, 54,* 191–196. doi: 10.2307/353286

Umberson, D., Williams, K., Powers, D. A., Liu, H., & Needham, B. (2006). You make me sick: Marital quality and health over the life course. *Journal of Health and Social Behavior, 47,* 1–16. doi: 10.1177/002214650604700101

Waite, L., & Gallagher, M. (2000). *The Case for Marriage: Why Married People are Happier, Healthier, and Better off Financially.* New York, NY: Broadway Books.

Wickrama, K. A. S., Lorenz, F. O., & Conger, R. D. (1997). Marital quality and physical illness: A latent growth curve analysis. *Journal of Marriage and the Family, 59*, 143–155. doi: 10.2307/353668

Yorgason, J. B., Booth, A., & Johnson, D. (2008). Health, disability, and marital quality: Is the association different for younger versus older cohorts? *Research on Aging, 30*, 623–648. doi: 10.1177/0164027508322570

Address correspondence to: Christine M. Proulx, University of Missouri, Department of Human Development and Family Studies, 314 Gentry Hall, Columbia, MO 65211, USA. Email: proulxc@missouri.edu

Exercise for Review 1

Directions: Answer the following questions based on your opinions. While there are no right or wrong answers, be prepared to explain the bases for your answers in classroom discussions.

1. Did the reviewers convince you that the topic of the review is important? Explain.

2. Is the review an essay organized around topics (as opposed to a string of annotations)? Explain.

3. Is the number of headings and subheadings adequate? Explain.

4. Is the tone of the review neutral and nonemotional? Explain.

5. Overall, is the review logically organized? Explain.

6. If research objectives or hypotheses are stated near the end of the review, do they flow logically from the material presented in the review? Explain.

7. Are there any obvious weaknesses in this review? Explain.

8. Does this review have any special strengths? Explain.

9. What is your overall evaluation of this review on a scale from *Excellent* (10) to *Very Poor* (0)? Explain.

Notes:

Sample Literature Review 2

Effects of Random Student Drug Testing in High Schools

Originally published as DuPont, R. L., Campbell, M. D., Campbell, T. G., Shea, C. L., & DuPont, H. S. (2013). Self-reported drug and alcohol use and attitudes toward drug testing in high schools with random student drug testing. *Journal of Child & Adolescent Substance Abuse*, 22, 104–119. Copyright © 2013 by Taylor & Francis Group, LLC. Reprinted with permission.

Introduction

Preadolescence and adolescence are high-risk periods for drug and alcohol abuse. Early initiation of drug and alcohol use is associated with greater likelihood of
5 drug use later in life (National Institute on Drug Abuse, 2003); this higher susceptibility is one of the many reasons schools across the United States have implemented drug and alcohol education and prevention programs. Student drug testing programs and policies
10 are one strategy that has grown in popularity after two Supreme Court rulings (*Vernonia School District 47J v Acton*, 1995; *Board of Education of Independent School District of Pottawatomie County et al. v Earls et al.*, 2002) upheld the constitutionality of randomly
15 drug testing student athletes and participants in extracurricular activities.

There is controversy and concern about drug testing students. The American Academy of Pediatrics strongly advises against random drug testing of adoles-
20 cents and believes that any drug screen should be completely voluntary (American Academy of Pediatrics Committee on Substance Abuse, 1996; American Academy of Pediatrics Committee on Substance Abuse and Council on School Health, 2007). Based on their
25 clinical experiences of drug testing adolescents with substance abuse problems, Knight and Levy (2007) warn that schools run the risk of drug-using adolescents changing their patterns of drug use to avoid detection and also cite a study that found 10% of labora-
30 tory drug tests in an adolescent drug-testing program were susceptible to error (Levy, Vaughan, Angulo, & Knight, 2007).

Studies of the effects of student drug testing have not clearly differentiated between programs that use ran-
35 dom testing and those that rely on for-cause or voluntary testing. Program-specific studies analyzing the effects of drug testing have been hampered by short durations between program inception and study conclusion. There are also a number of methodological
40 limitations to the few research studies on random student drug testing (RSDT).

Literature Review

According to the School Health Policies and Programs Study (SHPPS) conducted by the Centers for
45 Disease Control and Prevention (Jones, Fisher, Greene, Hertz, & Pritzl, 2007) in 2006, 25.5% of all school districts with middle schools or high schools in the United States had drug testing policies; this figure includes 11.4% of all middle schools and 19.5% of all
50 high schools. Of the 25.5% of all schools with policies, 56.1% conducted random drug testing of specific student groups, 63.9% conducted tests based on suspicion of use, 37.6% had voluntary drug testing for all students, 3.6% had voluntary testing for specific student
55 groups, and 13.4% used other unspecified criteria. Ringwalt and colleagues (2008) also estimated that in the 2004–2005 academic year, 14% of U.S. school districts with students in high school grades conducted drug testing of students. Among those who conducted
60 testing, some randomly drug tested students throughout the year while others tested students only when there was suspicion of drug use.

Research on the effects of student drug testing is inconclusive. Yamaguchi, Johnston, and O'Malley
65 (2003) examined anonymous student surveys from approximately 76,000 eighth-, tenth-, and twelfth-grade students in more than 200 schools with and without drug-testing policies. Analyses found no differences in self-reported drug use between students in schools with
70 drug-testing policies and students in schools without testing policies; however, many students who reported attending a school that tested for drugs were not themselves subject to testing.

In a prospective pilot study of athletes subject to
75 RSDT in two rural schools, Goldberg and colleagues (2003) found that drug testing appeared to reduce drug use; however, drug use risk factors, including risky behavior, perceiving greater peer drug use, and believing peers and authorities were more tolerant of use,
80 increased during the year among students subject to testing. A two-year prospective study by the same researchers failed to show consistent deterrent effects among student athletes in schools that were randomized to a drug-testing program compared to students in
85 schools without a drug-testing program (Goldberg et al., 2007). Similar to the pilot study, athletes in schools that mandated drug testing reported an increase in drug use risk factors.

90 Research has indicated that students in athletics and extracurricular activities differ from those who do not participate in such activities in ways that may influence behaviors like drug and alcohol use. For example, students who participate in non-athletic extracurriculars tend to have greater academic success than those who 95 do not (Mahoney & Cairns, 1997; Mahoney, Cairns, & Farmer, 2003), and participation in extracurriculars inside and outside of school can be a protective factor against drug use (Liu, 2012). However, some studies of middle school, high school, and older adolescent male 100 athletes show that they are more likely to be engaged in heavy drinking and performance-enhancing drug use (Garry & Morrissey, 2000; Patel & Luckstead, 2000; Wetherill & Fromme, 2007; Yusko, Buckman, White, & Pandina, 2008).

105 A small study that surveyed students in grades 6 through 12 in 3 rural northwestern schools found that fewer students involved in after-school activities (11%) frequently used drugs than those who did not participate (19%) (Russell, Jennings, & Classey, 2005). Rates 110 of frequent alcohol use were similar between these groups. However, student attitudes toward drug testing were mixed. Students who frequently used drugs or alcohol were less likely to support drug testing. Most students believed that drug testing would be a violation 115 of privacy but agreed that, if it were implemented in their schools, they would not be embarrassed to take a drug test, nor would testing deter them from participating in after-school activities.

In another study of student attitudes toward drug 120 testing, Evans, Reader, Liss, Wiens, and Roy (2006) surveyed ninth-, tenth-, and eleventh-grade students in two rural Florida high schools prior to the implementation of an aggressive RSDT program. Under its policy, students who tested positive on random drug tests were 125 given the choice between ineligibility for all extracurricular activities and parking privileges for 1 year and a 10-day minimum suspension from activities and privileges with completion of a minimum of 6 substance abuse counseling sessions. The majority (74.1%) of 130 surveyed students agreed that testing would be effective in deterring drug use and 46.3% believed there was a drug problem at their school. Nearly half (45.4%) of the students thought the RSDT was a "good idea" and one-quarter (25.5%) had no strong opinion. However, 135 many students (40%) mistakenly believed that there were minimal or no consequences to testing positive on a drug test. Had more students been familiar with the policy and the consequences for a positive drug test, positive perceptions of fairness (43.2%) may have been 140 lower. Unfortunately, these studies assessed student populations that were not subject to drug testing; answers were based on hypothesis and conjecture rather than on experience.

Purpose

145 The primary purpose of the demonstration project was to examine through semiannual surveys whether program modifications, such as increasing the frequency of drug testing or adding an educational component, altered students' self-reported substance use.

References

American Academy of Pediatrics Committee on Substance Abuse (1996). Testing for drugs of abuse in children and adolescents. *Pediatrics, 98*(1), 305–307.

American Academy of Pediatrics Committee on Substance Abuse and Council on School Health (2007). Testing for drugs of abuse in children and adolescents: Addendum-testing in schools and at home. *Pediatrics, 119*(3), 627–630.

Board of Education of Independent School District of Pottawatomie County et al. v Earls et al., 536 US 822. (2002).

Evans, G., Reader, S., Liss, H., Wiens, B., & Roy, A. (2006). Implementation of an aggressive random drug-testing policy in a rural school district: Student attitudes regarding program fairness and effectiveness. *Journal of School Health, 76*(9), 452–458.

Garry, J. P., & Morrissey, S. L. (2000). Team sports participation and risk-taking behaviors among a biracial middle school population. *Clinical Journal of Sport Medicine, 10*(3), 185–190.

Goldberg, L., Elliot, D., MacKinnon, D., Moe, E., Kuehl, K., Nohre, L., & Lockwood, C. (2003). Drug testing athletes to prevent substance abuse: Background and pilot study results of the SATURN (Student Athlete Testing Using Random Notification) study. *Journal of Adolescent Health, 32*(1), 16–25.

Goldberg, L., Elliot, D., MacKinnon, D., Moe, E., Kuehl, K., Yoon, M., Williams, J. (2007). Outcomes of a prospective trial of student-athlete drug testing: The Student Athlete Testing Using Random Notification (SATURN) study. *Journal of Adolescent Health, 41*(5), 421–429.

Jones, S. E., Fisher, C. J., Greene, B. Z., Hertz, M. F., & Pritzl, J. (2007). SHPPS 2006: School Health Policies and Programs Study. *Journal of School Health, 77*(8), 522–543.

Knight, J. R., & Levy, S. (2007). The national debate on drug testing in schools. *Journal of Adolescent Health, 41*(5), 419–420.

Levy, S., Vaughan, B. L., Angulo, M., & Knight, J. R. (2007). Results of random testing program in an adolescent substance abuse program. *Pediatrics, 119*(4), e843–e848.

Liu, L. Y. (2012). *Texas school survey of substance use among adolescents: Grades 7–12, 2010.* Austin, TX: Texas Department of State Health Services, Mental Health and Substance Abuse Division.

Mahoney, J. L., Cairns, B. D., & Farmer, T. W. (2003). Promoting interpersonal competence and educational success through extracurricular activity participation. *Journal of Educational Psychology, 95*(2), 409–418.

Mahoney, J. L., & Cairns, R. B. (1997). Do extracurricular activities protect against early school dropout? *Developmental Psychology, 33*(2), 241–253.

National Institute on Drug Abuse. (2003). *Preventing drug use among children and adolescents: A research-based guide for parents, educators, and community leaders* (NIH Publication No. 04-4212[A]). Bethesda, MD: National Institute on Drug Abuse.

Patel, D. R., & Luckstead, E. F. (2000). Sport participation, risk taking and health risk behaviors. *Archives of Pediatrics & Adolescent Medicine, 11*(1), 141–155.

Ringwalt, C., Vincus, A. A., Ennett, S. T., Hanley, S., Bowling, J. M., Yacoubian, G. S., Jr., & Rohrbach, L. A. (2008). Random drug testing in U.S. public school districts. *American Journal of Public Health, 98*(5), 3–5.

Russell, B., Jennings, B., & Classey, S. (2005). Adolescent attitudes toward random drug testing in schools. *Journal of Drug Education, 35*(3), 167–184.

Vernonia School District 47J v Acton, 515 U.S. 646 (1995).

Wetherill, R. R., & Fromme, K. (2007). Alcohol use, sexual activity, and perceived risk in high school athletes and non-athletes. *Journal of Adolescent Health, 41*(3), 294–301.

Yamaguchi, R., Johnston, L. D., & O'Malley, P. M. (2003). Relationship between student illicit drug use and school drug-testing policies. *Journal of School Health, 73*(4), 159–164.

Yusko, D. A., Buckman, J. F., White, H. R., & Pandina, R. J. (2008). Alcohol, tobacco, illicit drugs, and performance enhancers: A comparison of use by college student athletes and nonathletes. *Journal of American College Health, 57*(3), 281–290.

Notes: (1) One of the original eight school districts recruited for the demonstration project withdrew prior to project onset; however, there were two participating high schools in one school district, leaving eight high schools (grades 9 to 12) to participate in the study. Schools were located in Alabama, Idaho, Indiana (3), Kentucky (2), and Michigan. (2) There were no significant demographic differences between students included and excluded from the study in regard to gender, grade level, race/ethnicity, or percentage participating in athletics and/or other extracurricular activities. (3) Because all schools tested student athletes, it was not possible to make compari-

sons within this population. Also, students participating in both athletics and extracurriculars were excluded from these two subgroups.

Address correspondence to: Robert L. DuPont, MD, Principal Investigator, President, Institute for Behavior and Health, Inc., 6191 Executive Boulevard, Rockville, MD 20852, USA. Email: BobDuPont@aol.com

Exercise for Review 2

Directions: Answer the following questions based on your opinions. While there are no right or wrong answers, be prepared to explain the bases for your answers in classroom discussions.

1. Did the reviewers convince you that the topic of the review is important? Explain.

2. Is the review an essay organized around topics (as opposed to a string of annotations)? Explain.

3. Is the number of headings and subheadings adequate? Explain.

4. Is the tone of the review neutral and nonemotional? Explain.

5. Overall, is the review logically organized? Explain.

6. If research objectives or hypotheses are stated near the end of the review, do they flow logically from the material presented in the review? Explain.

7. Are there any obvious weaknesses in this review? Explain.

8. Does this review have any special strengths? Explain.

9. What is your overall evaluation of this review on a scale from *Excellent* (10) to *Very Poor* (0)? Explain.

Notes:

Sample Literature Review 3

College Students' Perceptions of Their Grandparents and Communication Technology Use

Introduction

A heightened interest in grandchild–grandparent relationships over the past several decades is likely due to an increase in average lifespan and longevity of this
5 relationship. The U.S. projected life expectancy at birth in 2010 was 75.7 years for men and 80.8 for women (U.S. Census Bureau, 2011). Globally, life expectancy is equivalent or greater than that of the United States in most of the European Union, Australia, New Zealand,
10 and other countries, such as Israel, Japan, and Jordan (AARP International, 2011). Today, adult grandchildren may have surviving grandparents into middle age; however, little is known about this relationship for grandchildren in college.

15 The Internet Generation defines a majority of today's college students who are more technologically savvy than previous generations (Mitchell, 2008). Concurrently, adults over age 50 are using technology more frequently in their daily lives (Madden & Zickuhr,
20 2011; Purcell, 2011; Rainie, 2010). Technology may facilitate or impede communication between grandparents and grandchildren. The Internet may facilitate communication for long-distance relatives with sensory impairments. A grandmother with a hearing deficit
25 may be better able to communicate with a grandchild using e-mail rather than a telephone. However, technology may diminish the amount of face-to-face contact among grandchildren and grandparents (Hoge-boom, McDermott, Perrin, Osman, & Bell-Ellison,
30 2010).

Although several studies have examined the attitudes of college students about aging and older adults, there is a paucity of research on college students' perceptions of their grandparents, specifically within the east-
35 ern United States. This study sought to address a gap in the literature and gain an understanding of modern grandchild–grandparent relationships. Therefore, the purpose of this study was to explore and describe the perceptions of college students about their
40 grandparents. Specifically, we sought to understand how college students view their relationships and communication with their grandparents and the factors that influence relationships between college student grandchildren and their grandparents.

45 ### Literature Review

The study purpose guided a literature review of grandchild–grandparent relationships and communication and organizes this section.

Grandchild–Grandparent Relationships

50 Lineage (Boon & Brussoni, 1998; Brown, 2003; Yi, Pan, Chang, & Chan, 2006), parents of grandchildren (Brown, 2003; Kemp, 2007), physical and cognitive impairment in grandparents (Boon & Shaw, 2007a, 2007b), and age/longevity of grandparents (AARP In-
55 ternational, 2011; Kirmeyer & Hamilton, 2011; Rempusheski, 1990; Szinovacz, 1998; U.S. Census Bureau, 2011) emerged from the literature as the most salient and relevant issues and factors that influence the nature of a grandchild–grandparent relationship. Undergradu-
60 ate college participants in western Canada reported their maternal grandmothers as their closest grandparent (Boon & Brussoni, 1998). However, Thai adolescent grandchildren were more likely to report closer relationships with paternal grandparents with whom
65 48% lived between birth and age three (Yi, Pan, Chang, & Chan, 2006). Kemp (2007) reported that grandchildren who are closer with their parents and whose parents have positive relationships with their own parents tend to be closer with their grandparents,
70 whereas Brown (2003) reported grandparent caregiving rather than gender or lineage predicted grandchild–grandparent relationships.

When faced with the physical or cognitive impairment of a grandparent, some grandchildren reported
75 more frequent visits to spend time with grandparents while they had the chance, and other participants reported lack of a desire to visit to avoid seeing grandparents deteriorating (Boon & Shaw, 2007a). However, when Boon and Shaw (2007b) focused on the severity
80 of a grandparent's impairment they found that many more participants reported positive effects on their lives than reported negative or no effects. A grandchild's perceptions may be influenced by a grandparent's age. Age of mother at first birth influences the

age of first-time grandparents and varies by world events, such as war, sociologic trends such as women choosing careers before motherhood (Kirmeyer & Hamilton, 2011), childbearing differences globally, and
90 the life cycle stages of grandparents at birth of grandchildren (Rempusheski, 1990).

In addition to grandparent age, gender disparity of death rates (AARP International, 2011; U.S. Census Bureau, 2011) and a gender-lineage hierarchy of
95 grandparent survival wherein maternal grandmothers live the longest and paternal grandfathers the shortest (Szinovacz, 1998) may influence a grandchild's perceptions. Therefore, US grandchildren in college will have longer histories with surviving grandparents, most
100 of whom will likely be maternal grandmothers. Other factors that may influence the grandchild–grandparent relationship include divorce, step-grandparents (Soliz, 2007), or other stressful life events (Wood & Liossis, 2007). Entering college may be a stressful life event for
105 grandchildren and grandparents.

Grandchild–Grandparent Communication

Face-to-face visits, landline telephone, and letters/cards mailed by the postal service comprise the nontechnology or traditional modes of communication
110 between grandchildren and grandparents. Communication technology or new modes of communication include cellular or mobile phones and Internet access devices that transmit photo, voice, and text messages. The most frequent predictors of kinds of communica-
115 tion used in grandchild–grandparent interactions are computer access, grandparent gender, grandchild age, and distance between grandparents and grandchildren (Hurme, Westerback, & Quadrello, 2010; Quadrello et al., 2005). E-mail was the most frequent online activity
120 carried out by grandmothers and grandparents with higher levels of education in the UK, Spain, Finland, and Estonia (Quadrello et al., 2005). Access to computers ranged from 23% to 44% in these European countries (Quadrello et al., 2005) compared to 70%
125 reported access in the United States (Rainie, 2010).

Quadrello and colleagues (2005) reported that face-to-face visits were used most frequently, followed closely by landline phone use, particularly for grandparents living in close proximity to grandchildren. In
130 contrast, Hurme and colleagues (2010) reported that grandparents and grandchildren in close proximity to each other were more likely to use all forms of communication except cards/letters. Grandmothers and female grandchildren were more likely to use
135 cards/letters to communicate, and younger grandparents were more likely to use mobile phone and text messaging (Hurme et al., 2010).

Theoretical Framework

Intergenerational family systems theory or Bowen's
140 theory (Bowen, 1972; Brown, 1999) focuses on patterns that develop in families in order to defuse anxi-ety. Anxiety emerges as a result of competing perceptions of closeness and distance in a relationship, brought about by external stress and family themes
145 communicated from previous generations. Eleven interlocking concepts (differentiation of self, triangles, nuclear family emotional system, couple conflict, symptoms in a spouse, symptoms in a child, family projection process, emotional cutoff, multigenerational
150 transmission process, sibling positions, and evolution of society) define the theoretical elements. For families in which several generations coexist, each member's personal growth and development may be influenced by another. Bowen's theory references the influence
155 that the first generation (grandparents) has on the third generation (grandchildren), the bidirectional, mutual influence of both generations, and the intervening influence of the second generation. This theory informed the focus of the inquiry, scale selection, and develop-
160 ment of demographic questions. This study was designed to explore intergenerational influences for the current generation of college-age grandchildren and their grandparents by describing the grandchild's perceptions of the relationship with a grandparent.

References

AARP International. (2011). Aging everywhere; country profiles. Retrieved from http://www.aarpinternational.org/

Boon, S. D., & Brussoni, M. J. (1998). Popular images of grandparents: Examining young adults' views of their closest grandparents. *Personal Relationships, 5*, 105–119. Retrieved from http://onlinelibrary.wiley.com/journal/10.1111/%281SSN%291475-6811

Boon, S. D., & Shaw, M. J. (2007a). Grandchildren's perceptions of grandparents' health: Worries and impact on their own lives. *Journal of Intergenerational Relationships, 5*(1), 57–77. doi: 10.1300/J194v05n01_05

Boon, S. D., & Shaw, M. J. (2007b). Reasons young adults visit (and do not visit) impaired grandparents. *Canadian Journal on Aging, 26*, 357–366. doi: 10.3138/cja. 26.4.357

Bowen, M. (1972). On the differentiation of self. First published anonymously in J. Framo (Ed.), *Family Interaction: A Dialogue Between Family Researchers and Family Therapists* (pp. 111–173). New York: Springer. Reprinted in M. Bowen (1978). *Family Therapy in Clinical Practice*. New York: Jason Aronson.

Brown, J. (1999). Bowen family systems theory and practice: Illustration and critique. *Australian and New Zealand Journal of Family Therapy, 20*(2), 94–103. Retrieved from http://www.familysystemstraining.com/papers/bowen-illustration-and-critique.html

Brown, L. H. (2003). Intergenerational influences on perceptions of current relationships with grandparents. *Journal of Intergenerational Relationships, 1*(1), 95–112. Retrieved from http://jir.ucsur.pitt.edu

Hogeboom, D. L., McDermott, R. J., Perrin, K. M., Osman, H., & Bell-Ellison, B. A. (2010). Internet use and social networking among middle aged and older adults. *Educational Gerontology, 36*(2), 93–111. doi: 10.1080/036012 70903058507

Hurme, H., Westerback, S., & Quadrello, T. (2010). Traditional and new forms of contact between grandparents and grandchildren. *Journal of Intergenerational Relationships, 8*(3), 264–280. doi: 10.1080/15350770.2010.498739.

Kemp, C. L. (2007). Grandparent–grandchild ties: Reflections on continuity and change across three generations. *Journal of Family Issues, 28*(7), 855–881. doi: 10.1177/0192513X07299599

Kirmeyer, S. E., & Hamilton, B. E. (2011). *Childbearing differences among three generations of U.S. women.* Hyattsville, MD: National Center for Health Statistics. Retrieved from http://www.cdc.gov/nchc/data/databriefs/db68.pdf

Madden, M., & Zickuhr, K. (2011). 65% of online adults use social networking sites. Retrieved from http://pewinternet.org/Reports/2011/Social-Networking -Sites.aspx

Mitchell, D. A. (2008). Generation Z. Striking the balance: Healthy doctors for a health community. *Australian Family Physician, 37*(8), 665–667. Retrieved from http://www.racgp.org.au/afp

Purcell, K. (2011). Search and email still top the list of most popular online activities. Retrieved from http://pewinternet.org/Reports/2011/Search-and-email.aspx

Quadrello, T., Hurme, H., Menzinger, J., Smith, P. K., Veisson, M., Vidal, S., & Westerback, S. (2005). Grandparents use of new communication technologies in a European perspective. *European Journal of Ageing*, *2*, 200–207. doi: 10.1007/sl0433-005-0004-y

Rainie, L. (2010). Internet, broadband, and cell phone statistics. Retrieved from http://www.pewinternet.org/Reports/2010/Internet-broadband-and-cell-phone-statistics.aspx

Rempusheski, V. F. (1990). Role of the extended family in parenting: A focus on grandparents of preterm infants. *The Journal of Perinatal & Neonatal Nursing*, *4*(2), 43–55.

Soliz, J. (2007). Communicative predictors of a shared identity: Comparison of grandchildren's perceptions of family-of-origin grandparents and step grandparents. *Journal of Family Communication*, *7*(3), 177–194. Retrieved from http://www.tandf.co.uk/journals/HJFC

Szinovacz, M. E. (1998). Grandparents today: A demographic profile. *The Gerontologist*, *38*(1), 37–52. Retrieved from http://gerontologist.oxford journals.org

U.S. Census Bureau. (2011). Statistical abstract of the United States. Retrieved from http://www.census.gov/compendia/statab/2011/tables/11s0102.pdf

Wood, S., & Liossis, P. (2007). Potentially stressful life events and emotional closeness between grandparents and adult grandchildren. *Journal of Family Issues*, *28*(3), 380–398. doi: 10.1177/0192513X06293893

Yi, C., Pan, E., Chang, Y., & Chan, C. (2006). Grandparents, adolescents, and parents: Intergenerational relations of Taiwanese youth. *Journal of Family Issues*, *27*(8), 1042–1067. doi: 10.1177/0192513X06288119

Acknowledgments: This research was supported in part by the Jeanne K. Buxbaum Endowment and the Delaware INBRE program, with a grant from the National Center for Research Resources (P20 RR016472-06), National Institutes of Health.

Address correspondence to: Dr. Veronica F. Rempusheski, University of Delaware, 25 N. College Avenue, Newark, DE 19716, USA. Email: vrempush@udel.edu

Exercise for Review 3

Directions: Answer the following questions based on your opinions. While there are no right or wrong answers, be prepared to explain the bases for your answers in classroom discussions.

1. Did the reviewers convince you that the topic of the review is important? Explain.

2. Is the review an essay organized around topics (as opposed to a string of annotations)? Explain.

3. Is the number of headings and subheadings adequate? Explain.

4. Is the tone of the review neutral and nonemotional? Explain.

5. Overall, is the review logically organized? Explain.

6. If research objectives or hypotheses are stated near the end of the review, do they flow logically from the material presented in the review? Explain.

7. Are there any obvious weaknesses in this review? Explain.

8. Does this review have any special strengths? Explain.

9. What is your overall evaluation of this review on a scale from *Excellent* (10) to *Very Poor* (0)? Explain.

Notes:

Sample Literature Review 4

A Review of Interventions for Substance Use Among Homeless Youth

Originally published as Xiang, X. (2013). A review of interventions for substance use among homeless youth. *Research on Social Work Practice*, *23*(1), 34–45. Copyright © 2013 by The Author(s). Reprinted with permission.

Introduction

High prevalence of substance use, including the use of alcohol and other drugs, is a well-documented problem and a recurring concern for helping professionals working with homeless youth. The term *homeless youth* as used here refers to *unaccompanied youth* as it is defined in the McKinney-Vento Homeless Assistance Act—youth who lack a fixed, regular, and adequate residence and are not in the physical custody of a parent or guardian. Estimates of homeless youth in the United States range from 1.6 to 3 million (Sedlak, Finkelhor, Hammer, & Schultz, 2002; Whitbeck, 2009). The current review includes youth between the ages of 12 and 24 who fit the McKinney-Vento definition to allow review of the full array of relevant literature.

Substance use is both a precipitating factor and a consequence of homelessness (Zerger, 2002). High prevalence of substance use among homeless youth has been documented in national and regional representative surveys (Friedman et al., 2009; Greene, Ennett, & Ringwalt, 1997; O'Toole et al., 2004; Van Leeuwen et al., 2004). Greene, Ennett, and Ringwalt (1997) analyzed data from three national representative surveys and found that 75% of the street youth reported marijuana use; one third used hallucinogens, stimulants, and analgesics; 25% used crack cocaine, other cocaine, inhalants, and sedatives; and 17% engaged in injection drug use.

Homeless youth with substance use problems often suffer from other mental health problems. In a longitudinal study of comorbidities of substance use among homeless youth in eight cities, Johnson, Whitbeck, and Hoyt (2005) found that 93% of the youth in their sample who met substance abuse criteria also reported one other mental disorder, and half of their sample reported two or more mental disorders. In an intervention study, Slesnick and Prestopnik (2005) found that approximately 75% of the youth met *Diagnostic and Statistical Manual of Mental Disorders* (4th ed.) criteria for one or more Axis I diagnoses other than substance abuse. Research has also shown that homeless youth with drug addiction are more likely to engage in high-risk sexual practices (Friedman et al., 2009) and delinquent behaviors such as theft, property crimes, and drug trafficking in order to finance their addictions (Farabee, Shen, Hser, Grella, & Anglin, 2001).

To effectively address the high prevalence of substance use among homeless youth, an evidence-based approach is required to identify interventions that result in demonstrable health benefits for substance abusing homeless youth. Nevertheless, to the author's knowledge, only two comprehensive reviews of interventions for homeless youth exist to date (Altena, Brilleslijper-Kater, & Wolf, 2010; Slesnick, Dashora, Letcher, Erdem, & Serovich, 2009) and neither focuses on interventions for substance use. The primary goal of this review, therefore, is to summarize existing evidence on interventions for substance use among homeless youth. This information will help guide social service providers and agencies as they seek to identify effective treatments to assist this population with their substance use problems. Recognizing the myriad methodological complications associated with recruiting homeless youth to intervention studies (Zerger, Strehlow, & Gundlapalli, 2008), this review uses explicit and well-validated criteria to evaluate the quality of studies. Secondary goals of the review are to draw implications for practice, to provide a critical appraisal of the methodologies in existing literature, and to suggest avenues for future research.

Method

Data Sources

Multiple databases including PubMed, MEDLINE, PsychINFO, ERIC, Social Work Abstracts, Social Service Abstracts, Sociological Abstracts, and the Cochrane Central Register of Controlled Trials were searched from their inception through April 2012. Combinations of the following keywords were used: drug, substance, alcohol, homeless youth, homeless adolescents, street youth, runaways, intervention, treatment, programs, and services. The title and abstract of each article were reviewed to determine whether the publication should be included based on predetermined criteria. The bibliographies of relevant reviews and publications meeting final selection criteria were also searched to identify additional articles. A total of 1,829 articles was identified.

Study Selection

90   Studies were included if they examined the effectiveness of an intervention to improve substance use problems among homeless youth between the ages of 12 and 24. Interventions were broadly defined to include services provided by primary care providers and

95   to which homeless youth could be referred. Studies had to report data on substance use outcomes. Studies that only examined substance use knowledge and attitude without data on actual substance use outcomes were excluded. Studies that reported multiple health and

100   behavior outcomes were included only if they reported specific substance use outcomes. Given the challenges of adopting rigorous research designs in intervention studies with homeless youth, a wide range of study designs were accepted in this review, including ran-

105   domized controlled trials (RCTs), prospective longitudinal studies with nonrandomized control groups or no control group, and longitudinal or retrospective studies that compared substance use outcomes among people receiving different types or intensities of treatments.

110   Only articles published in English were included in this review. After reviewing the abstracts and titles, 1,692 were excluded and the remaining 137 were retrieved for a full-text review; 110 articles were further excluded for not meeting the selection criterion. The bib-

115   liographies of the retrieved articles and relevant reviews (Altena et al., 2010; Hwang, Tolomiczenko, Kouyoumdjian, & Garner, 2005; Slesnick & Prestopnik, 2009) were also searched. Results from articles that examined data from the same study were com-

120   bined. A total of 15 unique studies (18 articles) met the inclusion criteria and were included in this review. The results of the search and study selection process are presented in Figure 1.

Critical Appraisal

125   The quality of the studies was assessed using the guidelines developed by the U.S. Preventive Services Task Force Work Group (see Harris et al., 2001, for more information). In a modification of the guidelines, blinded outcome assessment was excluded from the

130   rating criteria because none of the selected studies utilized this assessment procedure. The detailed quality appraisal criteria used in this review is presented as follows (adapted from U.S. Preventive Services Task Force):

135   Studies were rated "good" if they met all of the following criteria (1) clear definition of interventions; (2) initial assembly of comparable groups, which refers to adequate randomization for RCTs and adjustment for potential confounders in the analysis for other types of

140   design; (3) proper maintenance of comparable groups throughout the study, which means there was ignorable attrition or comparable attrition rates across study groups; (4) a follow-up rate of at least 80% at the end of study (this cutoff criterion was used in Hwang et al.,

145   2005); (5) use of reliable and valid measurements; (6)

all important outcomes were considered; and (7) for RCTs, intent-to-treat analysis was performed. Studies received a "fair" rating if they failed to meet one or more of the criteria listed in the "good" category, and

150   had none of the fatal flaws noted in the "poor" category.

Studies were rated "poor" if they had any of the following fatal flaws (1) study groups were very different initially and/or the comparability across groups was not

155   properly maintained throughout the study; (2) the measurements were unreliable or invalid; (3) key confounders were not controlled for in the analysis for studies other than RCTs; (4) follow-up rate was less than 50% at the end of the study (this cutoff criterion

160   was used in Hwang et al., 2005); and (5) sample size was less than 50 per study group (this cutoff criterion was used in Hwang et al., 2005).

Results

The majority ($n = 12$) of the studies were conducted

165   in the United States, and three were conducted in foreign countries (two in Canada and one in Honduras). Substance use was the primary target behavior in seven studies. In one study, substance use was the secondary outcome to facilitate HIV reduction. The remaining

170   seven studies targeted multiple health outcomes. Of the 15 studies reviewed in this article, six (40%) were rated "fair" and the remaining nine (60%) were rated "poor"; no study received a "good" rating. The most common reasons for a study to receive a poor-quality rating

175   were low retention rates, initial incomparable groups, and unaccounted for potential confounders. Rating

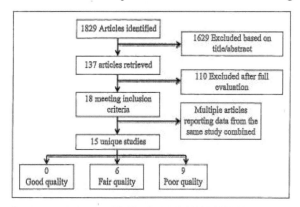

Figure 1. Summary of study research selection process.

results, reasons for fair or poor ratings, and detailed information on the reviewed studies are presented in Table 1.

180   *Brief Motivational Intervention*

Brief Motivational Intervention (BMI) is a technique that aims to increase clients' motivation to change. Utilizing strategies such as therapist empathy and reflective listening, the therapist involves the clients in

185   assessing their behavior and consequences, and pro-

vides feedback and direct advice as appropriate (Miller & Rollnick, 2002). BMI is a low-threshold and low-demand intervention, and has shown promising results for reducing substance abuse among adults (Stotts, Schmitz, Rhoades, & Grabowski, 2001). Two RCTs evaluated the effectiveness of BMI in reducing substance use among homeless youth. In the earlier study (Peterson, Baer, Wells, Ginzler, & Garrett, 2006), the treatment group reported a greater decrease in summed illicit drug use (other than marijuana) compared to the control group at the 1-month follow-up despite the small effect size; but this effect disappeared at the 3-month follow-up. No significant benefits of BMI on alcohol and marijuana use were found at either follow-up. As an attempt to improve the results from the earlier study, Baer, Garrett, Beadnell, Wells, and Peterson (2007) conducted a modified BMI featuring more sessions with a different sample of homeless youth. Although study participants reported overall reductions in alcohol, marijuana, and other drug use, there were no significant benefits of receiving the BMI intervention for the treatment group compared to the control group. Considering the relative rigor of the design in both studies, the findings indicate that BMI may be limited in its effectiveness as outreach for substance abusing homeless youth.

Community Reinforcement Approach

Community Reinforcement Approach (CRA) is a comprehensive behavioral treatment approach for substance abuse problems. CRA is based on the belief that environmental contingencies can play a powerful role in encouraging or discouraging substance use. Therefore, it seeks to rearrange these contingencies such that sober behavior is more rewarding than drinking or using drugs (Meyers & Smith, 1995). Two studies evaluated the effectiveness of CRA and mixed findings were reported. The first study adopted a rigorous RCT design (Slesnick, Prestopnik, Meyers, & Glassman, 2007). The results showed an overall improvement on substance use outcomes for all participants and a significantly greater improvement for the treatment group compared to the control group. The study results did not differ by age, gender, or ethnicity. The second study (Slesnick, Kang, Bonomi, & Prestopnik, 2008) examined the joint effectiveness of CRA and case management for homeless youth who requested the services through a drop-in center in Albuquerque, New Mexico. Results from a random coefficient model suggest that on average, participants' alcohol and drug use significantly decreased at 12-month follow-up. However, the number of treatment sessions attended did not predict participants' rate of change in alcohol or drug use across time. The findings should be interpreted with caution because of the relative weak design (i.e., no control group).

Knowledge and Skills Training

Two studies evaluated the efficacy of knowledge and skills training on substance use outcomes among homeless youth. One study (Booth, Zhang, & Kwiatkowski, 1999) utilized a crossover quasi-experiment design to examine an 8-hr knowledge and skills training based on a health belief and peer influence model in reducing drug and sex risk behaviors among runaways who were trained to act as peer educators. The training features role-playing, discussion, and practice of refusal skills when drugs were offered. Univariate analysis showed that participants in the treatment group decreased their use of heroin/cocaine by 7% while those in the control group reported no change. However, this change (i.e., 7% reduction) was not statistically significant. Similar results were found on the number of drugs used. Participants in the treatment group decreased the number of drugs used by 3% while those in the control group reported a slight increase of 1%. However, neither change was statistically significant. The authors argued that the changes, albeit statistically insignificant, might be substantially meaningful. The other study (Ferguson & Xie, 2008) pilot-tested the effectiveness of a social enterprise intervention (SEI) in improving the mental health and risk-behaviors among a small sample of homeless youth in a drop-in center in Los Angeles. The SEI model targets homeless youth aged from 18 to 24. It consists of vocational training and supportive mentorship with the aims to improve healthy behaviors, mental health status, service connections, and social support of street youth. While the treatment group experienced improvements in some mental health measures (e.g., depression and self-esteem), they reported a significantly greater increase in the number of days they had been drunk and using drugs in the past 6 months compared to those in the control group. It was unclear why the treatment group had a greater increase in substance use.

Case Management

Two studies examined the effectiveness of case management for reducing substance use among homeless youth. In a RCT, Cauce et al. (1994, 1998) evaluated the relative efficacy of intensive mental health case management compared to regular case management delivered in a drop-in center in downtown Seattle. The intensive case management features lower caseloads, more supervision, flexible funds, and higher educational qualifications of the caseworkers. The participants reported significant reductions in substance use over time, but there were no significant benefits for the participants receiving intensive case management compared to those who received regular services. The other study (Souza, Porten, Nicholas, Grais, & the Medecins Sans Frontiere-Honduras Team, 2011) evaluated multidisciplinary case management services delivered in a

Table 1. *Summary of Evaluations of Interventions for Substance Abusing Homeless Youth*

Study and Design	Quality Rating and Reasons	Study Settings and Participants	Intervention and Follow-up	Substance Use Outcomes
Brief motivational intervention (BMI)				
Peterson et al. (2006) RCT	Fair Follow up < 80% at end of study	Study settings: field-site offices in Seattle. Treatment: *n*=92; Control 1: *n*=99; Control 2: *n*=94. Age: 14–19 (*M*=17.4, *SD*=1.5). 55% Male. 72% White, 16% multiracial, 3% Native American, 3% Black, 3% Latino, 1% other.	Intervention: 1 session BMI; Control 1: same interview assessment protocol as the intervention group, without the feedback; Control 2: assessment at 1-month follow-up only. Follow-up at 1 month (82%) and 3 months (80%), overall follow-up rate 74.4%.	Significant reduction in summed illicit drug use other than marijuana for treatment group compared to control groups at 1-month follow-up. This effect disappeared at 3-month follow-up. No significant benefits for the treatment group on alcohol and marijuana use compared to the control groups. Intervention effects did not differ by age, gender, or ethnicity.
Baer et al. (2007) RCT	Fair Follow up < 80% at end of study	Study settings: field-site offices in Seattle. Treatment: *n*=75; Control: *n*=52. Age: 14–19 (*M*=17.90, *SD*=1.2). 56% Male. 58% White, 19% multiracial, 9% Native American, 8% Black, 4% Latino, 2% other.	Intervention: 4 sessions BMI; Control: treatment-as-usual. Follow-up at 1 month (82.9%) and 3 months (follow-up rate not reported), overall follow-up rate 76.1%.	Participants in both groups reported overall reductions in alcohol use at 3- but not 1-month follow-up, and reductions in marijuana and other drug use at both follow-ups. No significant benefits for treatment participants compared to the control.
Community reinforcement approach (CRA)				
Slesnick, Prestopnik, Meyers, et al. (2007) RCT	Fair Groups were initially different in number of other substance use diagnoses.	Study settings: drop-in center Albuquerque, NM. Treatment: *n*=96; Control: *n*=84. Age: 14–22 (*M*=19.2, *SD*=2.1). 60% Male. 41% White, 30% Latino, 13% Native American, 12% multiracial, 3% Black.	Intervention: 12-session CRA and 4-session HIV education/skill practice; Control: regular services provided by a drop-in center. Follow-up at 6 months (86%).	Participants in both groups had reductions in substance use over time including percent days of alcohol and drugs use, and number of categories of drug used. Treatment group had greater reduction in percent days of alcohol and drug use, but not number of categories of drug used, compared to those in the control. Intervention effects did not differ by age, gender, or ethnicity.
Slesnick, Kang, et al. (2008) Longitudinal study of outcomes with different types and intensities of treatment	Fair Follow-up < 80% at end of the study	Study settings: drop-in center in Albuquerque, NM. Recruited: *n*=172. Age: 14–20 (*M*=20, *SD* not reported). 59% Male. 37% White, 31% Latino, 12% Native American, 12% multiracial, 8% Black.	Intervention: case management and CRA. No control group. Follow-up at 6 months (73%) and 12 months (76%), overall follow-up rate 68%.	Results from random coefficient model suggested that on average, participants' alcohol and drug use significantly decreased at 12-month follow-up. However, time effect disappeared when other covariates were added in the model. Number of treatment sessions attended did not predict participants' rate of change in alcohol or drug use across time.

(continued)

Table 1. (continued)

Study and Design	Quality Rating and Reasons	Study Settings and Participants	Intervention and Follow-up	Substance Use Outcomes
Knowledge and skills training				
Booth et al. (1999) Crossover design	Fair Groups were initially different in substance use; follow up < 80% at end of study	Study settings: drop-in center in US. Treatment: n=72; Control: n=75. Age: range not reported (M=17.4, SD=1.5). 51% Male. 73% White, 12% Latino, 8% Black, 5% Native American, 3% other.	Intervention: 8-hour knowledge and skill training; Control: no training. Follow-up at 3 months (60%).	Participants did not report significant reduction in use of heroin/cocaine or number of drugs used.
Ferguson & Xie (2008) Prospective longitudinal study with non-randomized control group	Poor Sample size <50; follow up <80% at end of study; some confounders unaccounted for	Study settings: drop-in center in LA. Treatment: n=16; Control: n=12. Age: 18–24 (M=21, SD=1.4). 71% Male. 39% Black, 21% Latino, 21% White, 14% multiracial, 4% Asian.	Intervention: social enterprise intervention providing mentoring, job training, and clinical services; Control: usual care services. Follow-up at 9 months (68%)	Treatment group reported an increase in number of days they had been drunk in the past 6 months, whereas those in the control reported a decrease. Both groups reported an increase in the number of days of drug use in the past 6 months with the treatment group reporting a significant greater increase compared to the control group.
Case management (CM)				
Cauce et al. (1994, 1998) RCT	Poor Initial resemblance between groups not stated; follow-up <50% at end of study	Study settings: a multi-service center in downtown Seattle. Recruited: n=304; Treatment: n=78; Control: n=72 in the analysis. Age: 13–21 (M=17, SD not reported). 61% Male. 60% White, 16% Black, 6% Latino, 5% Native American.	Intervention: intensive case management; Control: regular case management. Follow-up at 3, 6, 9, and 12 months (specific follow-up rates not reported). 49% of the participants completed at least two follow-up assessments.	Participants reported significant reduction in substance use over time. No significant benefits for the treatment group compared to the control.
Souza et al. (2011) Longitudinal study of outcomes with different types and intensities of treatments	Poor Follow-up < 80% at end of the study; key confounders not accounted for	Study settings: drop-in center in Tegucigalpa, Honduras. Recruited: n=400. Age: <=25, (M=17.5, SD not reported). 62% Male.	Intervention: multidisciplinary CM Follow-up at 12, 24, and 36 months (specific follow-up rates not reported). 59% of the participants had baseline and at least one follow-up visit.	Cessation of substance use defined as more than 50% of follow-up visits without substance use. Survival analysis indicated probability of remaining on substance was .88 at 12-month and .82 at 24-month follow-up.
Peer support intervention				
Stewart et al. (2009) Prospective longitudinal study without a control group	Poor Confounders not accounted for; follow-up <50% at the end of study	Study settings: two agencies serving homeless and at-risk youths and one community center in Alberta, Canada Recruited: n=70. Age: 16–24 (M=19, SD=2.5). 54% Male. 60% Aboriginal, 27% White, 13% other.	Intervention: 20-week pilot peer support intervention. Follow-up at 12 weeks after the first intervention (41%), and at the end of intervention (20%).	Univariate analysis showed that 55% of participants at midpoint and 29% at post-test reported decreased use of drugs and alcohol or complete cessation of both.
Family therapy				
Slesnick, Bartle-Haring, & Gangamma, (2006); Slesnick & Prestopnik (2005, 2009) RCT	Fair Groups might not be comparable because of their different retention rates.	Study settings: runaway shelters in Albuquerque, NM. Treatment 1 (FFT): n=40; Treatment 2 (EBFT): n=102; Control: n=101. Age: 12–17 (M=15, SD=1.4). 43% Male. 41% Latino, 34% White, 7% Native American, 6% Black, 12% other.	Intervention: 16-session family therapy (FT), one provided in the office (FFT) and one in the home (EBFT) Control: shelter services. Follow-up at 3 months (88%), 9 months (82%), and 15 months (81%) for the treatment groups; at 3 (78%), 9 (81%), and 15 (82%) months for the control group.	Participants reported significant reduction in percent days of overall drug and alcohol use, with the FT groups showing significantly greater decrease compared to the control group. Participants' age and gender moderated the effects of FFT. Participants' history of sexual and physical abuse moderated the effects of EBFT.

(continued)

Table 1. (continued)

Study and Design	Quality Rating and Reasons	Study Settings and Participants	Intervention and Follow-up	Substance Use Outcomes
Milburn et al. (2012) RCT	Poor Groups differed by gender initially; overall follow-up <50%	Study settings: site selected by the family (usually their home) in LA and San Bernardino. Treatment: *n*=68; Control: *n*=83. Age: 12–17 (*M*=14.8, *SD*=1.4) 34% Male. 62% Latino, 21% Black, 11% White, 10% other.	Intervention: 5-session family-based intervention based on cognitive-behavioral theories; Control: regular care. Follow-up at 3 months (71%), 6 months (58%) and 12 months (46%).	Participants had overall reduction in alcohol and hard drug use over time, with the treatment group having greater reduction compared to the control group. However, treatment group reported an increase in marijuana use, whereas the control group reported a decrease.
Shelter services Steele & O'Keefe (2001) Longitudinal study of outcomes with different intensities of treatment	Poor Key confounders not accounted for; follow-up rate not reported.	Study settings: a residential comprehensive care center in New Orleans. Recruited: *n*=106. Age: 16–21 (*M* and *SD* not reported). 30% Male. Ethnic composition not reported.	Intervention: residential comprehensive health care services. Specific interventions related to drug abuse were screening and intensive counseling to modify high-risk behaviors. Follow-up at 9 months (follow-up rate not reported).	Percent of participants who had drug dependence decreased from 41% on admission to 3% during follow-up or at completion.
Rotheram-Borus et al. (2003) Prospective longitudinal studies with non-randomized control group	Poor This study meets all the criteria for "good" except for an overall follow-up rate <50%	Study settings: four shelters in New York City. Treatment *n*=101; Control: *n*=86 after matching. Age: 11–18 (*M*=15.6, *SD*=1.7). 51% Male. 59% Black, 26% Latino, 15% other.	Intervention: residential comprehensive care services including access to health resources, skill training; Control: regular services. Follow-up at 3 months (57%), 6 months (58%), 12 months (50%), 18 months (46%), and 24 months (70%).	Marijuana use and the number of drugs used were significantly lower in the treatment group among female participants at 6-month and 12-month follow-up. No significant benefits of the treatment for male participants. No significant benefits of the treatment beyond 12 months.
Pollio et al. (2006) Longitudinal study of outcomes with different types of treatments	Poor Follow-up <50% at end of study; potential confounders not accounted for.	Study settings: youth crisis shelters in a Midwestern city. Recruited: *n*=371. Age: range not reported (*M*=14.7, *SD*=1.5). 39% Male. 73% White, 27% other.	Intervention: emergency and crisis shelter services. Follow-up at 6 weeks, 3 months, and 6 months (25–30% attrition per time period).	Proportion of youth reporting substance use decreased significantly at all follow-ups compared to the baseline. There was an additional significant decrease from 6 weeks to 3 months, but then a significant increase from 3 months to 6 months, resulting in no significant differences between 6-week and 6-month follow-ups.
Supportive housing Kisely et al. (2008) Retrospective study comparing outcomes of people using different types of services	Poor Groups initially not comparable on years of education; sample size <50; key confounders not accounted for.	Study settings: a youth program in Halifax, Canada. Treatment: *n*=15; Control: *n*=30. Age: 16–25 (*M*=19.8, *SD*=2.52). 71% Male. Ethnic composition not reported.	Intervention: supportive housing with residential supervision, in-home counseling and support; Control: access to services but not housing. No follow-up as it was a retrospective study.	Univariate analysis showed that treatment participants had significantly lower level rates of current substance use compared to those in the control condition.

drop-in center in Tegucigalpa, Honduras. Survival analysis showed a lower probability of continuing substance use at the 1- and 2-year follow-ups. The study results should be interpreted with caution considering its low retention rate and weak design. Besides, the authors defined "stopped substance use" in the survival analysis if participants reported no substance use at more than 50% of their visits to the drop-in center. The results could be easily changed if a different criterion was used.

Peer Support Intervention

One study (Stewart, Reutter, Letourneau, & Makwarimba, 2009) pilot-tested the effectiveness of a peer support intervention in enhancing healthy behaviors among homeless youth in Alberta, Canada. The support intervention was developed on the theory that social support from peers and professionals can improve homeless youth's mental and physical health status, their coping skills, and abilities to deal with stressful events (Stewart et al., 2009). The intervention features group and dyad support delivered by both peer mentors who experienced homelessness themselves and professional mentors. The support groups met 3–4 hr per week for 5 months. Over half of the participants reported decreases in drug and alcohol use at 12 weeks after the first intervention, and 29% reported reduction in substance use or complete cessation of both at the end of the intervention. However, the findings should be interpreted with extra caution because the study quality was low as the retention rate was below 50% at the end of the study and potential confounders were not accounted for.

Family Therapy

Two studies evaluated the effectiveness of family-based interventions in reducing risk behaviors among homeless youth. One study (Slesnick, Bartle-Haring, & Gangamma, 2006; Slesnick & Prestopnik, 2005, 2009) utilized a rigorous RCT design and compared the effectiveness of office-based functional family therapy (FFT) and home-based ecologically based family therapy (EBFT) to usual shelter services. The interventions consisted of communication and parenting skills training, behavioral, cognitive, and environmental interventions, with the aim to alter dysfunctional family patterns that contribute to substance use, running away, and related individual problem behaviors (Slesnick, et al., 2006). Up to 16 family sessions were provided with each session lasting about 60 min. Participants reported a significant reduction in percent days of overall drug and alcohol use, with the two treatment groups experiencing greater decrease compared to the control group. Subgroup analysis revealed that participants with both sexual and physical abuse did better with EBFT than with treatment as usual on the number of drugs used in the past 90 days, while youth with neither sexual nor physical abuse did not differ between modalities. Age

and gender were found to moderate the effect of FFT, with significant reduction in percent of days of drug and alcohol use observed only for male and older (ages: 16–17) participants. The other study (Milburn et al., 2012) examined the effectiveness of a short family intervention in reducing risk behaviors and drug use among a sample of newly homeless youth. The intervention was specifically designed for newly homeless youth, and was based on the belief that running away from home was an ineffective attempt to resolve family conflict. Up to five sessions were provided, aiming to establish a positive family climate, improve family functioning, and help participants to learn problem-solving skills. Participants reported overall reductions in alcohol and hard drug use, and the treatment group reported greater reductions than the control group. However, marijuana use showed the opposite effect, with the treatment participants increasing times of use whereas those in the control group decreased use.

Shelter Services

Two studies evaluated the effectiveness of residential comprehensive care services addressing substance use, sexually transmitted diseases, and other health issues among homeless youth. In one study (Steele & O'Keefe, 2001), participants who had positive urine drug screens received a 28-day in-house drug treatment and individual counseling, in addition to the general health services provided at a residential comprehensive care center. Univariate analysis showed that percent of drug abusing homeless youth dropped from 41% on admission to 3% during follow-up or at completion. Despite the large percentage decrease in drug use, the efficacy of the treatment should be taken with caution considering the low quality of the study. There was no control group; and the results were merely descriptive, thus leaving out many uncontrolled confounders. The other study (Rotheram-Borus et al., 2003) followed a sample of homeless youth receiving shelter services for 2 years and found significant benefits of the shelter services for female participants, but not for male participants. Female participants in the treatment group reported a significant decrease in marijuana use and the number of drugs used at the 6- and 12-month follow-ups compared [to] those in the control condition.

Another study (Pollio, Thompson, Tobias, Reid, & Spitznagel, 2006) evaluated the effectiveness of emergency shelter and crisis services. Youth crisis shelters generally serve adolescents 12–18 years of age, with the priority of ensuring that youth are provided with the basic necessities. Alcohol/drug treatment was also available in these crisis shelters. Participants reported significant reductions in drug use at the 6-week, 3-, and 6-month follow-ups compared to the baseline. There was an additional significant reduction of substance use from 6-week to 3-month follow-ups, but this change reversed itself between 3- and 6-month follow-ups, resulting in no significant changes in substance use

410 between 6-week and 6-month follow-ups. The findings indicate that benefits of emergency shelter may be limited in the long run.

Supportive Housing

One study (Kisely et al., 2008) pilot-tested a supportive housing program, a combination of safe, affordable
415 housing with integrated support services, in Halifax, Canada. Participants in the housing program had stable supervised accommodation for a minimum of 3 months and had access to regular services in a drop-in center, whereas those in the control group had the same access
420 to drop-in center services but not the accommodation. Univariate analysis suggested that residents of supportive housing had significantly lower rates of current substance use than those in the control group. However, the study was retrospective and there was no
425 baseline test on substance use. The positive association between the supportive housing and lower rate of substance use could easily be explained away by differences in rates of substance use at the baseline or other systematic differences between the two groups.

430 **Discussion and Applications to Social Work**

Evidence on the effectiveness of interventions for substance abusing homeless youth is emerging as more formal evaluations are conducted. This review revealed that a variety of interventions with homeless youth
435 ranging from individual-focused therapies to shelter-based services have been examined. Common effects seemed evident as participants showed overall improvement in substance use outcomes in most of the studies. Differential effects were less common as par-
440 ticipants receiving the treatment of interest were rarely found to have greater improvement than those who received regular services. Only family therapy appeared to show signs of relative efficacy.

This review has certain limitations. Only articles
445 published in English were included. There might be relevant studies that either have never been published or published in other languages. Moreover, the working definition of homeless youth used in this review excluded homeless children under the age of 12 or those
450 who are homeless with their families. Findings of the review might not apply to these homeless populations. Another limitation of the working definition is its broad age limit of homeless youth (i.e., age 12–24). Although a broad age limit was needed for a fuller re-
455 view of evidence, it did not distinguish between the age groups of 12–18 and 18–24, an important determinant of service availability. Nevertheless, it seems that the participant's age has a limited role in moderating the treatment effects based on several studies reviewed
460 here (Peterson et al., 2006; Slesnick & Prestopnik, 2005; Slesnick et al., 2007).

Descriptive analysis of the sample characteristics of reviewed studies suggests that homeless youth are often troubled prior to becoming homeless. Participants

465 often reported being physically and/or sexually abused (Slesnick & Prestopnik, 2005), attempting suicide (Booth et al., 1999), experiencing school disruptions or dropping out at an early age (Stewart et al., 2009), and having multiple runaway episodes (Pollio et al., 2006)
470 prior to treatment. These findings indicate a need for prevention programs targeting household youth who are at high risk of becoming homeless.

For youth who are currently homeless, comprehensive substance use screening, assessment, and
475 treatment should be made accessible to them given the high prevalence of substance use in this population (Greene et al., 1997). Overall, this review indicates that study participants receiving some type of services (either in the treatment group or in the control group) im-
480 proved in substance use outcomes over time in most of the studies. When two different interventions were compared, however, differential effects were rarely found. These findings suggest that depending on the availability of resources and practice settings, practi-
485 tioners could offer a variety of services to homeless youth who abuse substances.

Another important implication drawn from the current review is that more effort should be made to encourage homeless youth to engage and remain in ther-
490 apy for their substance use and other mental health problems. A majority of the studies reviewed in this article had recruitment and retention issues (Cauce et al., 1998; Milburn et al., 2012; Pollio et al., 2006). The reluctance of homeless youth to engage in therapy has
495 also been well documented in the literature (see Slesnick, Meyers, Meade, & Segelken, 2000, for a review of this literature). Some strategies to engage homeless youth in substance use treatment include using and understanding language from the youth's cul-
500 ture, presenting the treatment in an appealing and nonthreatening way, emphasizing confidentiality, and identifying youths' motivations to enter therapy (Slesnick, Meyers, et al., 2000).

Moreover, there is some emerging evidence suggest-
505 ing moderation effects of certain youth characteristics on treatment outcomes. For example, Slesnick and Prestopnik (2005) found that homeless youth with a history of sexual and/or physical abuse benefited more from family therapy than those without any type of
510 abuse. In addition, another study evaluating the effects of residential comprehensive care services found reductions in substance use among females but not males (Rotheram-Borus et al., 2003). If systematic differences in treatment effects among subgroups of home-
515 less youth are consistently found in future research, service providers should explore intervention alternatives that are sensitive to client characteristics, such as life circumstances, gender, and culture.

Practitioners should note that this review was limited
520 to studies that evaluated interventions to decrease substance use among homeless youth. Many studies have evaluated substance use interventions with household

adolescents (see Weinberg, Rahdert, Colliver, & Glantz, 1998, for a review of this literature) or homeless adults (see Hwang et al., 2005, for a review of this literature), and some interventions appear to be effective for these populations. These interventions may also work well for homeless youth. Practitioners are advised to consult these studies and reviews for more information.

The review revealed several limitations in the current body of intervention research on substance use problems among homeless youth. Only 1% of the initial search results met the inclusion criteria. For each specific intervention, there were only two to three studies that examined its efficacy. These results indicate an insufficient number of studies that have evaluated treatment effectiveness among homeless youth who use substances. The paucity of empirical evidence will most likely impede the implementation of evidence-based substance use practice for homeless youth.

Of the 15 studies included, none appeared to have good quality, and the majority received a poor rating. The most common contributors to a poor rating for studies that adopted a design other than RCTs were the initial incomparability of study groups and failure to control for potential confounders caused by lack of randomization. When the study target is homeless youth, randomization is not always possible because of feasibility, ethical issues, and potential contaminations (Booth et al., 1999). As a result, several studies had incomparable study groups. Only one of the studies (Rotheram-Borus et al., 2003) utilized some statistical techniques (i.e., propensity score matching [PSM]) to address the initial incomparability between study groups.

It is also worth noting that three of the studies (Ferguson & Xie, 2008; Kisely et al., 2008; Stewart et al., 2009) were pilot work that tested the feasibility and effectiveness of SEI, peer-support intervention, and support housing respectively. Given the limited scope of pilot work, it is not surprising that all three received a poor rating. The poor ratings, however, do not necessarily translate into lack of effectiveness of those interventions. Nevertheless, more studies with larger scopes are needed to replicate the results from these pilot studies before they can be widely applied in practice settings.

The most significant methodological problem affecting the studies, including RCTs, is retention of participants. Two RCTs (Baer, Garrett, Beadnell, Wells, & Peterson, 2007; Peterson et al., 2006) were not rated "good" only because their retention rates were below 80%. In one study (Cauce et al., 1994, 1998), less than 50% of the participants initially recruited completed all the follow-up assessments. Retaining clients in substance use treatment is an important near-term outcome for service providers, and a potential mediator of subsequent client outcomes. Retaining homeless clients in interventions presents a particular challenge for sub-

stance use treatment providers. This is because homeless youth are difficult to engage in treatment initially, and consequently providing services can be more costly (Orwin, Garrison-Mogren, Jacobs, & Sonnefeld, 1999). Attrition may result in original comparable groups becoming incomparable at follow-up assessments, increasing the risk of selection bias that can greatly weaken internal validity. Many factors have been found to be associated with retention of homeless adults in longitudinal studies, including length of the treatment, nature and service components of the intervention, study site, clients' perceptions of the usefulness of the treatment, client satisfactions, therapeutic relationships, and responsiveness and friendliness of the staff (Orwin et al., 1999; Padgett, Henwood, Abrams, & Davis, 2008). High drop-out rate might also be due to youth's perceptions that the interventions are not effective.

Another issue that emerged from this review is the measurement of substance use outcomes and its implications for intervention studies. The most common measures of substance use in the studies reviewed here were the number of categories of drug used and percent days of overall alcohol and drug use in a specified period of time. A majority of the studies reported mixed findings regarding the effectiveness of the intervention when different measures of substance use outcomes were examined. In a study testing the effectiveness of CRA, for example, the treatment group had greater reduction than the control group in percent days of substance use but not number of drugs used (Slesnick et al., 2007). The findings also appeared to be different depending on the categories of drugs used. For instance, two studies (Milburn et al., 2012; Peterson et al., 2006) reported a significant treatment effect on the total number of drugs used (excluding marijuana); however, the effect did not extend to marijuana use. More studies are in need to replicate the findings. If differential effects on marijuana and other types of drugs are consistently found, efforts should be made to explore the underlying mechanisms; and new intervention strategies that are based on the types of drug used need to be developed.

Methodological problems set aside, studies rarely examined treatment experiences from the participants' perspectives with a few exceptions (e.g., Stewart et al., 2009). The effectiveness of a treatment may be of statistical significance when measured by standard instruments, but it might have little substantive significance for substance abusing homeless youth. Participants' perspectives may offer important insight on the substantive significance of the treatment. Seeking feedback from the participants may also facilitate the interpretations of unexpected findings. In one study (Ferguson & Xie, 2008), participants in the treatment group had more drunk and drug use episodes at follow-ups compared to the baseline. Exploring the participants' experiences through interviews or focus groups at follow-ups may help us understand these disturbing findings. Future intervention studies should explore clients' experiences. For example, in what ways are the treatments beneficial or harmful to them? Are they likely to maintain any treatment gains that they had made in stopping or reducing substance use? What part of the treatment could be enhanced to better meet their needs?

Finally, with a few exceptions (Peterson et al., 2006; Rotheram-Borus et al., 2003; Slesnick & Prestopnik, 2005; Slesnick et al., 2007), potential moderation effects of ethnicity, gender, age, and other youth characteristics on the treatment outcomes were rarely explored. Mixed findings were reported in studies that examined moderation's effects. In two studies, participants' outcomes did not differ by age, gender, or ethnicity (Peterson et al., 2006; Slesnick et al., 2007). However, being sexually and/or physically abused appeared to moderate the treatment effects in another study (Slesnick et al., 2006; Slesnick & Prestopnik, 2005, 2009). These findings have yet to be replicated.

Corresponding to these limitations identified, several suggestions for future research are presented here. To augment effect size in RCT studies, researchers may consider using control groups that receive minimum usual care services or temporarily withholding services for the control groups until after the study is finished. Another way to improve study findings is to maintain comparable study groups and high retention rates throughout the study. When dropout occurs, follow-up data should be collected to explore the reasons for dropout and to allow intent-to-treat analysis to be performed. For studies conducted in naturalistic settings or secondary analysis of routinely collected data from agencies, efforts should be made to address the threat of selection bias by examining the comparability of study groups and describing the differences between groups (if any). Statistical techniques such as PSM could be utilized when appropriate. Potential confounders should always be controlled in order to discern true treatment effect. Moreover, studies that explore systematic differences in treatment effects among subgroups of homeless youth are in great demand. Homeless youth is a diverse population. The effects of gender, ethnicity, age, and history of abuse have been explored in a few studies, but the findings are not conclusive. The potential impact of sexual orientation and duration of homelessness on treatment effects are rarely explored. More research is needed to examine these systematic differences in order to inform interventions that are sensitive to the specific characteristics of subgroups of homeless youth. This review also highlights the need for exploring participants' experiences of the treatment, their satisfaction, and how their perceptions influence their treatment outcomes. A mixed method approach that embeds focus groups and/or interviews within the larger quantitative experiment, as it was adopted in Ferguson and Xie's (2008) pilot study

of SEI, may be utilized to help develop recruitment strategies, improve treatment procedures, and better understand participants' perspectives. Additionally, multiple measures of substance use outcomes should be examined in a single study as a way to strengthen the robustness of the treatment effects. Separate analyses should be conducted for different categories of substance used (e.g., alcohol, cannabis, and narcotics) when appropriate.

In conclusion, although existing evidence on the effectiveness of substance use interventions for homeless youth is emerging, it is quite limited in informing evidence-based practice. Mixed findings are often reported for the same intervention. The heterogeneity of the interventions and the few studies conducted on each intervention make it difficult to determine the relative efficacy of a specific intervention. The quality of the studies was often poor, which further impedes drawing firm conclusions about the efficacy of interventions. Hopefully, the directions presented will assist the development of more high-quality intervention studies to strengthen the evidence base of substance use interventions for homeless youth.

References

Altena, A. M., Brilleslijper-Kater, S. N., & Wolf, J. R. L. M. (2010). Effective interventions for homeless youth: A systematic review. *American Journal of Preventive Medicine, 38*, 637–645. doi:10.1016/j.amepre.2010.02.017

Baer, J. S., Garrett, S. B., Beadnell, B., Wells, E. A., & Peterson, P. L. (2007). Brief motivational intervention with homeless adolescents: Evaluating effects on substance use and service utilization. *Psychology of Addictive Behaviors, 21*, 582–586. doi:10.1037/0893-164X.21.4.582

Booth, R. E., Zhang, Y. M., & Kwiatkowski, C. F. (1999). The challenge of changing drug and sex risk behaviors of runaway and homeless adolescents. *Child Abuse and Neglect, 23*, 1295–1306. doi: 10.1016/S0145-2134(99)00090-3

Cauce, A. M., Morgan, C. J., Wagner, V., Moore, H., Sy, J., Wurzbacher, K., Blanchard, T. (1994). Effectiveness of intensive case management for homeless adolescents: Results of a 3-month follow-up. *Journal of Emotional and Behavioral Disorders, 2*, 219–227.

Cauce, A. M., Paradise, M., Embry, L., Morgan, C. J., Lohr, Y., Theofelis, J., Wagner, V. (1998). Homeless youth in Seattle: Youth characteristics, mental health needs, and intensive case management. In M. H. Epstein, K. Kustash, & A. Duchnowski (Eds.), *Outcomes for children and youth with behavioral and emotional disorders and their families: Programs and evaluation best practices* (pp. 611–632). Austin, TX: Pro-ed.

Farabee, D., Shen, H., Hser, Y. I., Grella, C. E., & Anglin, M. D. (2001). The effect of drug treatment on criminal behavior among adolescents in DATOS-A. *Journal of Adolescent Research, 16*, 679–696. doi:10.1 177/07435584011 66009

Ferguson, K. M., & Xie, B. (2008). Feasibility study of the social enterprise intervention with homeless youth. *Research on Social Work Practice, 18*, 5–19. doi: 10.1177/1049731507303535

Friedman, M. S., Marshal, M. P., Stall, R., Kidder, D. P., Henny, K. D., Courtenay-Quirk, C., Holtgrave, D. R. (2009). Associations between substance use, sexual risk taking and HIV treatment adherence among homeless people living with HIV. *AIDS Care, 21*, 692–700. doi: 10.1080/0954012080 2513709

Greene, J. M., Ennett, S. T., & Ringwalt, C. L. (1997). Substance use among runaway and homeless youth in three national samples. *American Journal of Public Health, 87*, 229–235. Retrieved from http://ajph.aphapublications. org/doi/pdf/10.2105/AJPH.87.2.229

Harris, R. P., Helfand, M., Woolf, S. H., Lohr, K. N., Mulrow, C. D., Teutsch, S. M., & Atkins, D. (2001). Current methods of the U.S. preventive services task force: A review of the process. *American Journal of Preventive Medicine, 20*, 21–35. doi: 10.1016/ S07493797(01)00261-6

Hwang, S. W., Tolomiczenko, G., Kouyoumdjian, F. G., & Garner, R. (2005). Interventions to improve the health of homeless: A systematic review. *American Journal of Preventive Medicine, 29*, 311.el-311.e75. doi: 10.1016/ j.amepre.2005.06.017

Johnson, K. D., Whitbeck, L. B., & Hoyt, D. R. (2005). Substance abuse disorders among homeless and runaway adolescents. *Journal of Drug Issues, 35*, 799–816.

Kisely, S. R., Parker, J. K., Campbell, L. A., Karabanow, J., Hughes, J. M., & Gahagan, J. (2008). Health impacts of supportive housing for homeless youth: A pilot study. *Public Health, 122*, 1089–1092. doi: 10.1016/j.puhe.2008.01.009

Meyers, R. J., & Smith, J. E. (1995). *Clinical guide to alcohol treatment: The community reinforcement approach.* New York, NY: Guilford Press.

Milburn, N. G., Iribarren, F. J., Rice, E., Lightfoot, M., Solorio, R., Rotheram-Borus, M. J., ... Duan, N. (2012). A family intervention to reduce sexual risk behavior, substance use, and delinquency among newly homeless youth. *Journal of Adolescent Health, 50*, 358–364. doi:10.1016/j.jadohealth. 2011.08.009

Miller, W. R., & Rollnick, S. (2002). *Motivational interviewing: Preparing people to change addictive behavior* (2nd ed.). New York, NY: Guilford Press.

Orwin, R. G., Garrison-Mogren, R., Jacobs, M. L., & Sonnefeld, L. J. (1999). Retention of homeless clients in substance abuse treatment: Findings from the National Institute on Alcohol Abuse and Alcoholism Cooperative Agreement Program. *Journal of Substance Abuse Treatment, 17*, 45–66. doi: 10.1016/S0740-5472(98)00046-4

O'Toole, T. P., Gibbon, J. L., Hanusa, B. H., Freyder, P. J., Conde, A. M., & Fine, M. J. (2004). Self-reported changes in drug and alcohol use after becoming homeless. *American Journal of Public Health, 94*, 830–835. doi: 10.2105/AJPH.94.5.830

Padgett, P. K., Henwood, B., Abrams, C., & Davis, A. (2008). Engagement and retention in services among formerly homeless adults with co-occurring mental illness and substance abuse: Voices from the margins. *Psychiatric Rehabilitation Journal, 31*, 226–233. doi: 10.2975/31.3.2008.226.233

Peterson, P. L., Baer, J. S., Wells, E. A., Ginzler, J. A., & Garrett, S. B. (2006). Short-term effects of a brief motivational intervention to reduce alcohol and drug risk among homeless adolescents. *Psychology of Addictive Behaviors, 20*, 254–264. doi: 10.1037/0893-164X.20.3.254

Pollio, D. E., Thompson, S. J., Tobias, L., Reid, D., & Spitznagel, E. (2006). Longitudinal outcomes for youth receiving runaway/homeless shelter services. *Journal of Youth and Adolescence, 35*, 859–866. doi: 10.1007/s 10964-006-9098-6

Rotheram-Borus, M. J., Song, J., Gwadz, M., Lee, M., Rossem, R. V., & Koopman, C. (2003). Reductions in HIV risk among runaway youth. *Prevention Science, 4*, 173–186. doi:10.1023/A:1024697706033

Sedlak, A. J., Finkelhor, D., Hammer, H., & Schultz, D. J. (2002). *National estimates of missing children: An overview.* Washington, DC: U.S. Department of Justice, Office of Justice Programs, Office of Juvenile Justice and Delinquency Prevention.

Slesnick, N., Bartle-Haring, S., & Gangamma, R. (2006). Predictors of substance use and family therapy outcome among physically and sexually abused runaway adolescents. *Journal of Marital and Family Therapy, 32*, 261–281. doi:10.1111/j.1752-0606.2006.tb01606.x

Slesnick, N., Dashora, P., Letcher, A., Erdem, G., & Serovich, J. (2009). A review of services and interventions for runaway and homeless youth: Moving forward. *Children and Youth Services Review, 31*, 732–742. doi:10.1016/j.childyouth.2009.01.006

Slesnick, N., Kang, M. J., Bonomi, A. E., & Prestopnik, J. L. (2008). Six- and twelve-month outcomes among homeless youth accessing therapy and case management services through an urban drop-in center. *Health Services Research, 43*, 211–229. doi:10.1111/j.1475-6773.2007.00755.x

Slesnick, N., Meyers, R. J., Meade, M., & Segelken, D. H. (2000). Bleak and hopeless no more: Engagement of reluctant substance-abusing runaway youth and their families. *Journal of Substance Abuse Treatment, 19*, 215–222. doi:10.1016/S0740-5472 (00) 00100-8

Slesnick, N., & Prestopnik, J. L. (2005). Ecologically based family therapy outcome with substance abusing runaway adolescents. *Journal of Adolescence, 28*, 277–298. doi:10.1016/ j.adolescence.2005.02.008

Slesnick, N., & Prestopnik, J. L. (2009). Comparison of family therapy outcome with alcohol-abusing, runaway adolescents. *Journal of Marital and Family Therapy, 35*, 255–277. doi: 10.1111/j.1752-0606.2009.00121.x

Slesnick, N., Prestopnik, J. L., Meyers, R. J., & Glassman, M. (2007). Treatment outcomes for street-living, homeless youth. *Addictive Behaviors, 32*, 1237–1251. doi:10.1016/j.addbeh.2006.08.010

Souza, R., Porten, K., Nicholas, S., & Grais, R., & the Medecins Sans Frontiere-Honduras Team. (2011). Outcomes for street children and youth under multidisciplinary care in a drop-in centre in Tegucigalpa, Honduras. *International Journal of Social Psychiatry, 57*, 619–626. doi:10.1 177/0020764010382367

Steele, R. W., & O'Keefe, M. A. (2001). A program description of health care interventions for homeless teenagers. *Clinical Pediatrics, 40*, 259–263. doi: 10.1177/000992280104000504

Stewart, M., Reutter, L., Letourneau, N., & Makwarimba, E. (2009). A support intervention to promote health and coping among homeless youth. *Canadian Journal of Nursing Research, 41*, 54–77.

Stotts, A. L., Schmitz, J. M., Rhoades, H. M., & Grabowski, J. (2001). Motivational interviewing with cocaine-dependent patients: A pilot study. *Journal of Consulting and Clinical Psychology, 69*, 858–862. doi:10.1037/0022-006X.69.5.858

Van Leeuwen, J. M., Hopfer, C., Hooks, S., White, R., Peterson, J., & Pirkopf, J. (2004). A snapshot of substance abuse among homeless and runaway youth in Denver, Colorado. *Journal of Community Health, 29*, 217–299. doi: 10.1023/B: JOHE.0000022028.50989.aa

Weinberg, N. Z., Rahdert, E., Colliver, J. D., & Glantz, M. D. (1998). Adolescent substance abuse: A review of the past 10 years. *Journal of the American Academy of Child and Adolescent Psychiatry, 37*, 252–261. doi: 10.1097/00004583-199803000-00009

Whitbeck, L. B. (2009*). Mental health and emerging adulthood among homeless young people.* New York, NY: Psychology Press.

Zerger, S. (2002). *Substance abuse treatment: What works for homeless people? A review of the literature.* Nashville, TN: National Health Care for the Homeless Council.

Zerger, S., Strehlow, A. J., & Gundlapalli, A. V. (2008). Homeless young adults and behavioral health: An overview. *American Behavioral Scientist, 51*, 824–841. doi: 10.1177/0002764207311990

Acknowledgments: The author would like to thank Dr. Mary Keegan Eamon for her comments that helped improve the article.

Address correspondence to: Xiaoling Xiang, School of Social Work, University of Illinois at Urbana-Champaign, 1010 West Nevada Street, Urbana, IL 61801, USA. Email: xxiang3@illinois.edu

Exercise for Review 4

Directions: Answer the following questions based on your opinions. While there are no right or wrong answers, be prepared to explain the basis for your answers in classroom discussions.

1. Did the reviewer convince you that the topic of the review is important? Explain.

2. Is the review an essay organized around topics (as opposed to a string of annotations)? Explain.

3. Is the number of headings and subheadings adequate? Explain.

4. Is the tone of the review neutral and nonemotional? Explain.

5. Overall, is the review logically organized? Explain.

6. If research objectives or hypotheses are stated near the end of the review, do they flow logically from the material presented in the review? Explain.

7. Are there any obvious weaknesses in this review? Explain.

8. Does this review have any special strengths? Explain.

9. What is your overall evaluation of this review on a scale from *Excellent* (10) to *Very Poor* (0)? Explain.

Table 1
Table of Random Numbers

Row #						
1	2 1 0	4 9 8	0 8 8	8 0 6	9 2 4	8 2 6
2	0 7 3	0 2 9	4 8 2	7 8 9	8 9 2	9 7 1
3	4 4 9	0 0 2	8 6 2	6 7 7	7 3 1	2 5 1
4	7 3 2	1 1 2	0 7 7	6 0 3	8 3 4	7 8 1
5	3 3 2	5 8 3	1 7 0	1 4 0	7 8 9	3 7 7
6	6 1 2	0 5 7	2 4 4	0 0 6	3 0 2	8 0 7
7	7 0 9	3 3 3	7 4 0	4 8 8	9 3 5	8 0 5
8	7 5 1	9 0 9	1 5 2	6 5 0	9 0 3	5 8 8
9	3 5 6	9 6 5	0 1 9	4 6 6	7 5 6	8 3 1
10	8 5 0	3 9 4	3 4 0	6 5 1	7 4 4	6 2 7
11	0 5 9	6 8 7	4 8 1	5 5 0	5 1 7	1 5 8
12	7 6 2	2 6 9	6 1 9	7 1 1	4 7 1	6 2 0
13	3 8 4	7 8 9	8 2 2	1 6 3	8 7 0	4 6 1
14	1 9 1	8 4 5	6 1 8	1 2 4	4 4 2	7 3 4
15	1 5 3	6 7 6	1 8 4	3 1 8	8 7 7	6 0 4
16	0 5 5	3 6 0	7 1 3	8 1 4	6 7 0	4 3 5
17	2 2 3	8 6 0	9 1 9	0 4 4	7 6 8	1 5 1
18	2 3 3	2 5 5	7 6 9	4 9 7	1 3 7	9 3 8
19	8 5 5	0 5 3	7 8 5	4 5 1	6 0 4	8 9 1
20	0 6 1	1 3 4	8 6 4	3 2 9	4 3 8	7 4 1
21	9 1 1	8 2 9	0 6 9	6 9 4	2 9 9	0 6 0
22	3 7 8	0 6 3	7 1 2	6 5 2	7 6 5	6 5 1
23	5 3 0	5 1 2	1 0 9	1 3 7	5 6 1	2 5 0
24	7 2 4	8 6 7	9 3 8	7 6 0	9 1 6	5 7 8
25	0 9 1	6 7 0	3 8 0	9 1 5	4 2 3	2 4 5
26	3 8 1	4 3 7	9 2 4	5 1 2	8 7 7	4 1 3

Notes:

Table 2

Table of Recommended Sample Sizes (n) for Populations (N) with Finite Sizes[1]

N	n	N	n	N	n
10	10	220	140	1,200	291
15	14	230	144	1,300	297
20	19	240	148	1,400	302
25	24	250	152	1,500	306
30	28	260	155	1,600	310
35	32	270	159	1,700	313
40	36	280	162	1,800	317
45	40	290	165	1,900	320
50	44	300	169	2,000	322
55	48	320	175	2,200	327
60	52	340	181	2,400	331
65	56	360	186	2,600	335
70	59	380	191	2,800	338
75	63	400	196	3,000	341
80	66	420	201	3,500	346
85	70	440	205	4,000	351
90	73	460	210	4,500	354
95	76	480	214	5,000	357
100	80	500	217	6,000	361
110	86	550	226	7,000	364
120	92	600	234	8,000	367
130	97	650	242	9,000	368
140	103	700	248	10,000	370
150	108	750	254	15,000	375
160	113	800	260	20,000	377
170	118	850	265	30,000	379
180	123	900	269	40,000	380
190	127	950	274	50,000	381
200	132	1,000	278	75,000	382
210	136	1,100	285	100,000	384

---

[1] Adapted from: Krejcie, R. V., & Morgan, D. W. (1970). Determining sample size for research activities. *Educational and Psychological Measurement, 30*, 607–610.

Notes:

Subject Index

T

V

Notes:

Notes:

Notes:

Notes:

Notes:

Notes:

Notes:

Notes:

Notes: